X·MEN

FIRST TO LAST

X-MEN: FIRST TO LAST. Contains material originally published in magazine form as X-MEN #12-15 and X-MEN GIANT-SIZE #1. First printing 2011. Hardcover ISBN# 978-0-7851-5287-3. Softcover ISBN# 978-0-7851-5288-0. Published by MARVEL WORLDWIDE, INC., a subsidiary of MARVEL ENTERTAINMENT, LLC. OFFICE OF PUBLICATION: 135 West 50th Street, New York, NY 10020. Copyright © 2011 and 2012 Marvel Characters, Inc. All rights reserved. Hardcover: $19.99 per copy in the U.S. and $21.99 in Canada (GST #R127032852). Softcover: $15.99 per copy in the U.S. and $17.99 in Canada (GST #R127032852). Canadian Agreement #40668537. All characters featured in this issue and the distinctive names and likenesses thereof, and all related indicia are trademarks of Marvel Characters, Inc. No similarity between any of the names, characters, persons, and/or institutions in this magazine with those of any living or dead person or institution is intended, and any such similarity which may exist is purely coincidental. **Printed in the U.S.A.** ALAN FINE, EVP - Office of the President, Marvel Worldwide, Inc. and EVP & CMO Marvel Characters B.V.; DAN BUCKLEY, Publisher & President - Print, Animation & Digital Divisions; JOE QUESADA, Chief Creative Officer; JIM SOKOLOWSKI, Chief Operating Officer; DAVID BOGART, SVP of Business Affairs & Talent Management; TOM BREVOORT, SVP of Publishing; C.B. CEBULSKI, SVP of Creator & Content Development; DAVID GABRIEL, SVP of Publishing Sales & Circulation; MICHAEL PASCIULLO, SVP of Brand Planning & Communications; JIM O'KEEFE, VP of Operations & Logistics; DAN CARR, Executive Director of Publishing Technology; SUSAN CRESPI, Editorial Operations Manager; ALEX MORALES, Publishing Operations Manager; STAN LEE, Chairman Emeritus. For information regarding advertising in Marvel Comics or on Marvel.com, please contact John Dokes, SVP Integrated Sales and Marketing, at jdokes@marvel.com. For Marvel subscription inquiries, please call 800-217-9158. Manufactured between 8/8/2011 and 9/5/2011 (hardcover), and 8/8/2011 and 3/5/2012 (softcover), by R.R. DONNELLEY INC., SALEM, VA, USA.

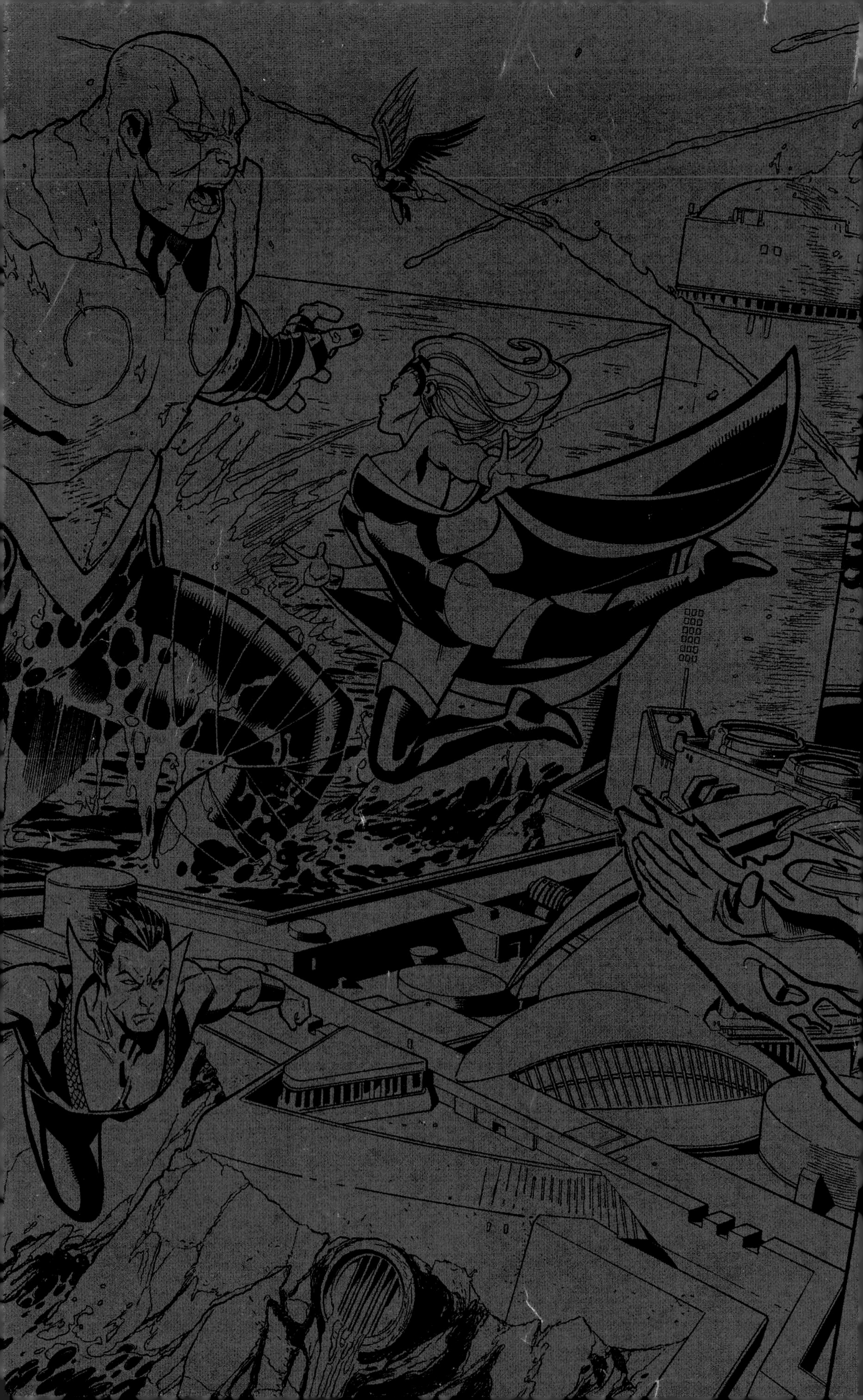

X-MEN

FIRST TO LAST

WRITER
CHRISTOPHER YOST
PENCILER
PACO MEDINA (NOW)
INKER
JUAN VLASCO (NOW)
ARTIST
DALABOR TALAJIC (THEN)
COLORISTS
MARTE GRACIA (NOW) &
JUAN VLASCO (THEN)
LETTERER
VIRTUAL CALLIGRAPHY'S
JOE CARAMAGNA
COVER ART
ED McGUINNESS & VAL STAPLES
WITH DEXTER VINES (#15)
ASSISTANT EDITOR
JORDAN D. WHITE
ASSOCIATE EDITOR
DANIEL KETCHUM
EDITORS
AXEL ALONSO & NICK LOWE

COLLECTION EDITOR: JENNIFER GRÜNWALD
EDITORIAL ASSISTANTS: JAMES EMMETT & JOE HOCHSTEIN
ASSISTANT EDITORS: ALEX STARBUCK & NELSON RIBEIRO
EDITOR, SPECIAL PROJECTS: MARK D. BEAZLEY
SENIOR EDITOR, SPECIAL PROJECTS: JEFF YOUNGQUIST
SENIOR VICE PRESIDENT OF SALES: DAVID GABRIEL
SVP OF BRAND PLANNING & COMMUNICATIONS: MICHAEL PASCIULLO
BOOK DESIGN: JEFF POWELL

EDITOR IN CHIEF: AXEL ALONSO
CHIEF CREATIVE OFFICER: JOE QUESADA
PUBLISHER: DAN BUCKLEY
EXECUTIVE PRODUCER: ALAN FINE

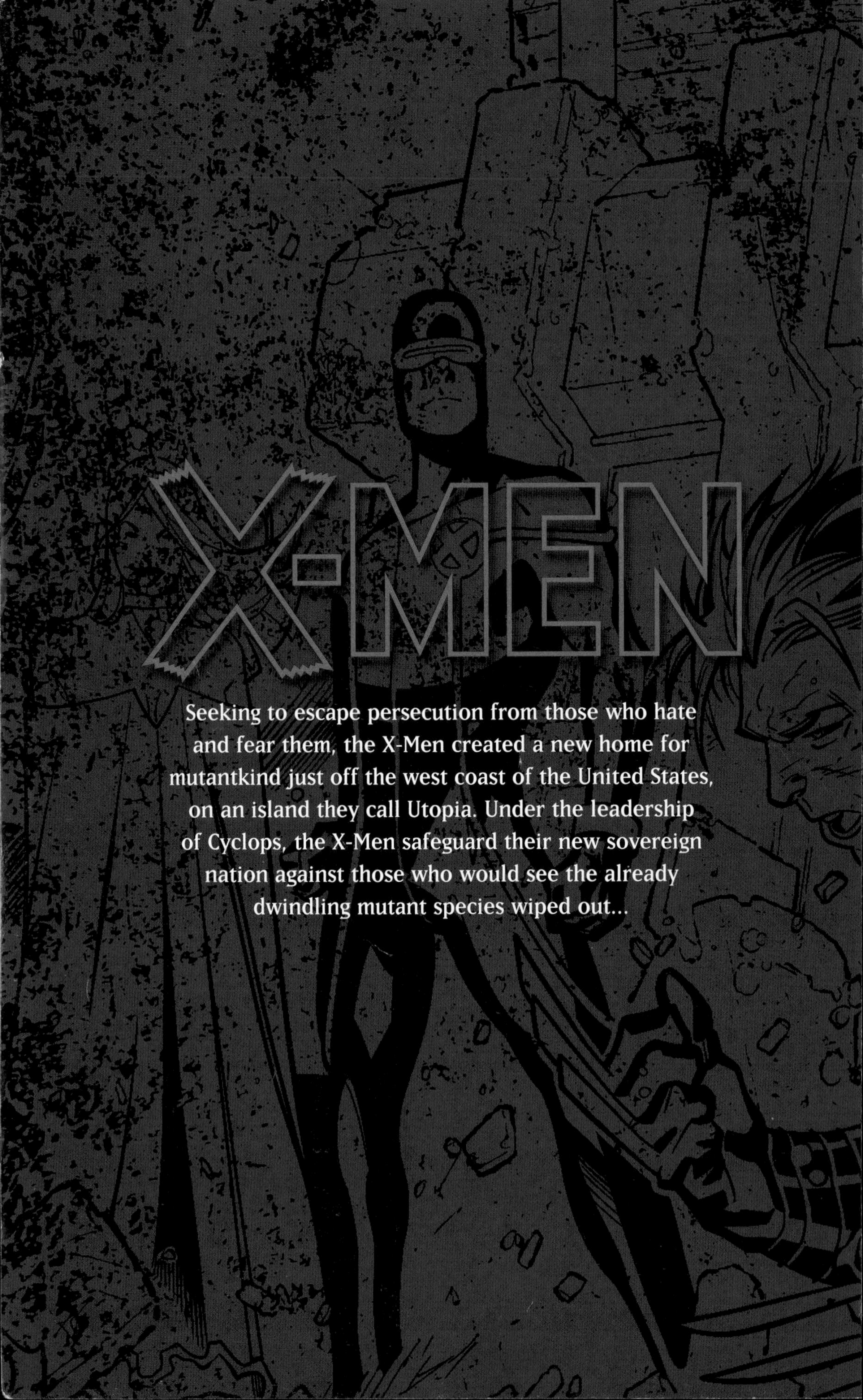

X-MEN

Seeking to escape persecution from those who hate and fear them, the X-Men created a new home for mutantkind just off the west coast of the United States, on an island they call Utopia. Under the leadership of Cyclops, the X-Men safeguard their new sovereign nation against those who would see the already dwindling mutant species wiped out...

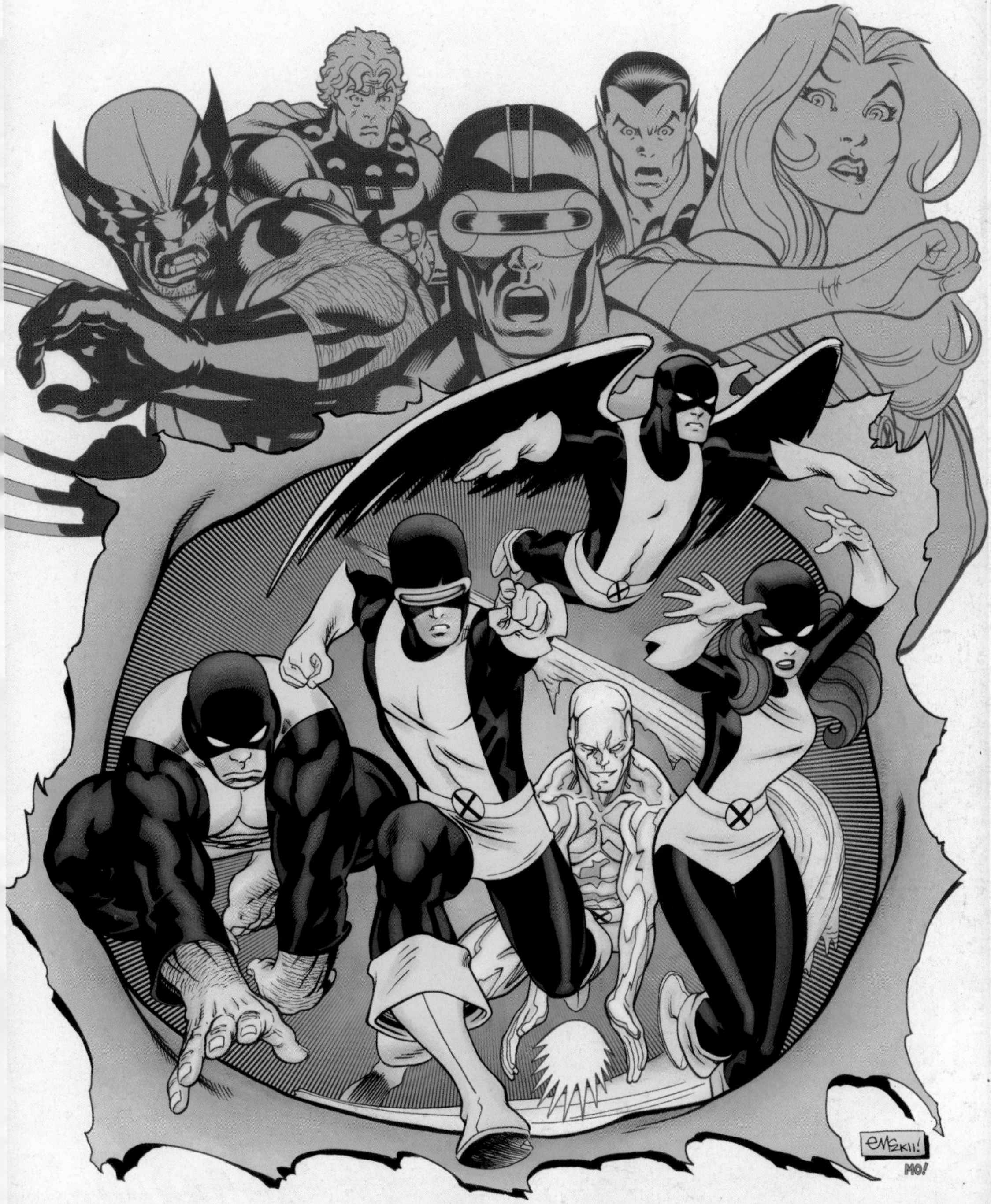

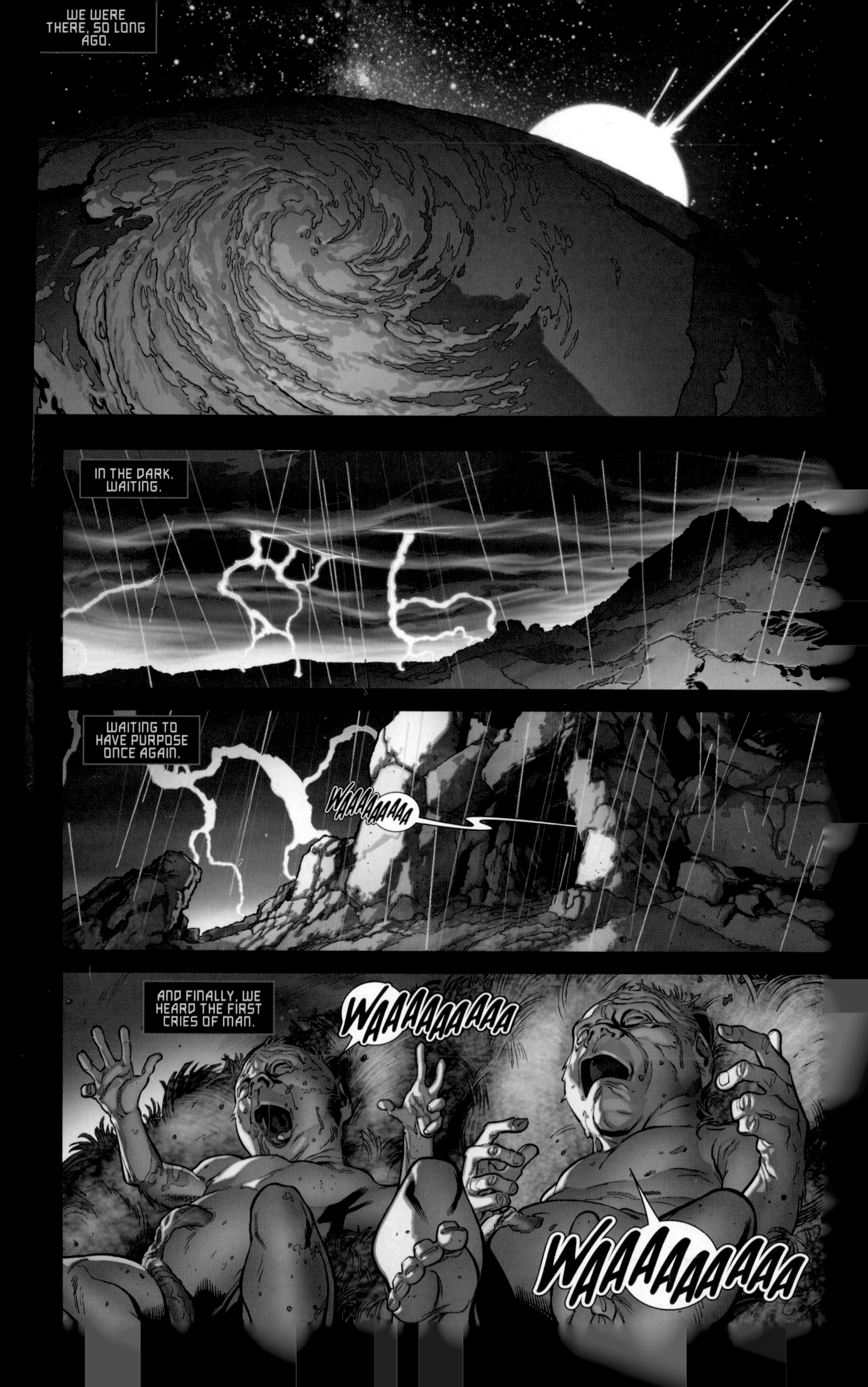
WE WERE THERE, SO LONG AGO.
IN THE DARK. WAITING.
WAITING TO HAVE PURPOSE ONCE AGAIN.
WAAAAAAAAA
AND FINALLY, WE HEARD THE FIRST CRIES OF MAN.
WAAAAAAAAA
WAAAAAAAAAA

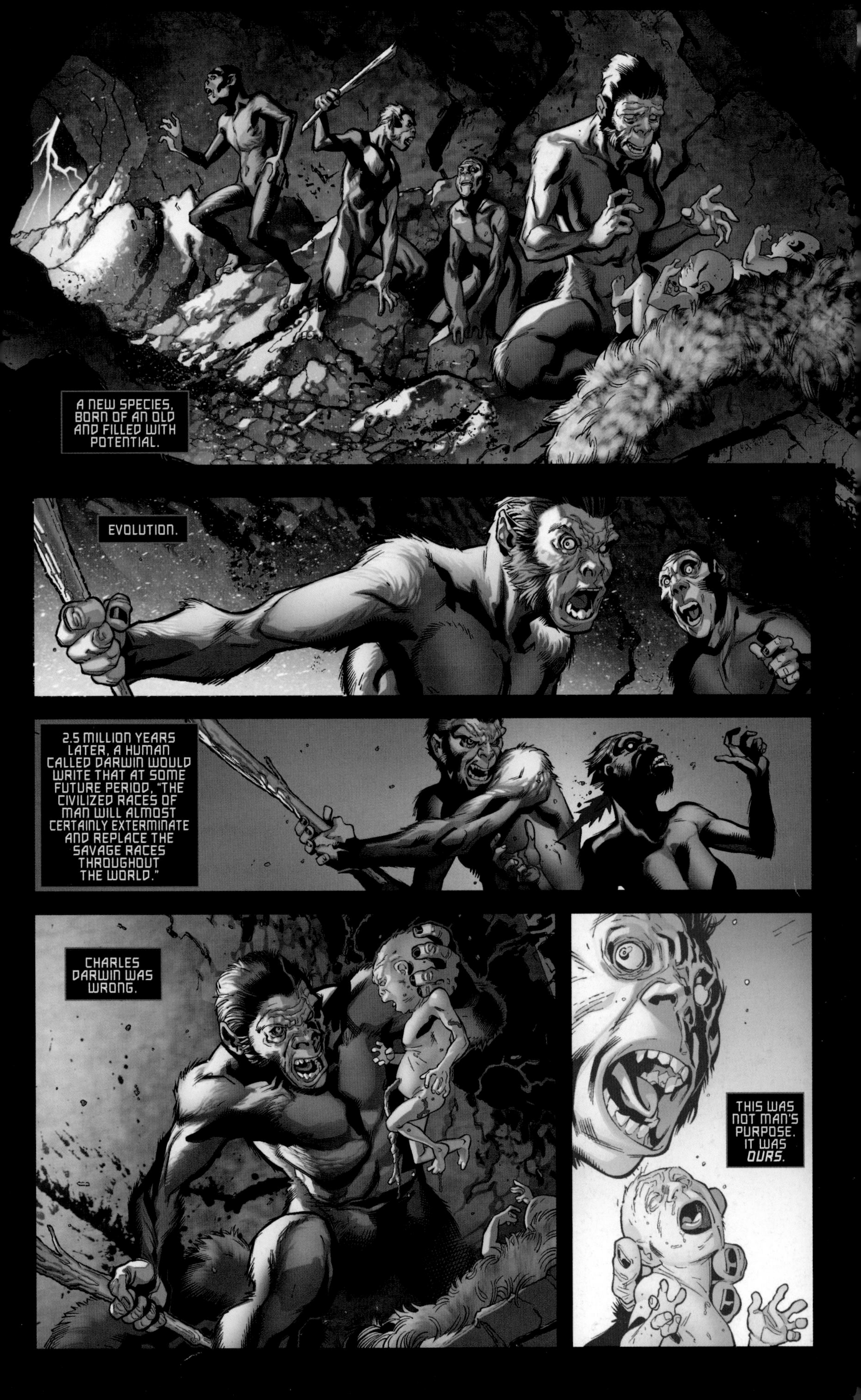
A NEW SPECIES, BORN OF AN OLD AND FILLED WITH POTENTIAL.
EVOLUTION.
2.5 MILLION YEARS LATER, A HUMAN CALLED DARWIN WOULD WRITE THAT AT SOME FUTURE PERIOD, "THE CIVILIZED RACES OF MAN WILL ALMOST CERTAINLY EXTERMINATE AND REPLACE THE SAVAGE RACES THROUGHOUT THE WORLD."
CHARLES DARWIN WAS WRONG.
THIS WAS NOT MAN'S PURPOSE. IT WAS *OURS*.

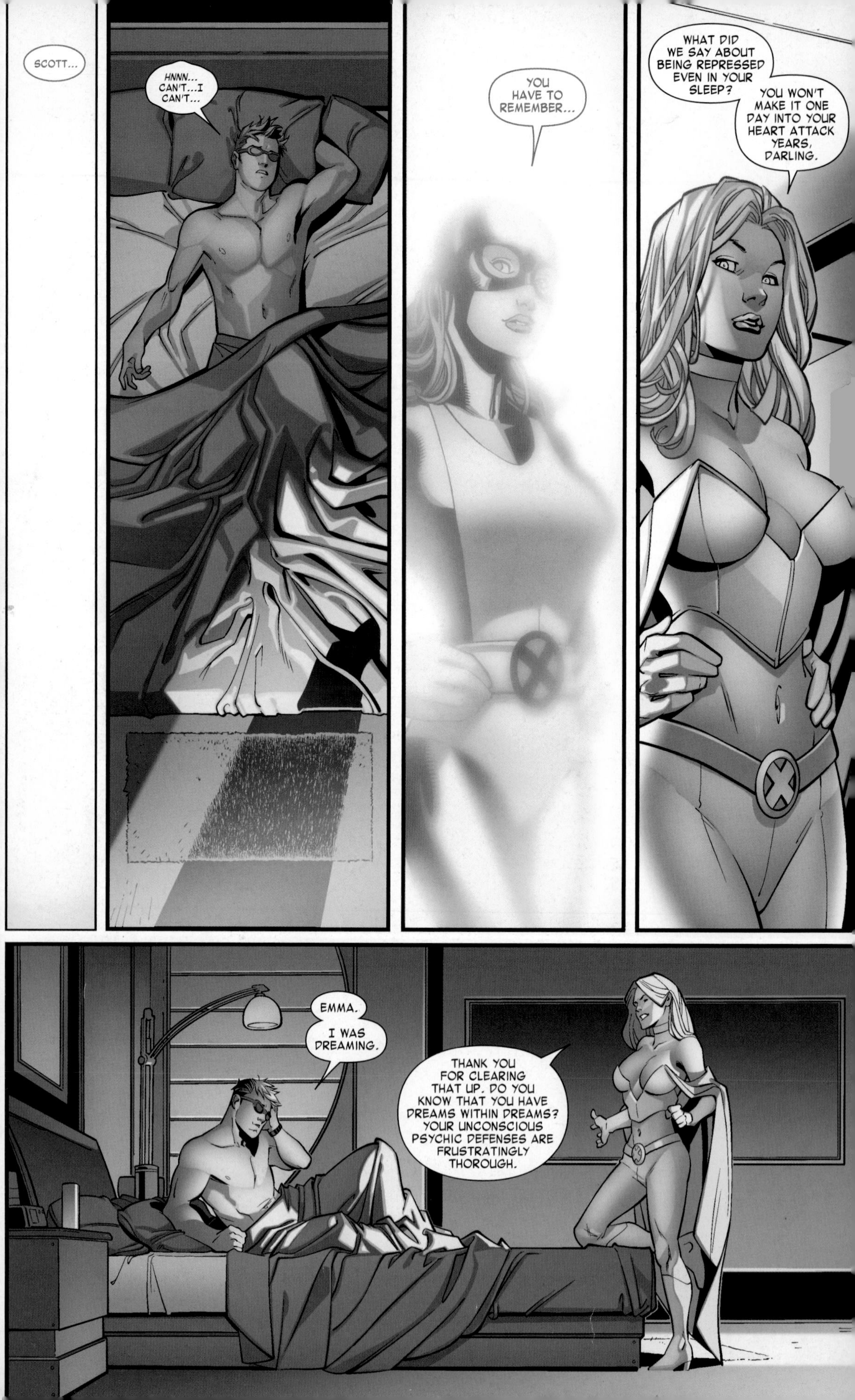
SCOTT...
HNNN... CAN'T...I CAN'T...
YOU HAVE TO REMEMBER...
WHAT DID WE SAY ABOUT BEING REPRESSED EVEN IN YOUR SLEEP?
YOU WON'T MAKE IT ONE DAY INTO YOUR HEART ATTACK YEARS, DARLING.
EMMA.
I WAS DREAMING.
THANK YOU FOR CLEARING THAT UP. DO YOU KNOW THAT YOU HAVE DREAMS WITHIN DREAMS? YOUR UNCONSCIOUS PSYCHIC DEFENSES ARE FRUSTRATINGLY THOROUGH.

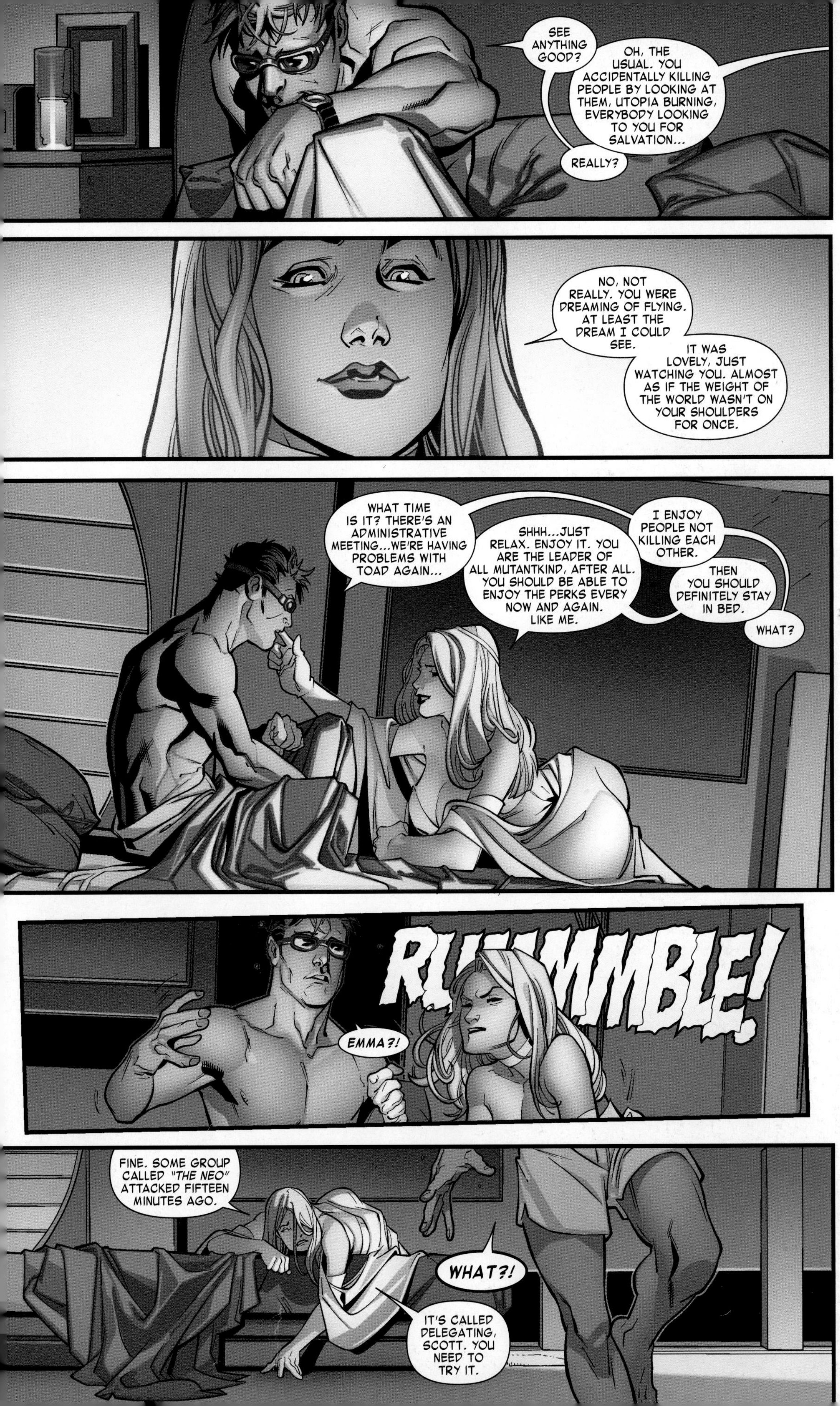
SEE ANYTHING GOOD?
OH, THE USUAL. YOU ACCIDENTALLY KILLING PEOPLE BY LOOKING AT THEM, UTOPIA BURNING, EVERYBODY LOOKING TO YOU FOR SALVATION...
REALLY?
NO, NOT REALLY. YOU WERE DREAMING OF FLYING. AT LEAST THE DREAM I COULD SEE.
IT WAS LOVELY, JUST WATCHING YOU. ALMOST AS IF THE WEIGHT OF THE WORLD WASN'T ON YOUR SHOULDERS FOR ONCE.
WHAT TIME IS IT? THERE'S AN ADMINISTRATIVE MEETING...WE'RE HAVING PROBLEMS WITH TOAD AGAIN...
SHHH...JUST RELAX. ENJOY IT. YOU ARE THE LEADER OF ALL MUTANTKIND, AFTER ALL. YOU SHOULD BE ABLE TO ENJOY THE PERKS EVERY NOW AND AGAIN. LIKE ME.
I ENJOY PEOPLE NOT KILLING EACH OTHER.
THEN YOU SHOULD DEFINITELY STAY IN BED.
WHAT?
RUMMMBLE!
EMMA?!
FINE. SOME GROUP CALLED "THE NEO" ATTACKED FIFTEEN MINUTES AGO.
WHAT?!
IT'S CALLED DELEGATING, SCOTT. YOU NEED TO TRY IT.

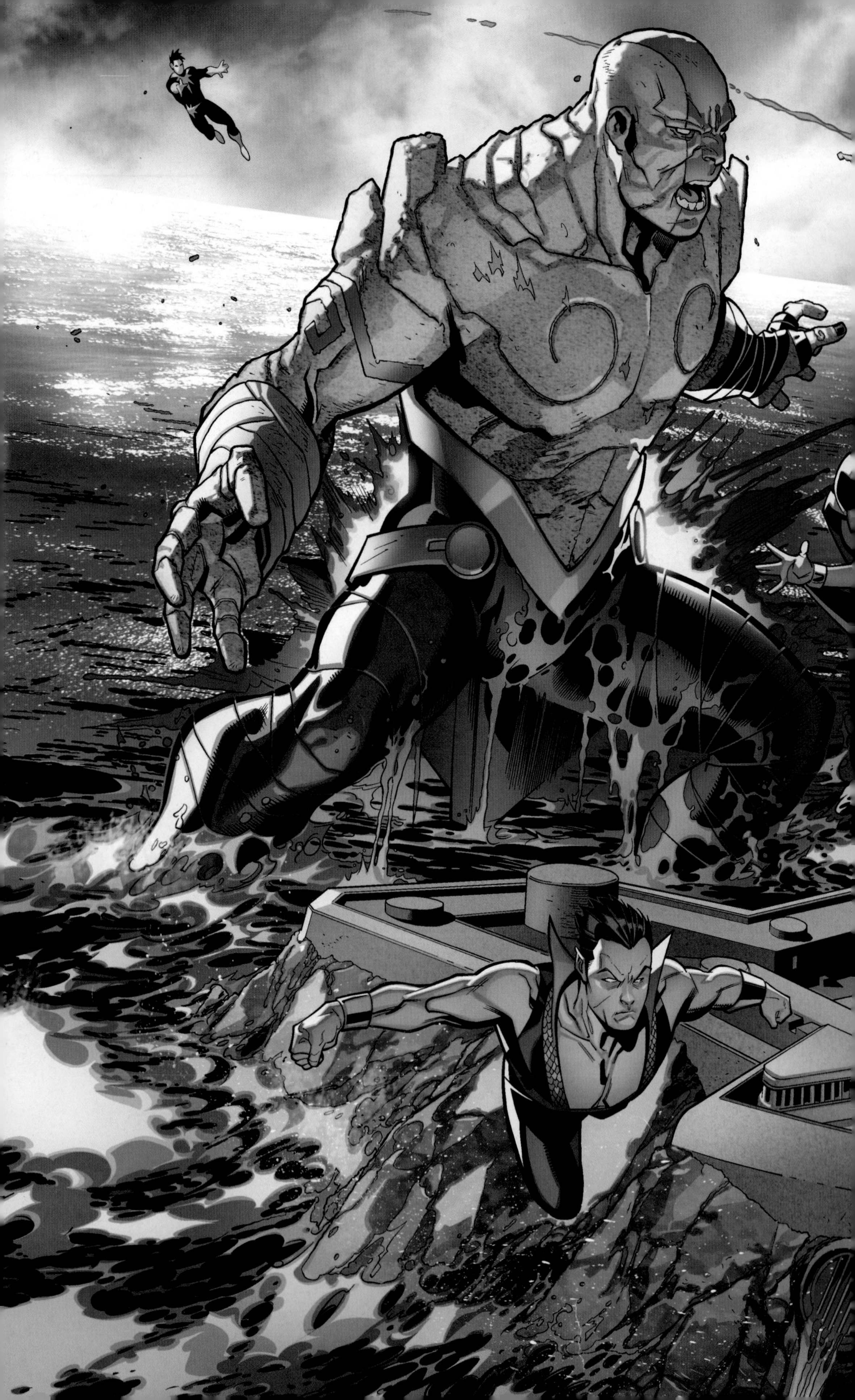

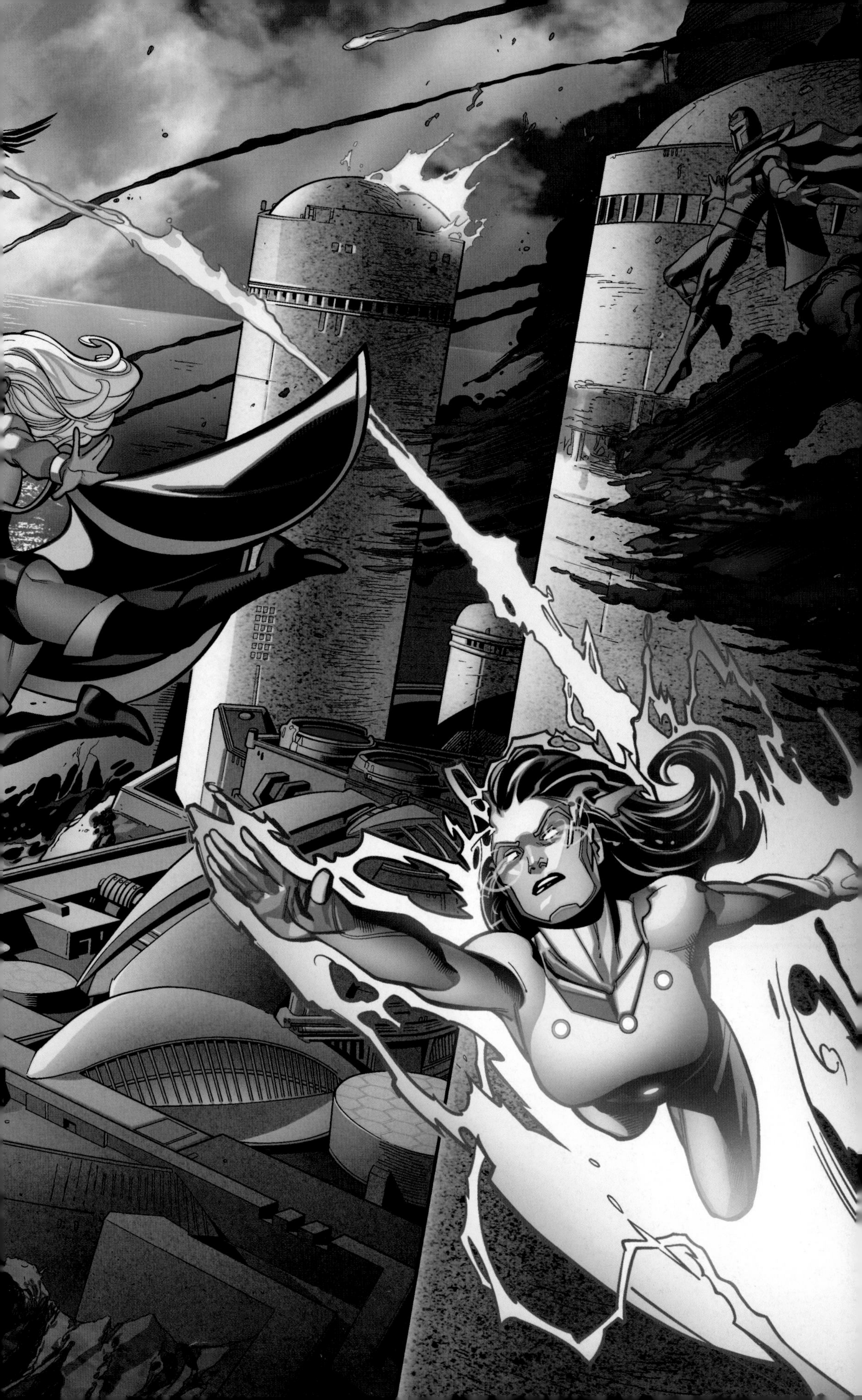

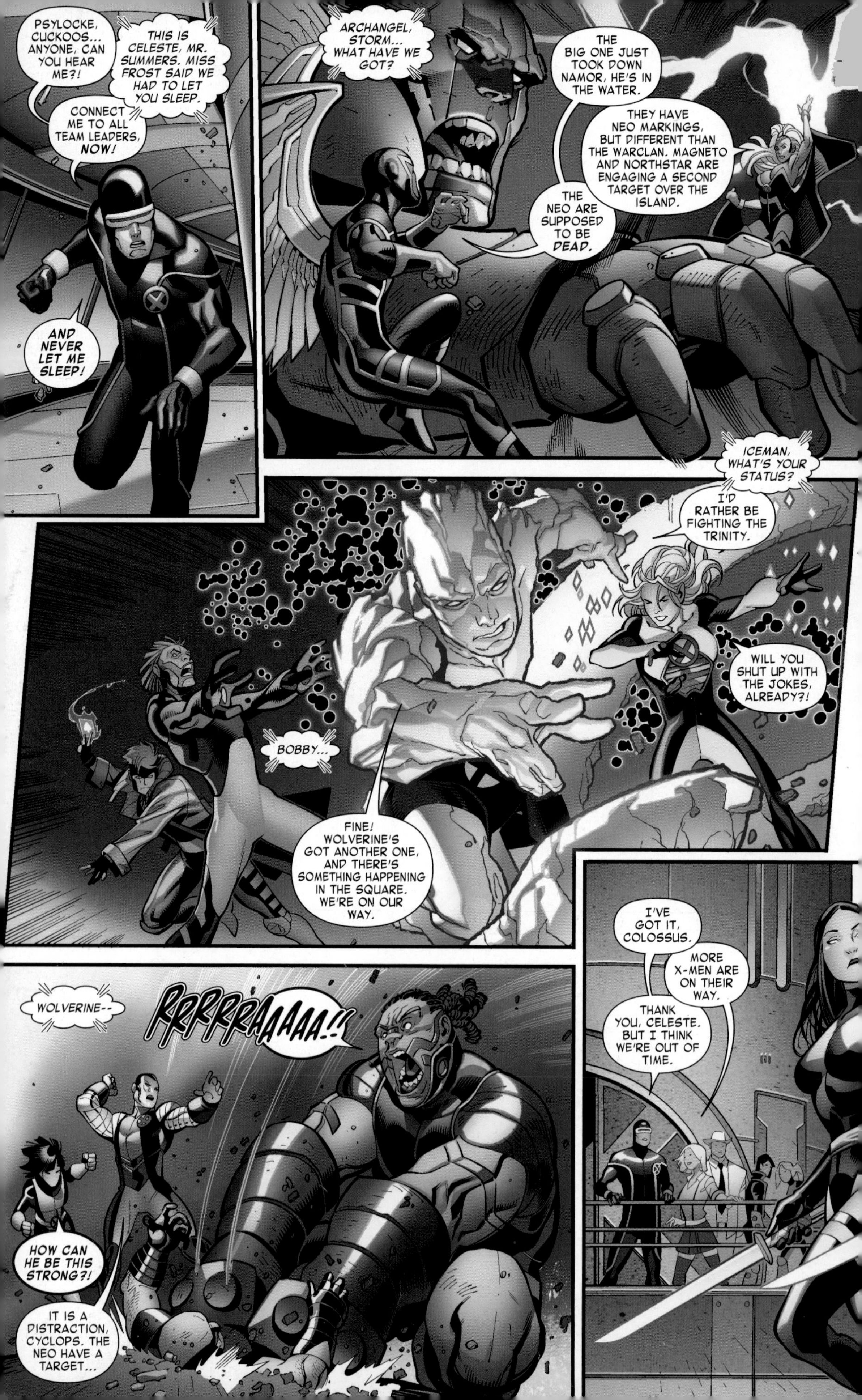
PSYLOCKE, CUCKOOS... ANYONE, CAN YOU HEAR ME?!
THIS IS CELESTE, MR. SUMMERS. MISS FROST SAID WE HAD TO LET YOU SLEEP.
CONNECT ME TO ALL TEAM LEADERS, NOW!
AND NEVER LET ME SLEEP!
ARCHANGEL, STORM... WHAT HAVE WE GOT?
THE BIG ONE JUST TOOK DOWN NAMOR, HE'S IN THE WATER.
THEY HAVE NEO MARKINGS, BUT DIFFERENT THAN THE WARCLAN. MAGNETO AND NORTHSTAR ARE ENGAGING A SECOND TARGET OVER THE ISLAND.
THE NEO ARE SUPPOSED TO BE DEAD.
ICEMAN, WHAT'S YOUR STATUS?
I'D RATHER BE FIGHTING THE TRINITY.
WILL YOU SHUT UP WITH THE JOKES, ALREADY?!
BOBBY...
FINE! WOLVERINE'S GOT ANOTHER ONE, AND THERE'S SOMETHING HAPPENING IN THE SQUARE. WE'RE ON OUR WAY.
WOLVERINE--
RRRRRAAAAA!!
HOW CAN HE BE THIS STRONG?!
IT IS A DISTRACTION, CYCLOPS. THE NEO HAVE A TARGET...
I'VE GOT IT, COLOSSUS.
MORE X-MEN ARE ON THEIR WAY.
THANK YOU, CELESTE. BUT I THINK WE'RE OUT OF TIME.

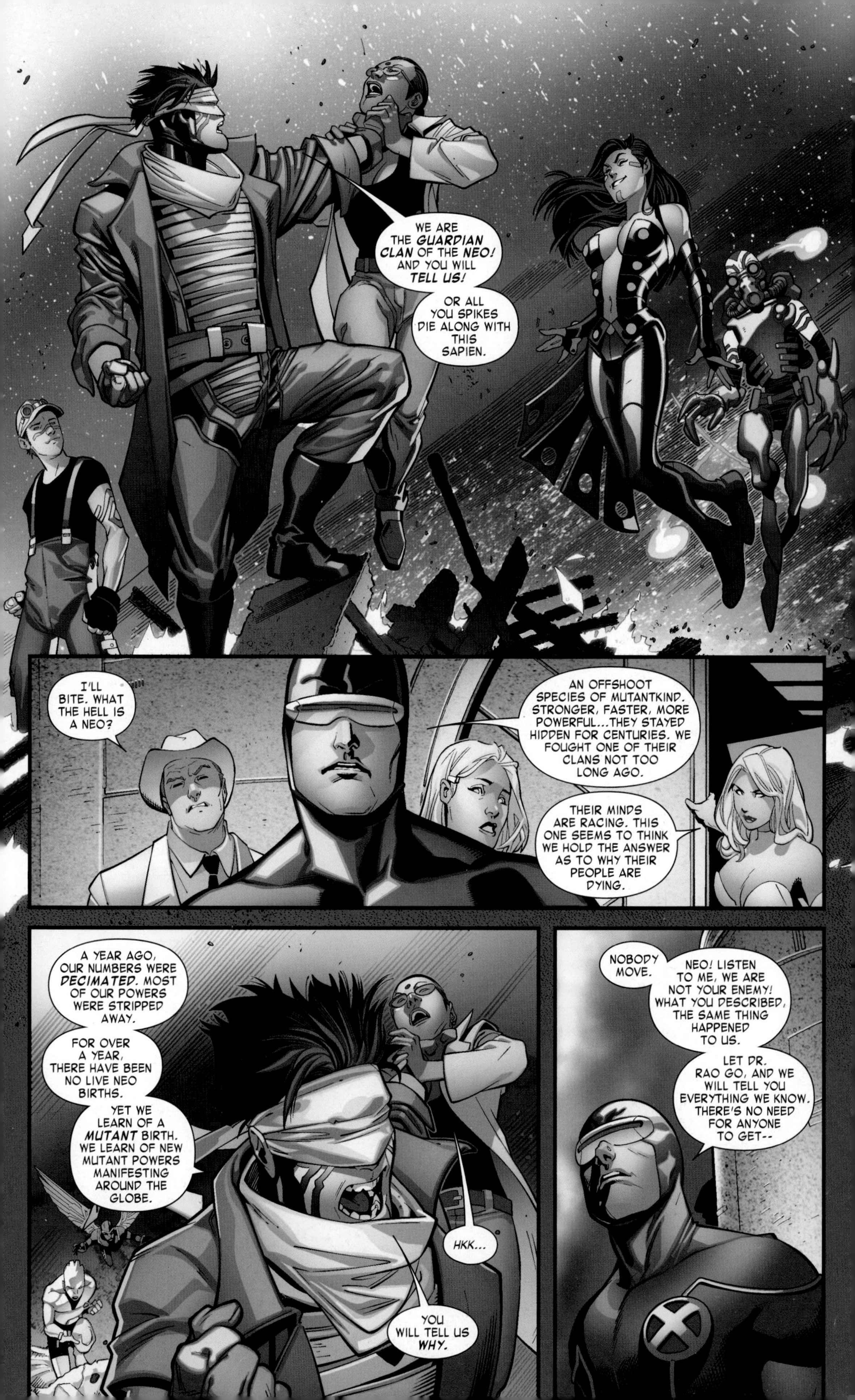
WE ARE THE GUARDIAN CLAN OF THE NEO! AND YOU WILL TELL US!
OR ALL YOU SPIKES DIE ALONG WITH THIS SAPIEN.
I'LL BITE. WHAT THE HELL IS A NEO?
AN OFFSHOOT SPECIES OF MUTANTKIND. STRONGER, FASTER, MORE POWERFUL...THEY STAYED HIDDEN FOR CENTURIES. WE FOUGHT ONE OF THEIR CLANS NOT TOO LONG AGO.
THEIR MINDS ARE RACING. THIS ONE SEEMS TO THINK WE HOLD THE ANSWER AS TO WHY THEIR PEOPLE ARE DYING.
A YEAR AGO, OUR NUMBERS WERE DECIMATED. MOST OF OUR POWERS WERE STRIPPED AWAY.
FOR OVER A YEAR, THERE HAVE BEEN NO LIVE NEO BIRTHS.
YET WE LEARN OF A MUTANT BIRTH. WE LEARN OF NEW MUTANT POWERS MANIFESTING AROUND THE GLOBE.
HKK...
YOU WILL TELL US WHY.
NOBODY MOVE.
NEO! LISTEN TO ME, WE ARE NOT YOUR ENEMY! WHAT YOU DESCRIBED, THE SAME THING HAPPENED TO US.
LET DR. RAO GO, AND WE WILL TELL YOU EVERYTHING WE KNOW. THERE'S NO NEED FOR ANYONE TO GET--

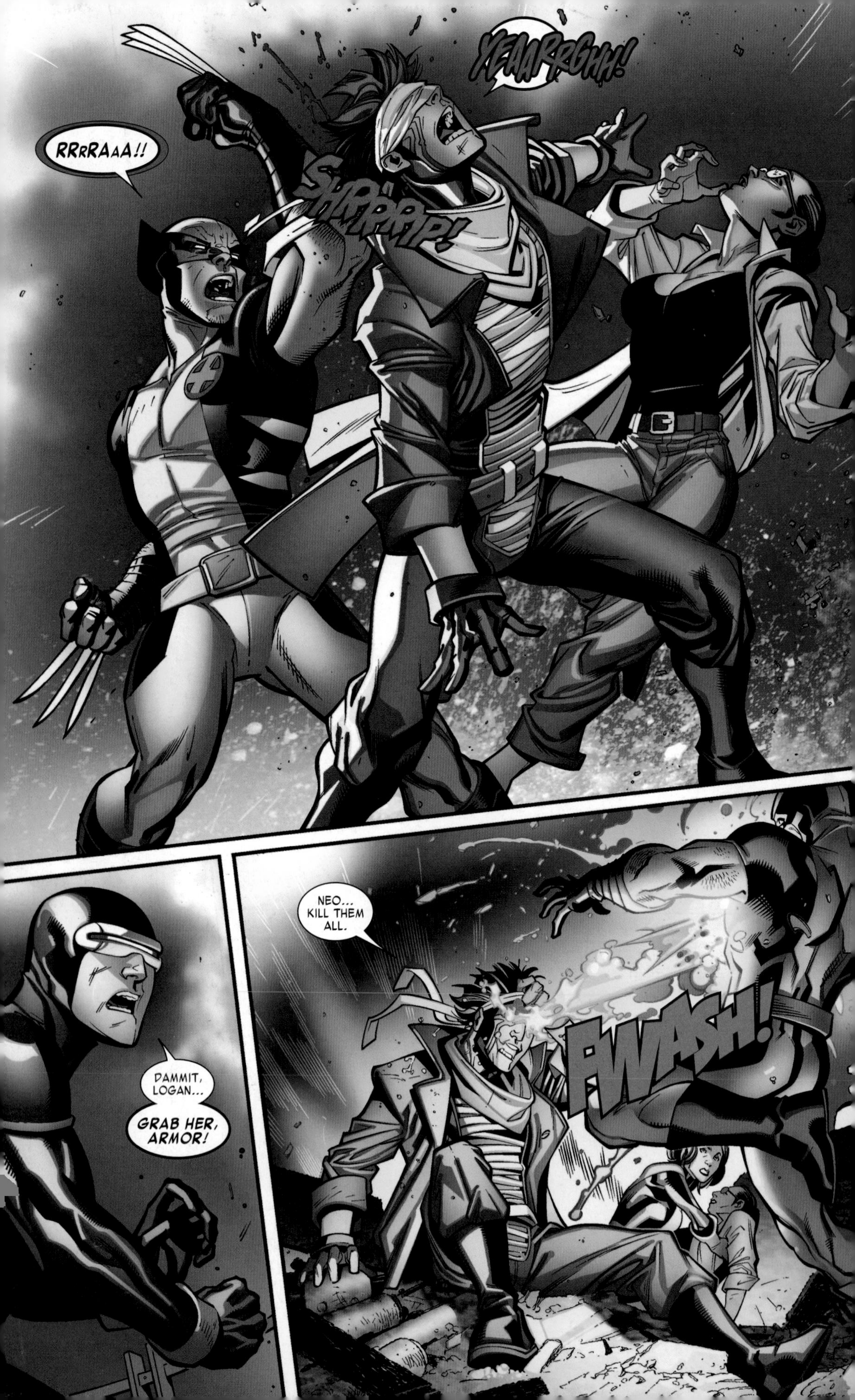

YEAARRGHH!
RRRRAAA!!
SHRRRIP!
NEO... KILL THEM ALL.
DAMMIT, LOGAN...
GRAB HER, ARMOR!
PWASH!

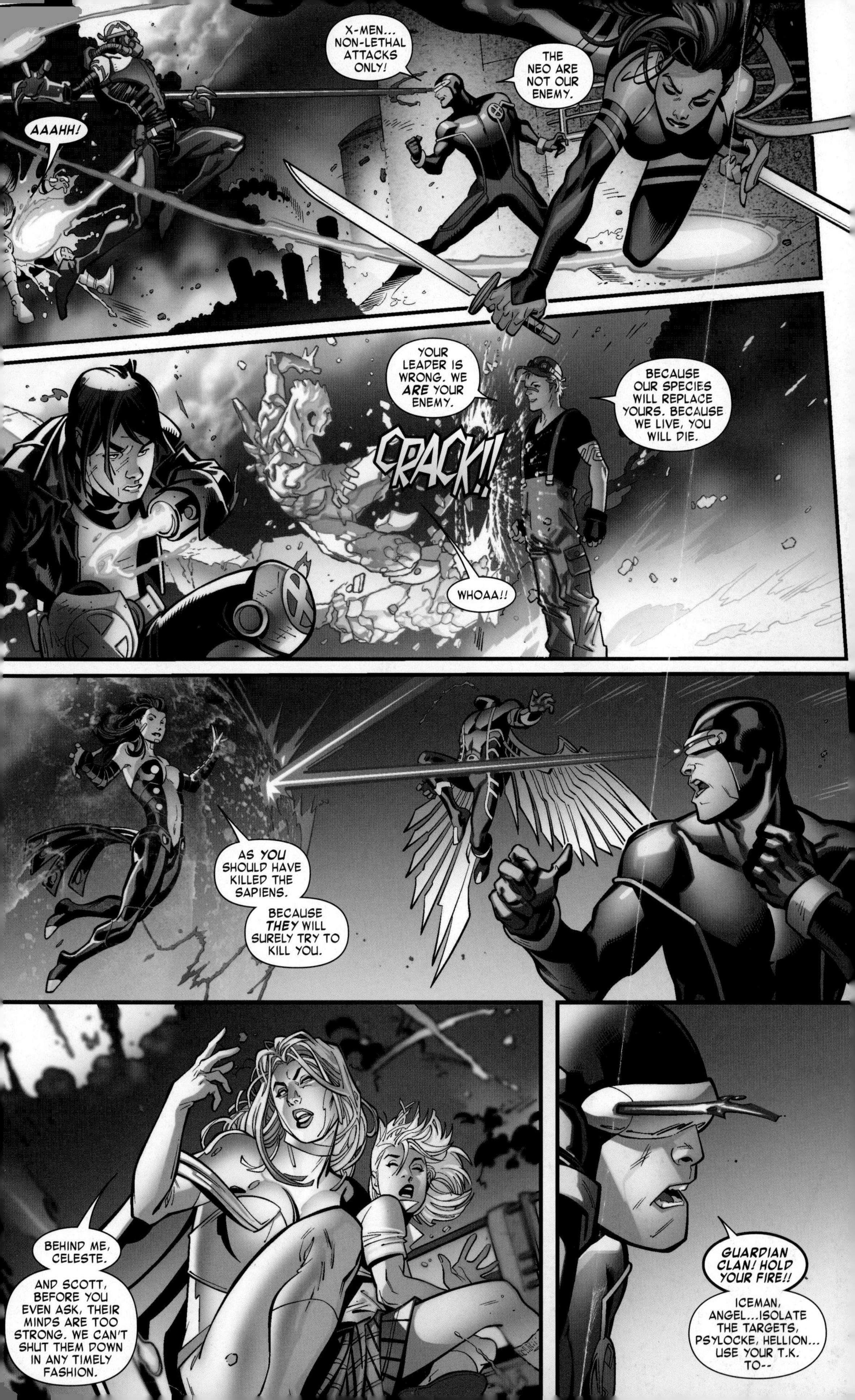
X-MEN... NON-LETHAL ATTACKS ONLY!
THE NEO ARE NOT OUR ENEMY.
AAAHH!
YOUR LEADER IS WRONG. WE ARE YOUR ENEMY.
BECAUSE OUR SPECIES WILL REPLACE YOURS. BECAUSE WE LIVE, YOU WILL DIE.
CRACK!!
WHOAA!!
AS YOU SHOULD HAVE KILLED THE SAPIENS.
BECAUSE THEY WILL SURELY TRY TO KILL YOU.
BEHIND ME, CELESTE.
AND SCOTT, BEFORE YOU EVEN ASK, THEIR MINDS ARE TOO STRONG. WE CAN'T SHUT THEM DOWN IN ANY TIMELY FASHION.
GUARDIAN CLAN! HOLD YOUR FIRE!!
ICEMAN, ANGEL...ISOLATE THE TARGETS, PSYLOCKE, HELLION... USE YOUR T.K. TO--

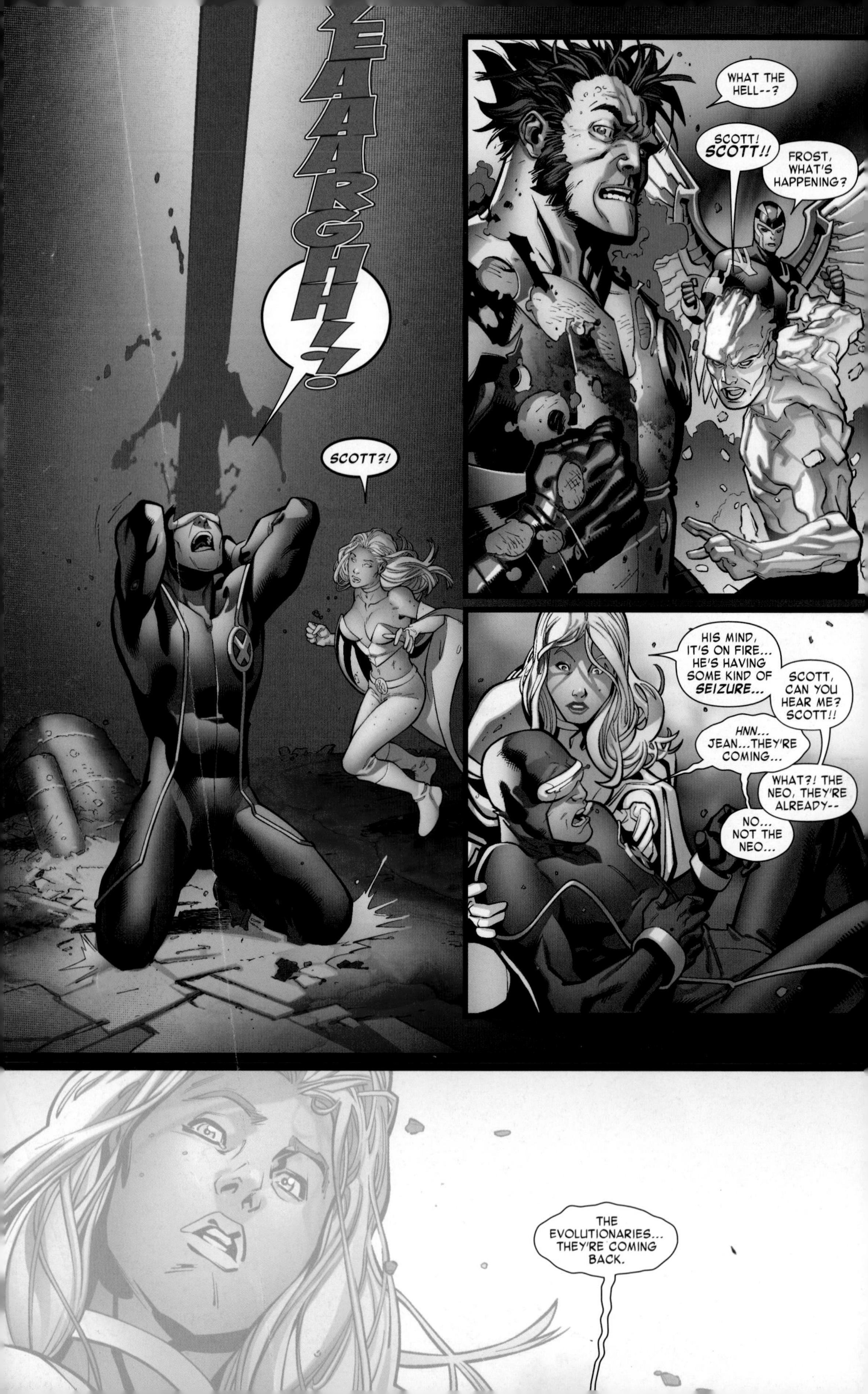
EEAAARGHH?!
SCOTT?!
WHAT THE HELL--?
SCOTT! SCOTT!!
FROST, WHAT'S HAPPENING?
HIS MIND, IT'S ON FIRE... HE'S HAVING SOME KIND OF SEIZURE...
SCOTT, CAN YOU HEAR ME? SCOTT!!
HNN... JEAN...THEY'RE COMING...
WHAT?! THE NEO, THEY'RE ALREADY--
NO... NOT THE NEO...
THE EVOLUTIONARIES... THEY'RE COMING BACK.

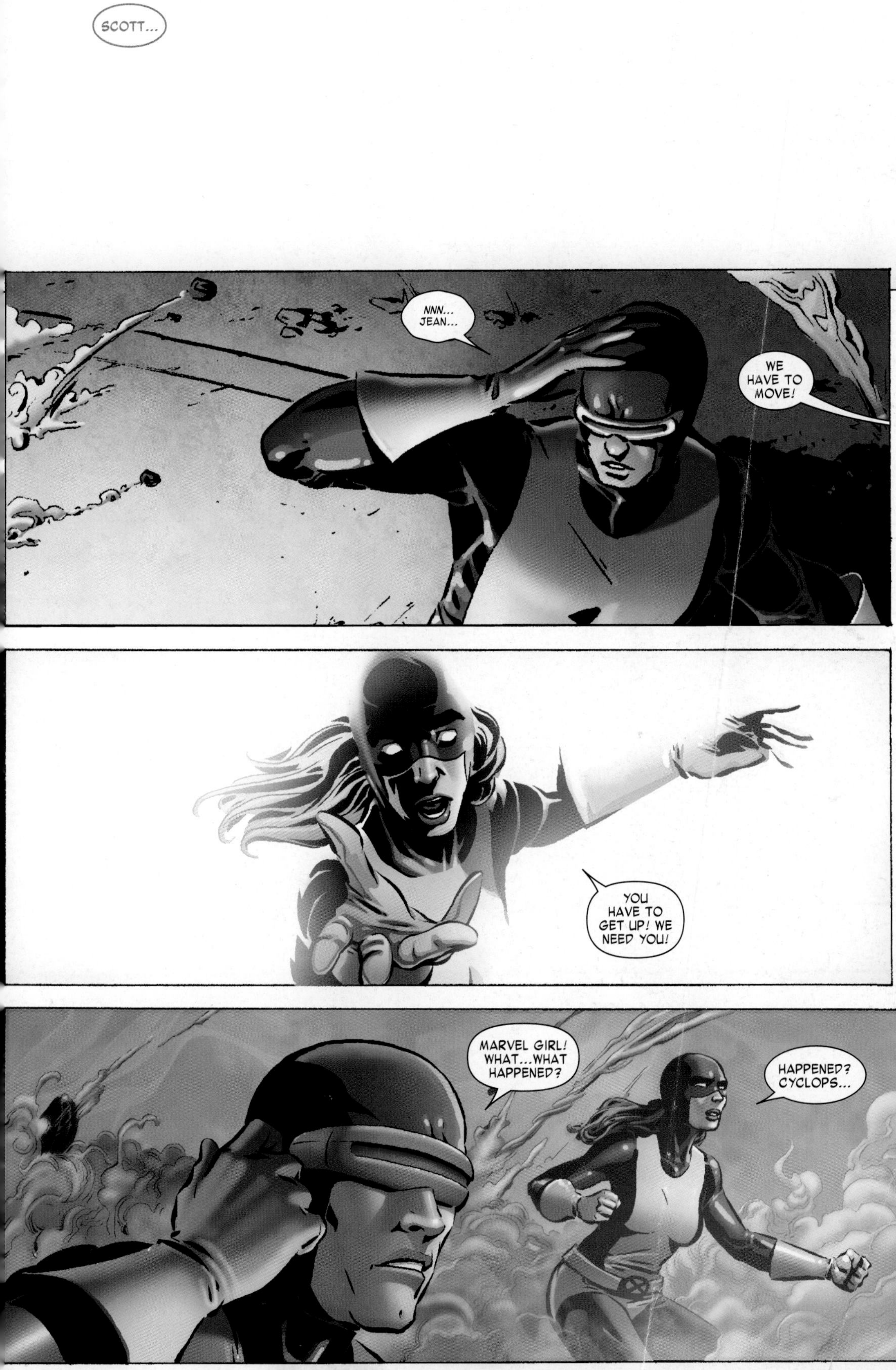
SCOTT...
NNN... JEAN...
WE HAVE TO MOVE!
YOU HAVE TO GET UP! WE NEED YOU!
MARVEL GIRL! WHAT...WHAT HAPPENED?
HAPPENED? CYCLOPS...

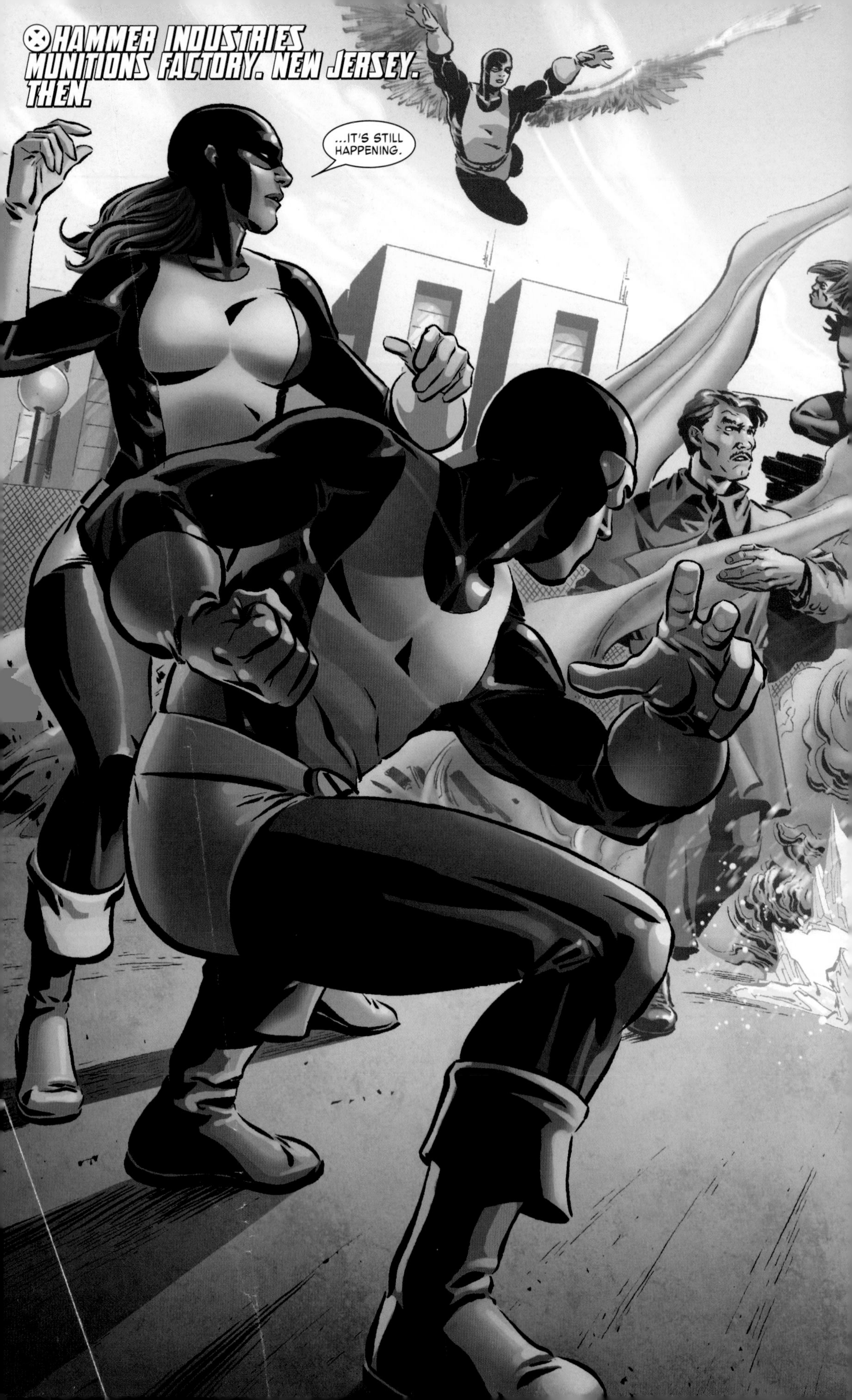
HAMMER INDUSTRIES MUNITIONS FACTORY. NEW JERSEY. THEN.
...IT'S STILL HAPPENING.

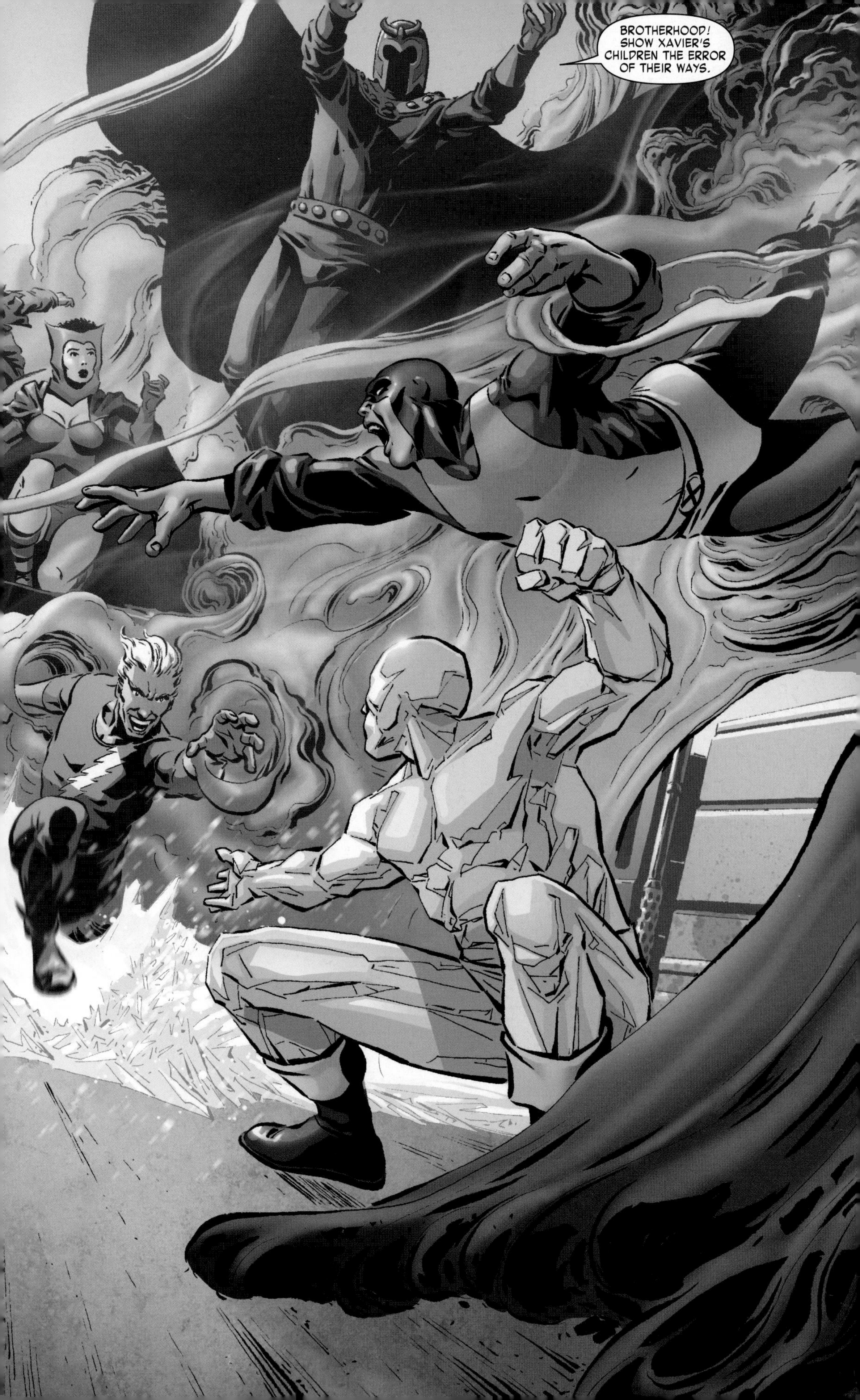
BROTHERHOOD! SHOW XAVIER'S CHILDREN THE ERROR OF THEIR WAYS.

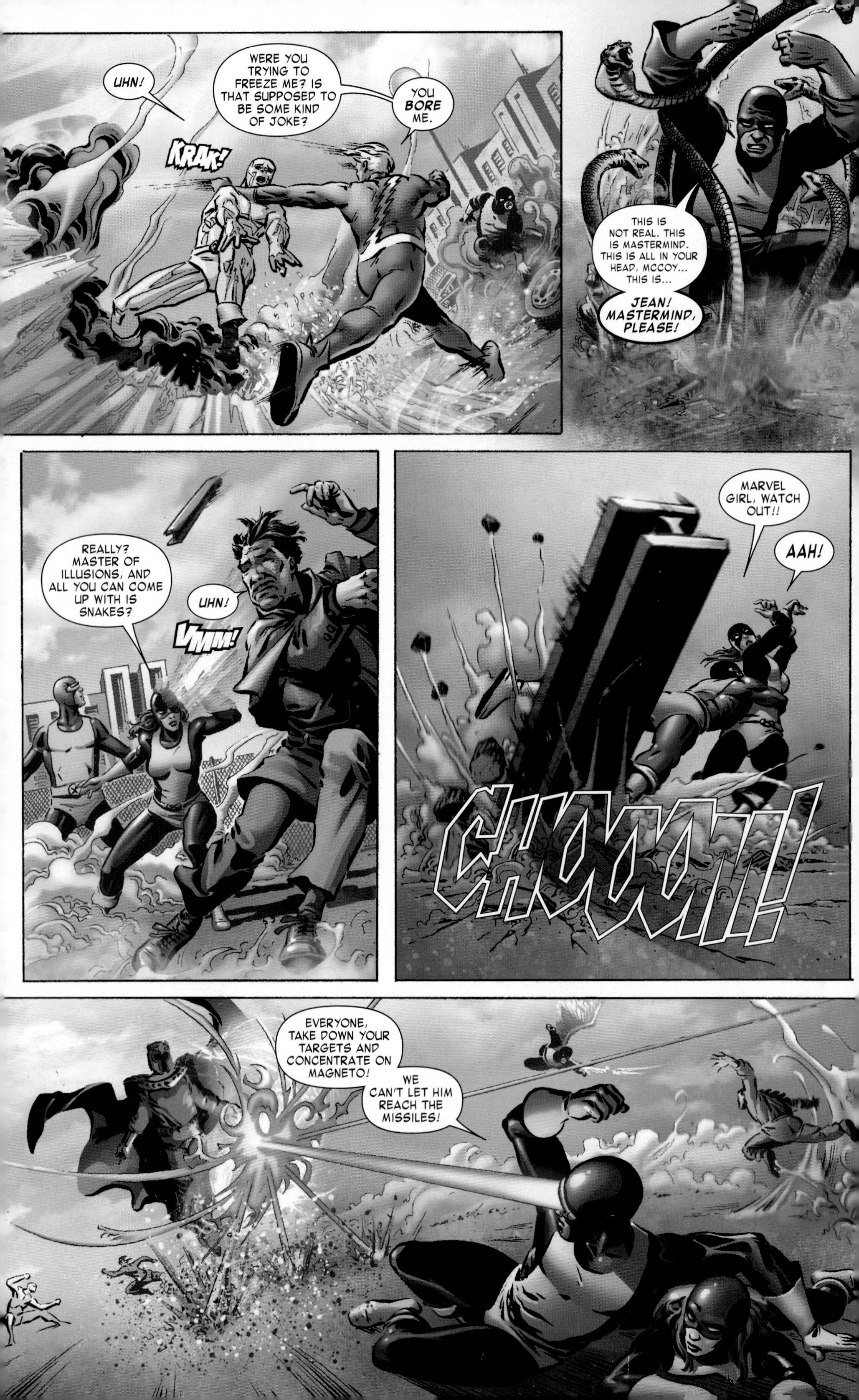

UHN!
WERE YOU TRYING TO FREEZE ME? IS THAT SUPPOSED TO BE SOME KIND OF JOKE?
YOU BORE ME.
KRAK!
THIS IS NOT REAL. THIS IS MASTERMIND. THIS IS ALL IN YOUR HEAD, MCCOY... THIS IS...
JEAN! MASTERMIND, PLEASE!
REALLY? MASTER OF ILLUSIONS, AND ALL YOU CAN COME UP WITH IS SNAKES?
UHN!
VMM!
MARVEL GIRL, WATCH OUT!!
AAH!
CHOOM!
EVERYONE, TAKE DOWN YOUR TARGETS AND CONCENTRATE ON MAGNETO!
WE CAN'T LET HIM REACH THE MISSILES!

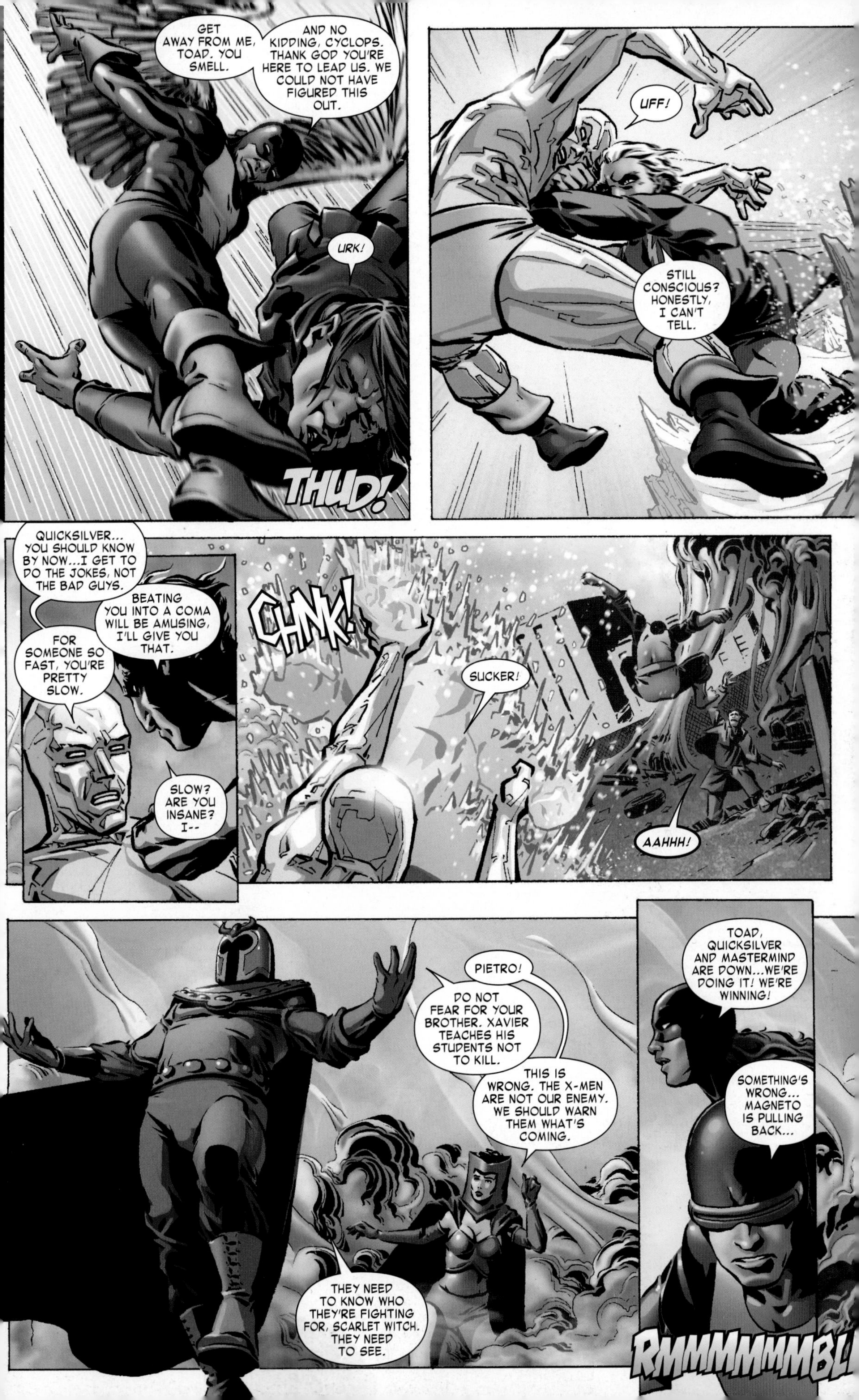
GET AWAY FROM ME, TOAD. YOU SMELL.
AND NO KIDDING, CYCLOPS. THANK GOD YOU'RE HERE TO LEAD US. WE COULD NOT HAVE FIGURED THIS OUT.
URK!
THUD!
UFF!
STILL CONSCIOUS? HONESTLY, I CAN'T TELL.
QUICKSILVER... YOU SHOULD KNOW BY NOW...I GET TO DO THE JOKES, NOT THE BAD GUYS.
BEATING YOU INTO A COMA WILL BE AMUSING, I'LL GIVE YOU THAT.
FOR SOMEONE SO FAST, YOU'RE PRETTY SLOW.
SLOW? ARE YOU INSANE? I--
CHNK!
SUCKER!
AAHHH!
PIETRO!
DO NOT FEAR FOR YOUR BROTHER. XAVIER TEACHES HIS STUDENTS NOT TO KILL.
THIS IS WRONG. THE X-MEN ARE NOT OUR ENEMY. WE SHOULD WARN THEM WHAT'S COMING.
THEY NEED TO KNOW WHO THEY'RE FIGHTING FOR, SCARLET WITCH. THEY NEED TO SEE.
TOAD, QUICKSILVER AND MASTERMIND ARE DOWN...WE'RE DOING IT! WE'RE WINNING!
SOMETHING'S WRONG... MAGNETO IS PULLING BACK...
RMMMMMMMBL

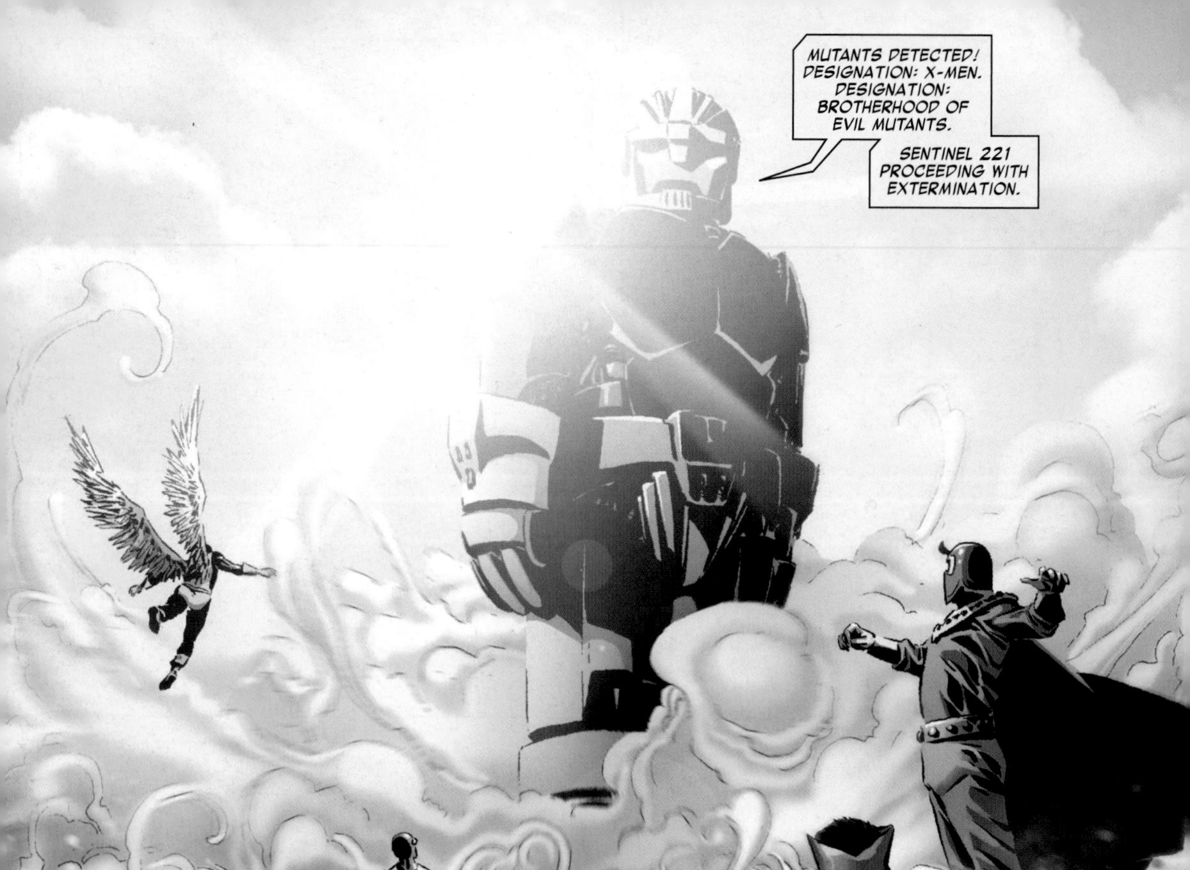
MUTANTS DETECTED! DESIGNATION: X-MEN. DESIGNATION: BROTHERHOOD OF EVIL MUTANTS.
SENTINEL 221 PROCEEDING WITH EXTERMINATION.

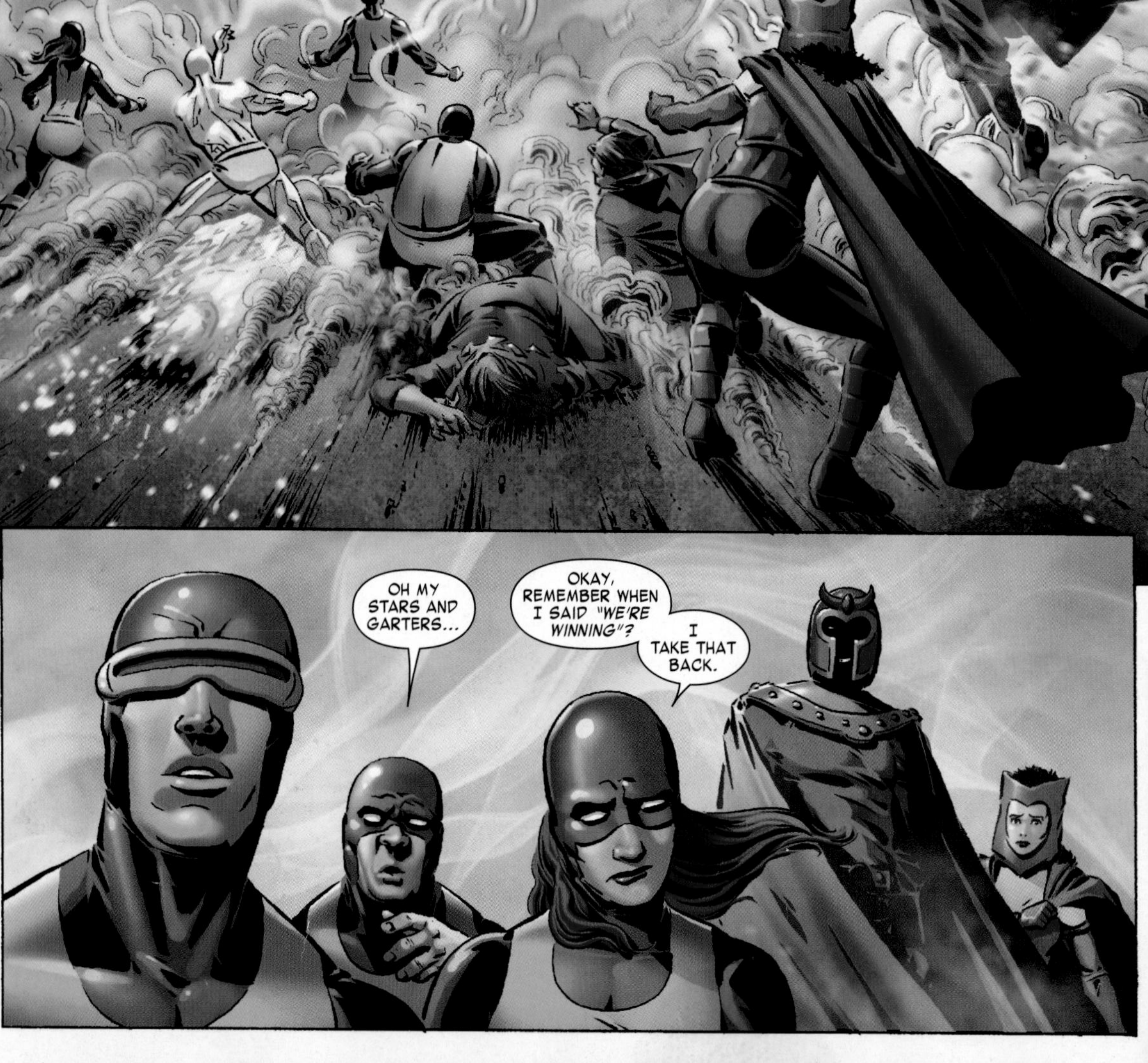
OH MY STARS AND GARTERS...
OKAY, REMEMBER WHEN I SAID "WE'RE WINNING"?
I TAKE THAT BACK.

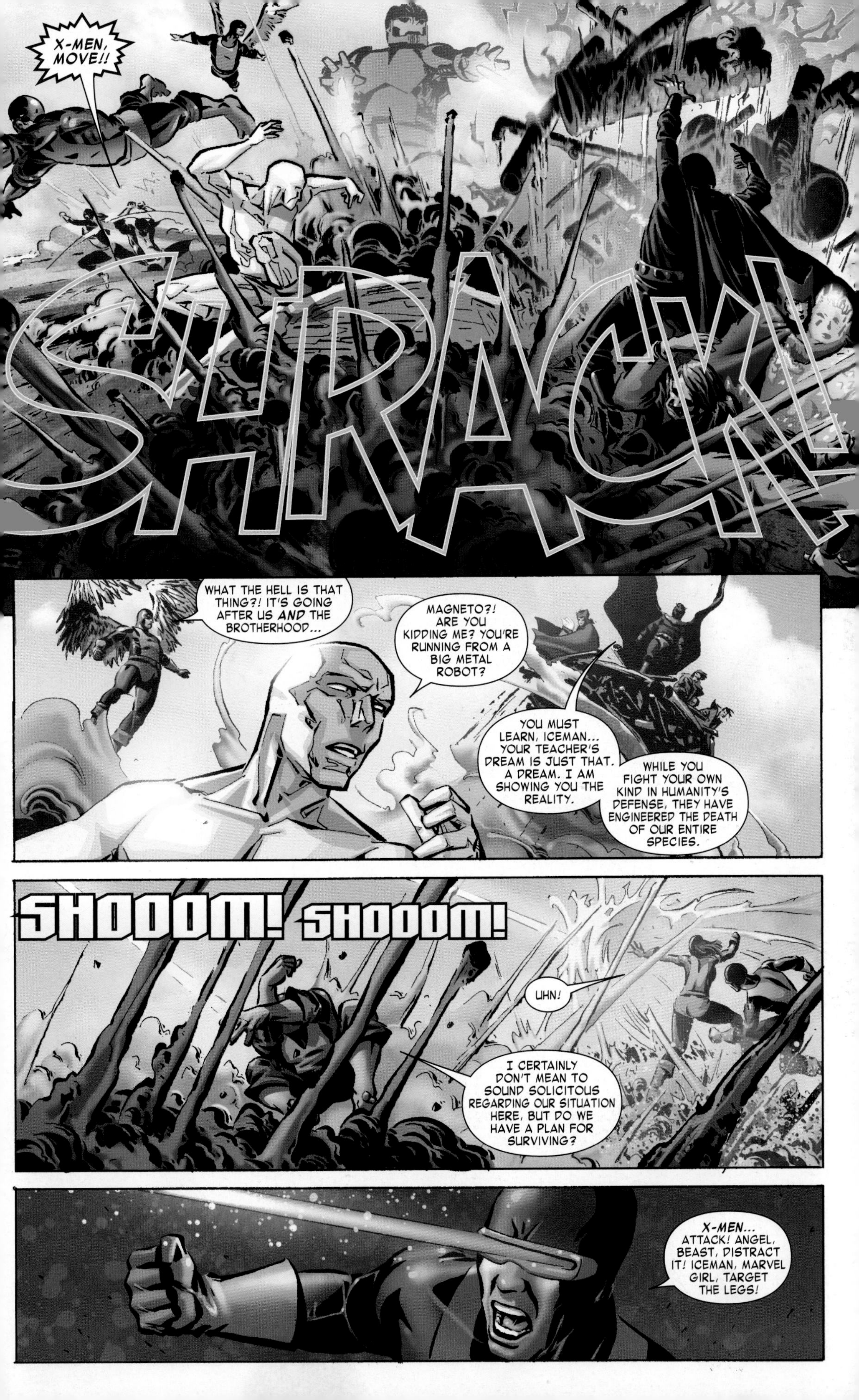
X-MEN, MOVE!!
SHRACK!
WHAT THE HELL IS THAT THING?! IT'S GOING AFTER US AND THE BROTHERHOOD...
MAGNETO?! ARE YOU KIDDING ME? YOU'RE RUNNING FROM A BIG METAL ROBOT?
YOU MUST LEARN, ICEMAN... YOUR TEACHER'S DREAM IS JUST THAT. A DREAM. I AM SHOWING YOU THE REALITY.
WHILE YOU FIGHT YOUR OWN KIND IN HUMANITY'S DEFENSE, THEY HAVE ENGINEERED THE DEATH OF OUR ENTIRE SPECIES.
SHOOOM! SHOOOM!
UHN!
I CERTAINLY DON'T MEAN TO SOUND SOLICITOUS REGARDING OUR SITUATION HERE, BUT DO WE HAVE A PLAN FOR SURVIVING?
X-MEN... ATTACK! ANGEL, BEAST, DISTRACT IT! ICEMAN, MARVEL GIRL, TARGET THE LEGS!

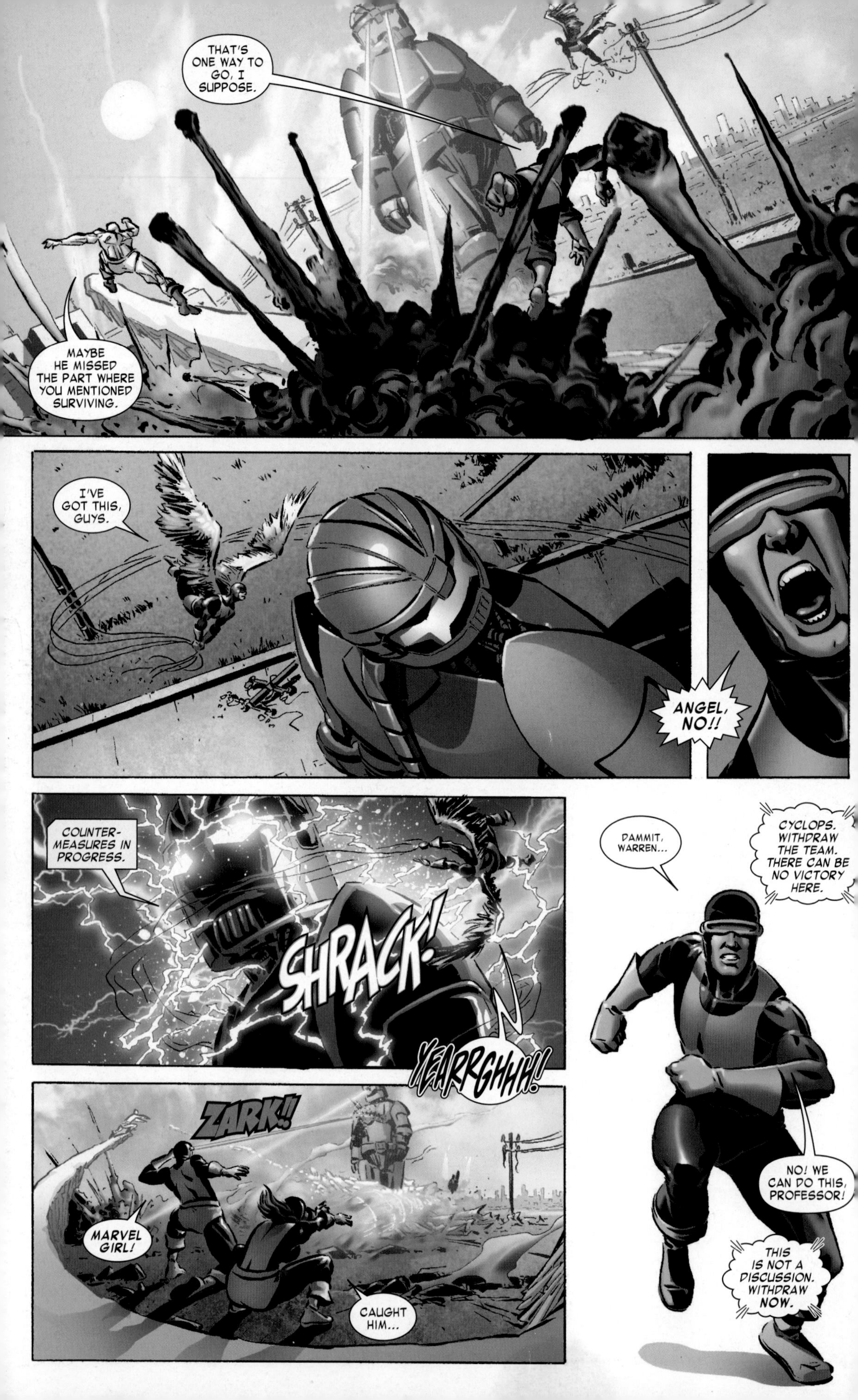

THAT'S ONE WAY TO GO, I SUPPOSE.
MAYBE HE MISSED THE PART WHERE YOU MENTIONED SURVIVING.
I'VE GOT THIS, GUYS.
ANGEL, NO!!
COUNTER-MEASURES IN PROGRESS.
SHRACK!
YEARRGHHH!
ZARK!!
MARVEL GIRL!
CAUGHT HIM...
DAMMIT, WARREN...
CYCLOPS. WITHDRAW THE TEAM. THERE CAN BE NO VICTORY HERE.
NO! WE CAN DO THIS, PROFESSOR!
THIS IS NOT A DISCUSSION. WITHDRAW NOW.

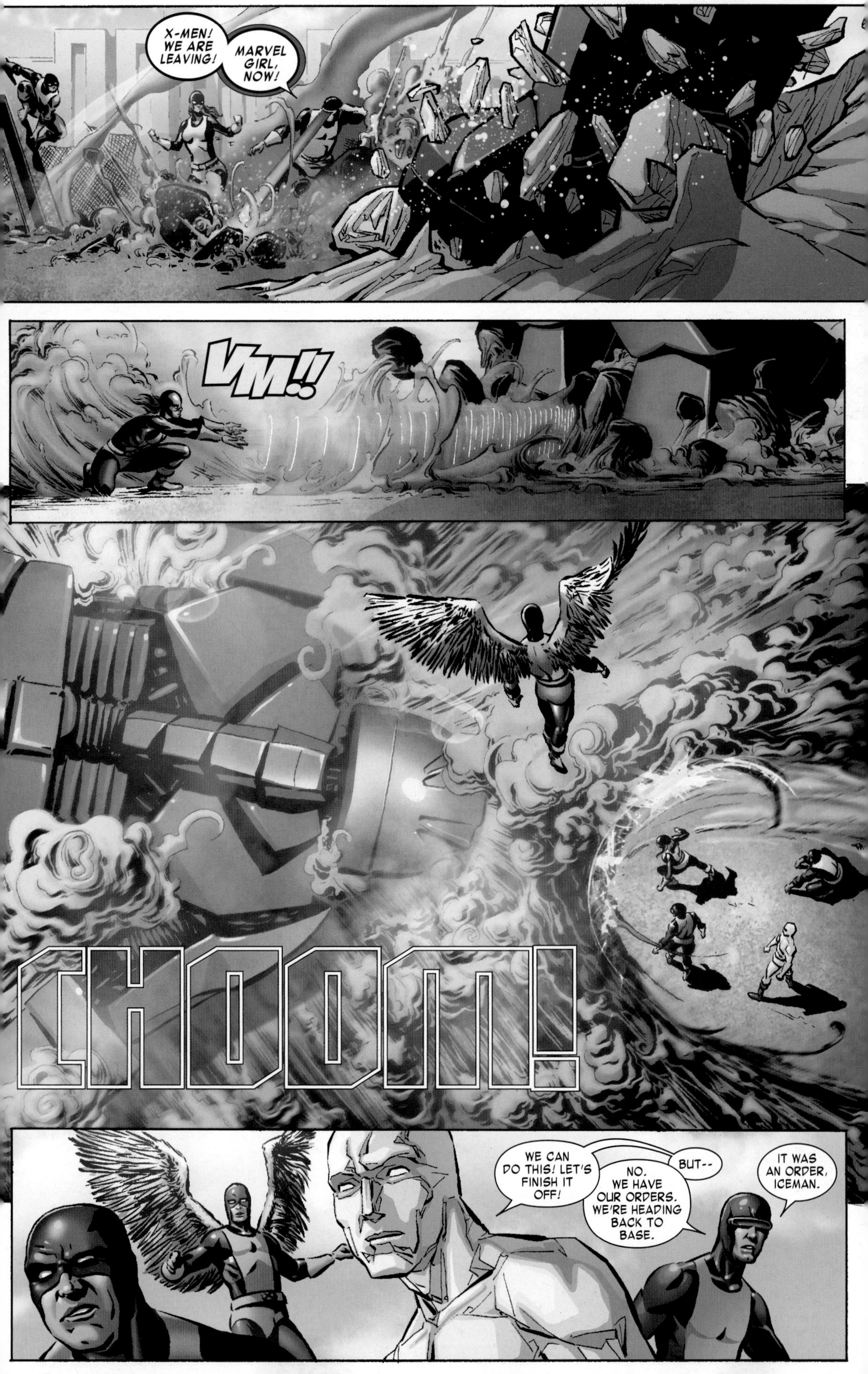
X-MEN! WE ARE LEAVING!
MARVEL GIRL, NOW!
VM!!
CHOOM!
WE CAN DO THIS! LET'S FINISH IT OFF!
BUT--
NO. WE HAVE OUR ORDERS. WE'RE HEADING BACK TO BASE.
IT WAS AN ORDER, ICEMAN.

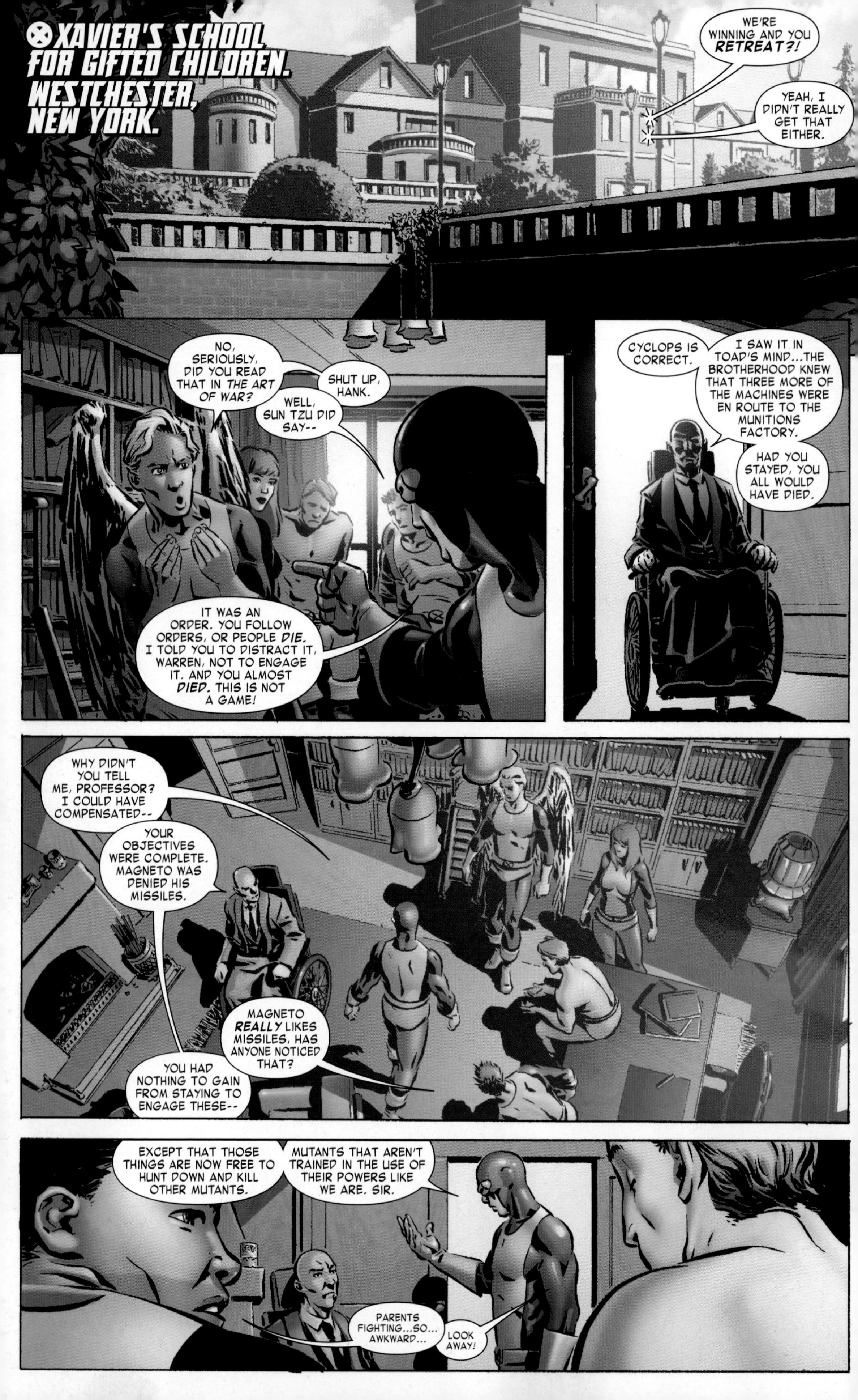
XAVIER'S SCHOOL FOR GIFTED CHILDREN. WESTCHESTER, NEW YORK.
WE'RE WINNING AND YOU RETREAT?!
YEAH, I DIDN'T REALLY GET THAT EITHER.
NO, SERIOUSLY, DID YOU READ THAT IN THE ART OF WAR?
WELL, SUN TZU DID SAY--
SHUT UP, HANK.
IT WAS AN ORDER. YOU FOLLOW ORDERS, OR PEOPLE DIE. I TOLD YOU TO DISTRACT IT, WARREN, NOT TO ENGAGE IT. AND YOU ALMOST DIED. THIS IS NOT A GAME!
CYCLOPS IS CORRECT.
I SAW IT IN TOAD'S MIND...THE BROTHERHOOD KNEW THAT THREE MORE OF THE MACHINES WERE EN ROUTE TO THE MUNITIONS FACTORY.
HAD YOU STAYED, YOU ALL WOULD HAVE DIED.
WHY DIDN'T YOU TELL ME, PROFESSOR? I COULD HAVE COMPENSATED--
YOUR OBJECTIVES WERE COMPLETE. MAGNETO WAS DENIED HIS MISSILES.
YOU HAD NOTHING TO GAIN FROM STAYING TO ENGAGE THESE--
MAGNETO REALLY LIKES MISSILES, HAS ANYONE NOTICED THAT?
EXCEPT THAT THOSE THINGS ARE NOW FREE TO HUNT DOWN AND KILL OTHER MUTANTS.
MUTANTS THAT AREN'T TRAINED IN THE USE OF THEIR POWERS LIKE WE ARE. SIR.
PARENTS FIGHTING...SO... AWKWARD...
LOOK AWAY!

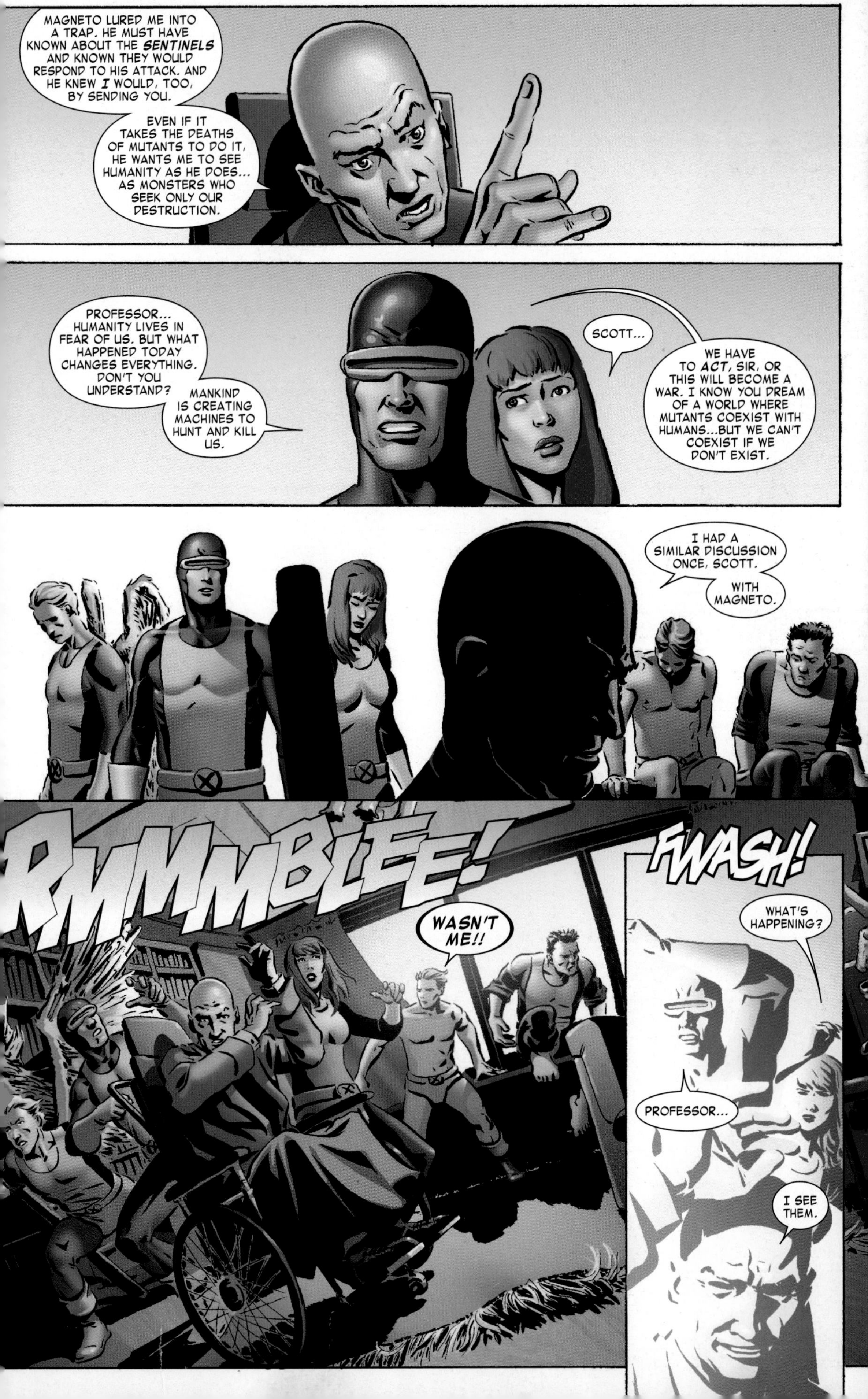
MAGNETO LURED ME INTO A TRAP. HE MUST HAVE KNOWN ABOUT THE SENTINELS AND KNOWN THEY WOULD RESPOND TO HIS ATTACK. AND HE KNEW I WOULD, TOO, BY SENDING YOU.
EVEN IF IT TAKES THE DEATHS OF MUTANTS TO DO IT, HE WANTS ME TO SEE HUMANITY AS HE DOES... AS MONSTERS WHO SEEK ONLY OUR DESTRUCTION.
PROFESSOR... HUMANITY LIVES IN FEAR OF US. BUT WHAT HAPPENED TODAY CHANGES EVERYTHING. DON'T YOU UNDERSTAND?
MANKIND IS CREATING MACHINES TO HUNT AND KILL US.
SCOTT...
WE HAVE TO ACT, SIR, OR THIS WILL BECOME A WAR. I KNOW YOU DREAM OF A WORLD WHERE MUTANTS COEXIST WITH HUMANS...BUT WE CAN'T COEXIST IF WE DON'T EXIST.
I HAD A SIMILAR DISCUSSION ONCE, SCOTT.
WITH MAGNETO.
RMMMBLEE!
WASN'T ME!!
FWASH!
WHAT'S HAPPENING?
PROFESSOR...
I SEE THEM.

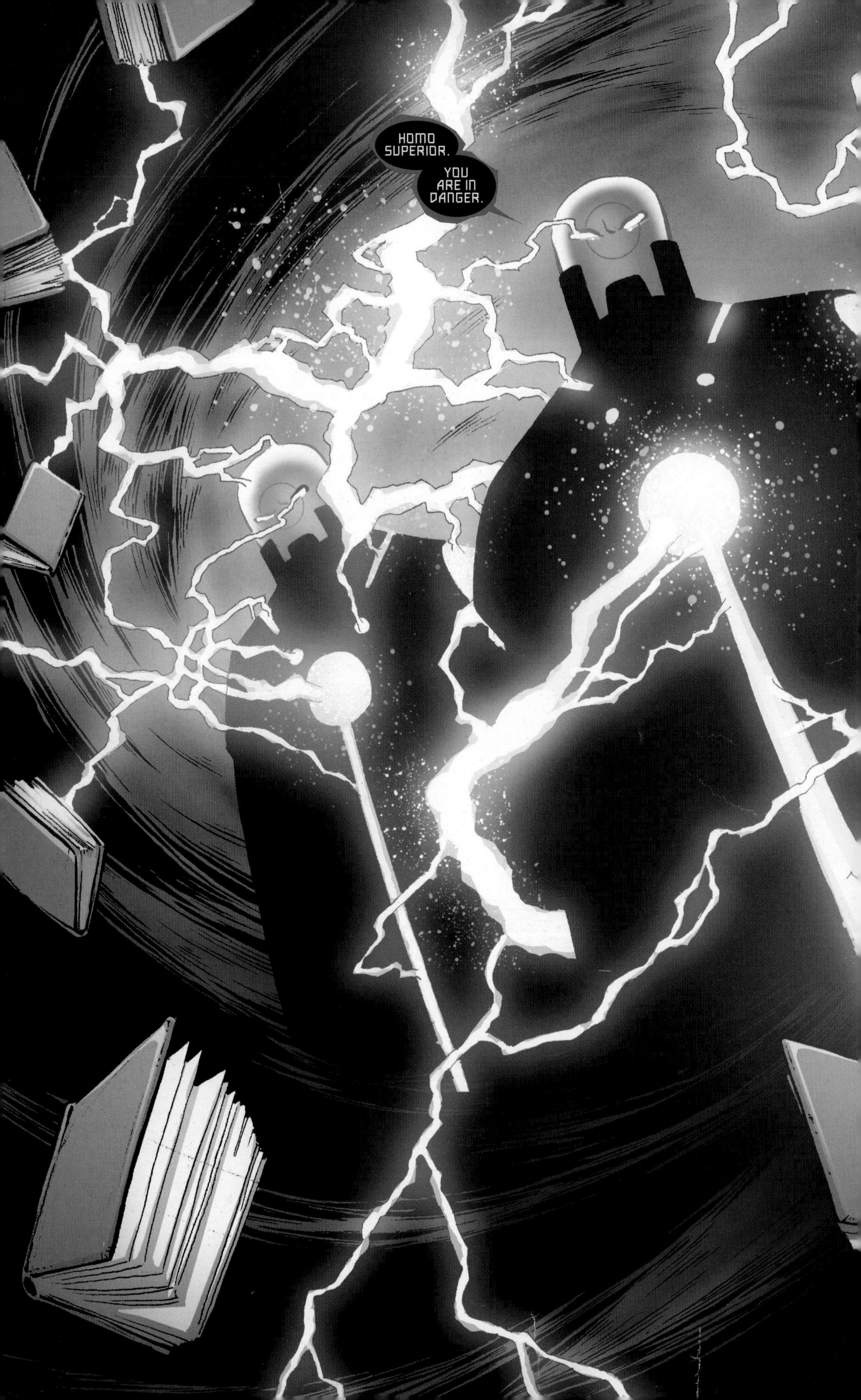
HOMO SUPERIOR.
YOU ARE IN DANGER.

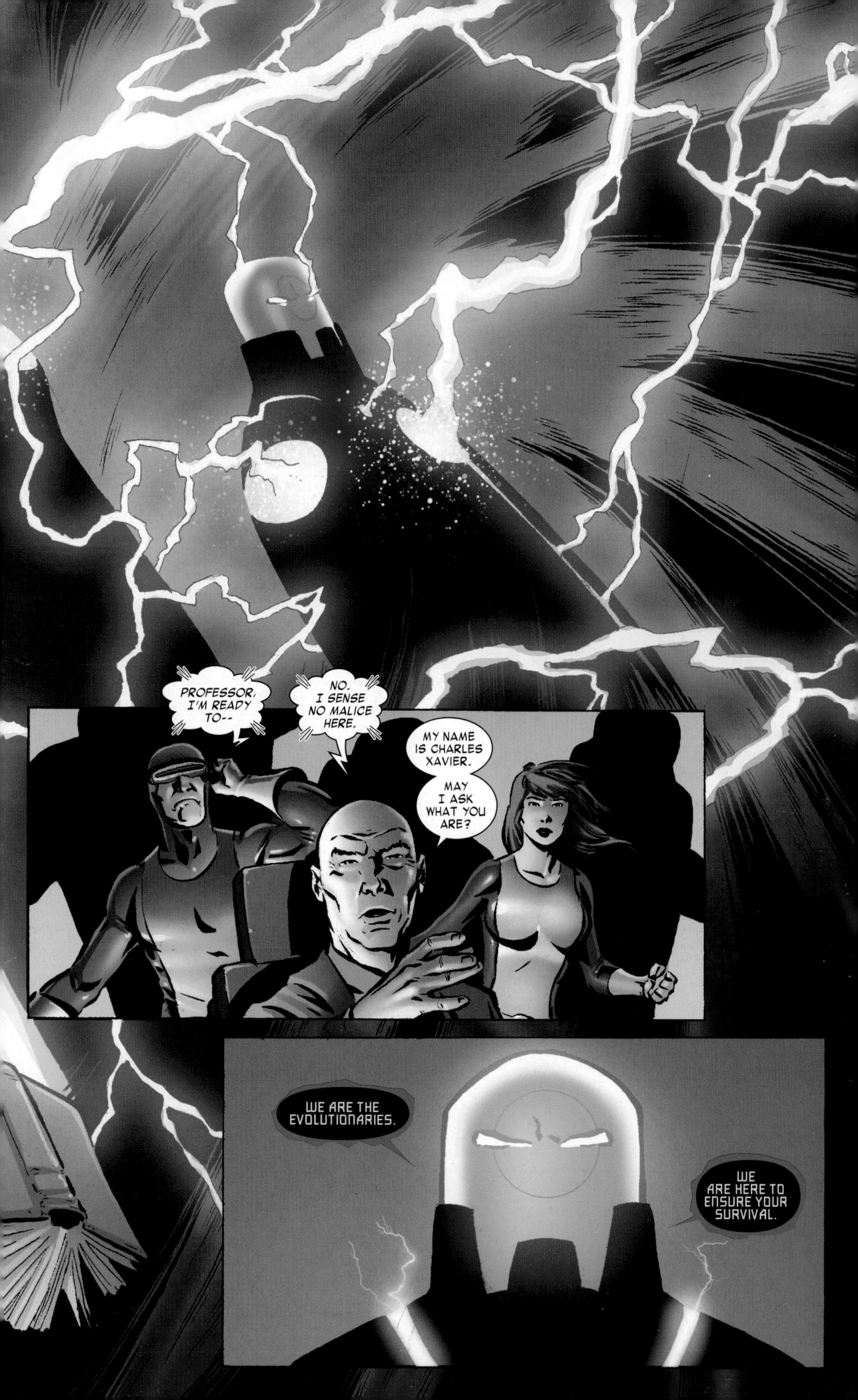
PROFESSOR, I'M READY TO--
NO. I SENSE NO MALICE HERE.
MY NAME IS CHARLES XAVIER.
MAY I ASK WHAT YOU ARE?
WE ARE THE EVOLUTIONARIES.
WE ARE HERE TO ENSURE YOUR SURVIVAL.

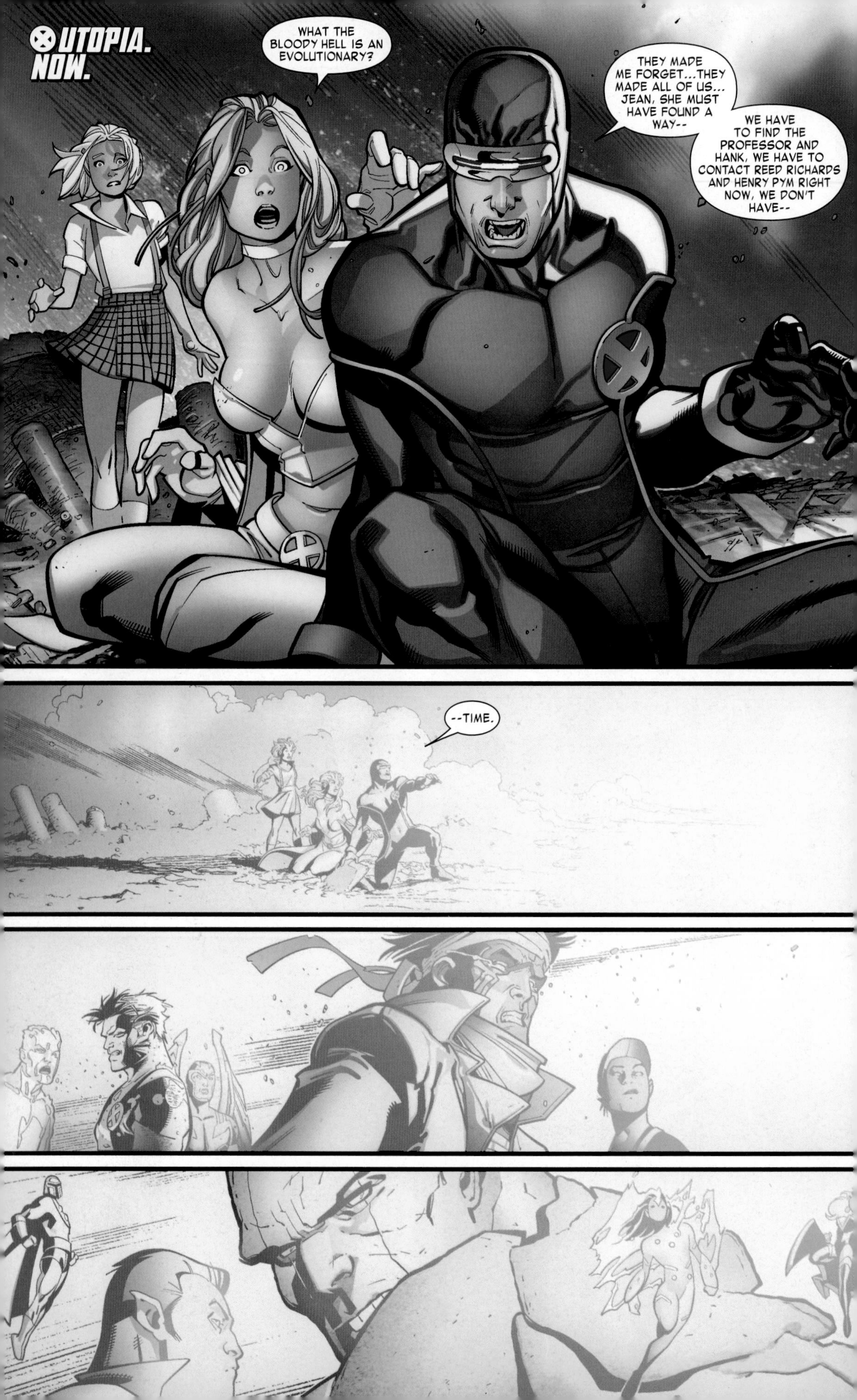
UTOPIA. NOW.
WHAT THE BLOODY HELL IS AN EVOLUTIONARY?
THEY MADE ME FORGET...THEY MADE ALL OF US... JEAN, SHE MUST HAVE FOUND A WAY--
WE HAVE TO FIND THE PROFESSOR AND HANK, WE HAVE TO CONTACT REED RICHARDS AND HENRY PYM RIGHT NOW, WE DON'T HAVE--
--TIME.

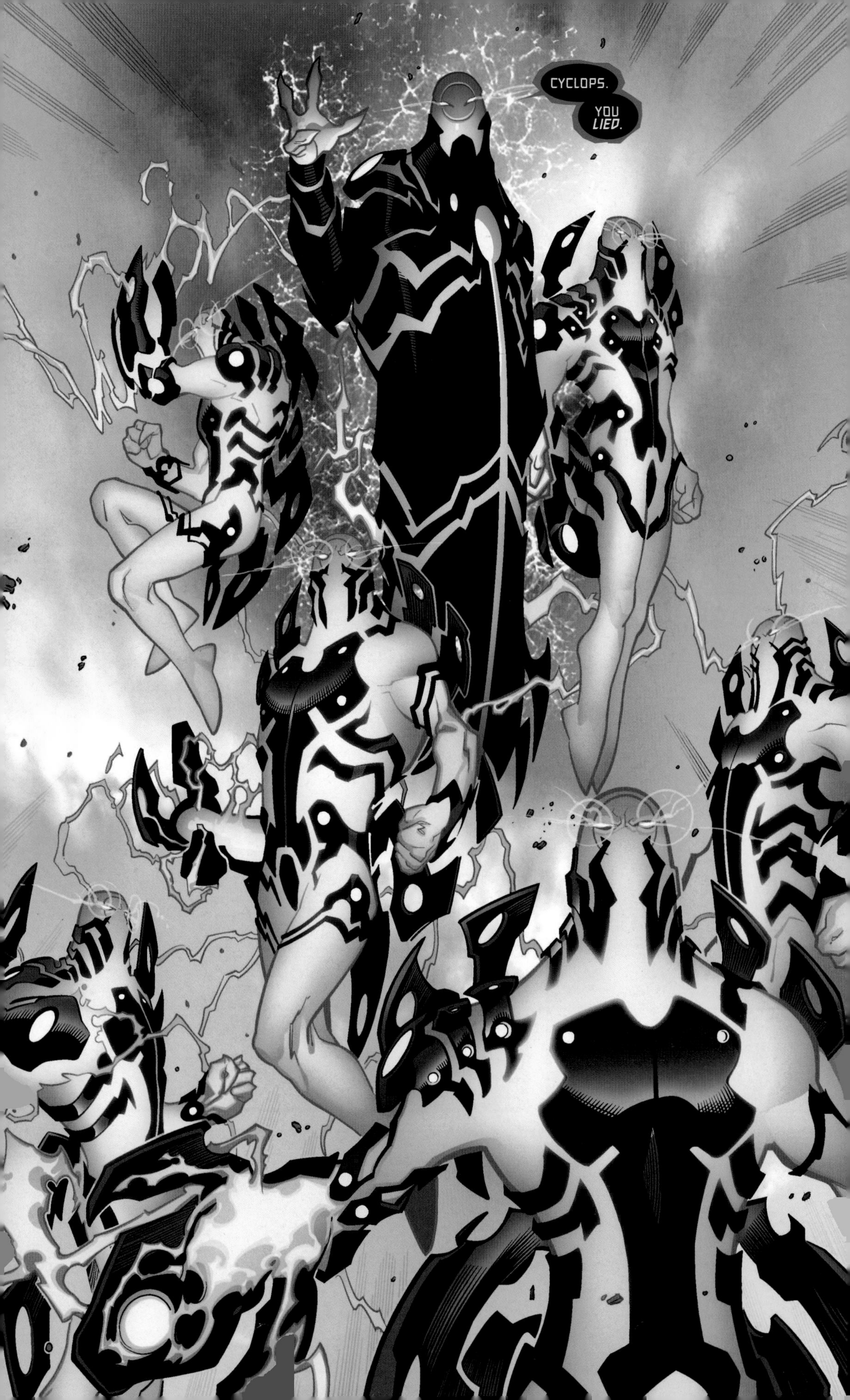
CYCLOPS.
YOU LIED.

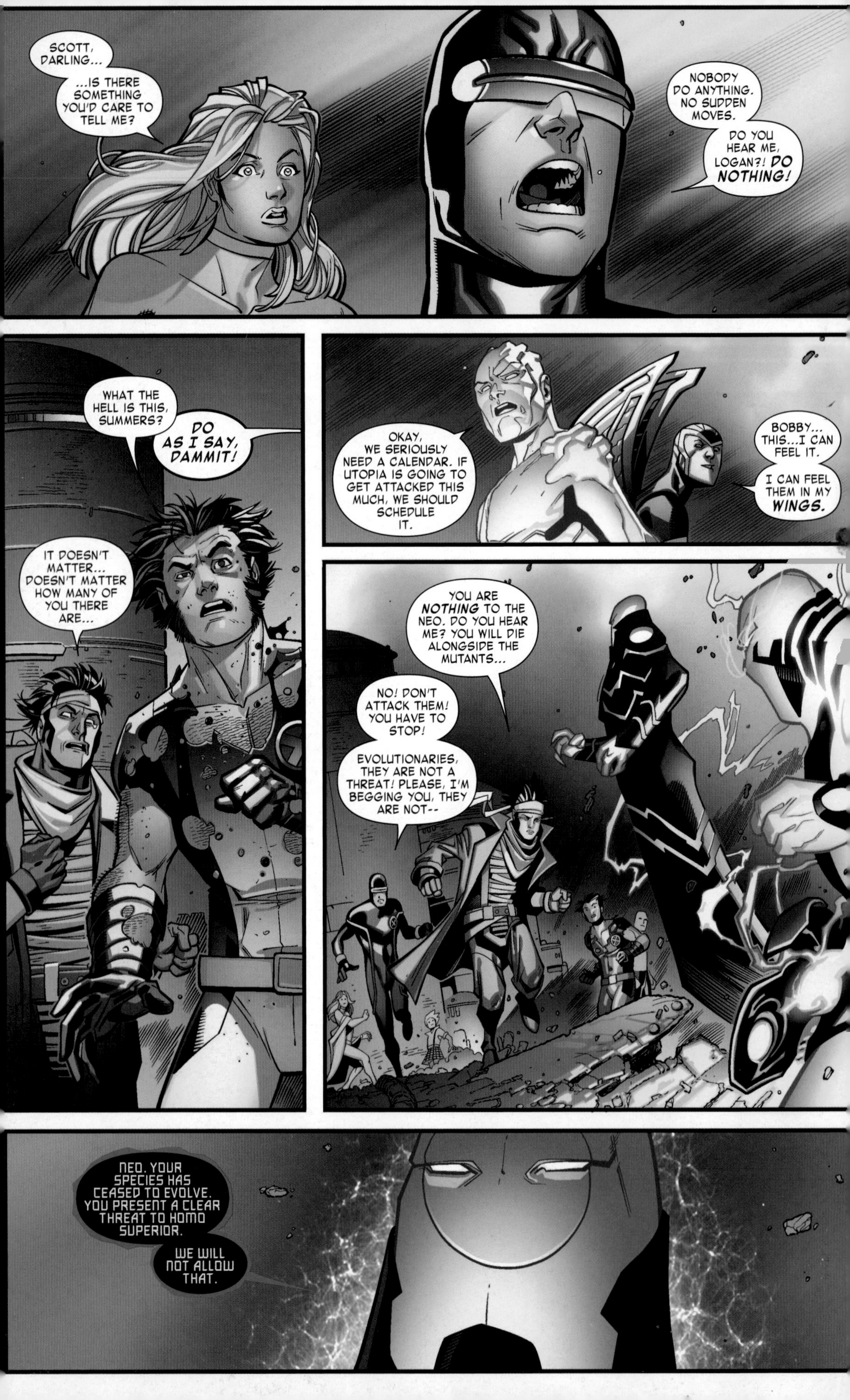
SCOTT, DARLING...
...IS THERE SOMETHING YOU'D CARE TO TELL ME?
NOBODY DO ANYTHING. NO SUDDEN MOVES.
DO YOU HEAR ME, LOGAN?! DO NOTHING!
WHAT THE HELL IS THIS, SUMMERS?
DO AS I SAY, DAMMIT!
IT DOESN'T MATTER... DOESN'T MATTER HOW MANY OF YOU THERE ARE...
OKAY, WE SERIOUSLY NEED A CALENDAR. IF UTOPIA IS GOING TO GET ATTACKED THIS MUCH, WE SHOULD SCHEDULE IT.
BOBBY... THIS...I CAN FEEL IT.
I CAN FEEL THEM IN MY WINGS.
YOU ARE NOTHING TO THE NEO. DO YOU HEAR ME? YOU WILL DIE ALONGSIDE THE MUTANTS...
NO! DON'T ATTACK THEM! YOU HAVE TO STOP!
EVOLUTIONARIES, THEY ARE NOT A THREAT! PLEASE, I'M BEGGING YOU, THEY ARE NOT--
NEO. YOUR SPECIES HAS CEASED TO EVOLVE. YOU PRESENT A CLEAR THREAT TO HOMO SUPERIOR.
WE WILL NOT ALLOW THAT.

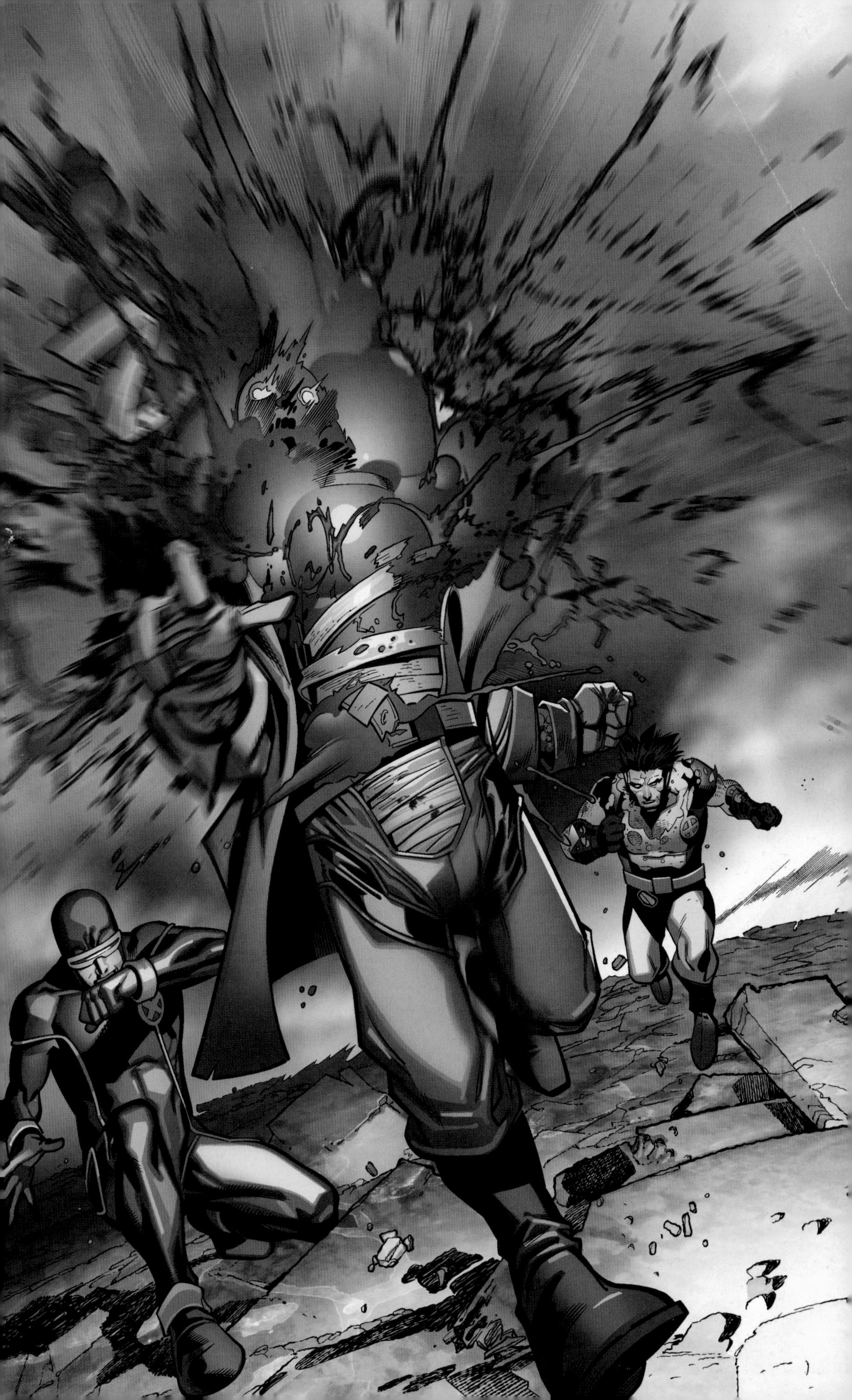

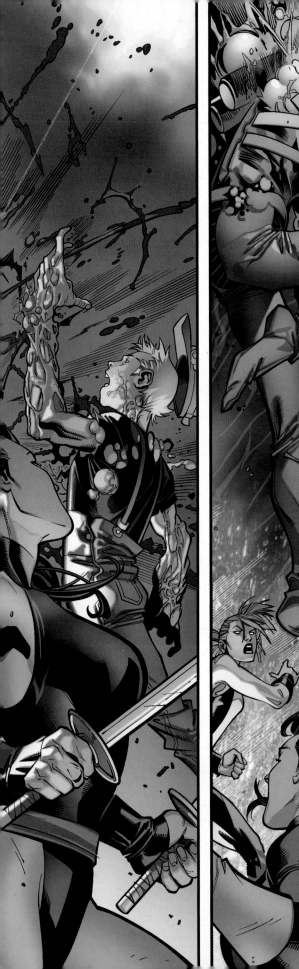

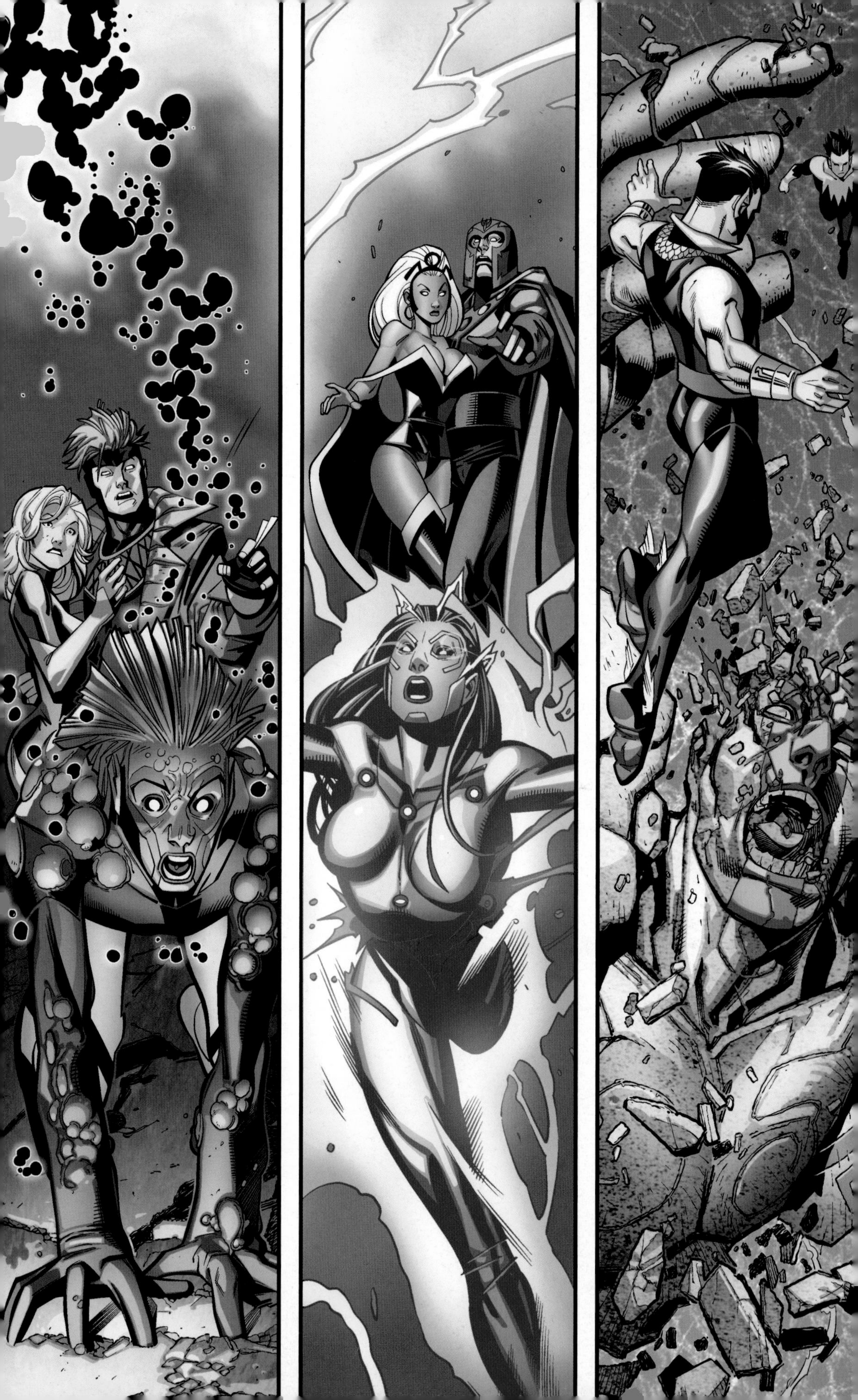

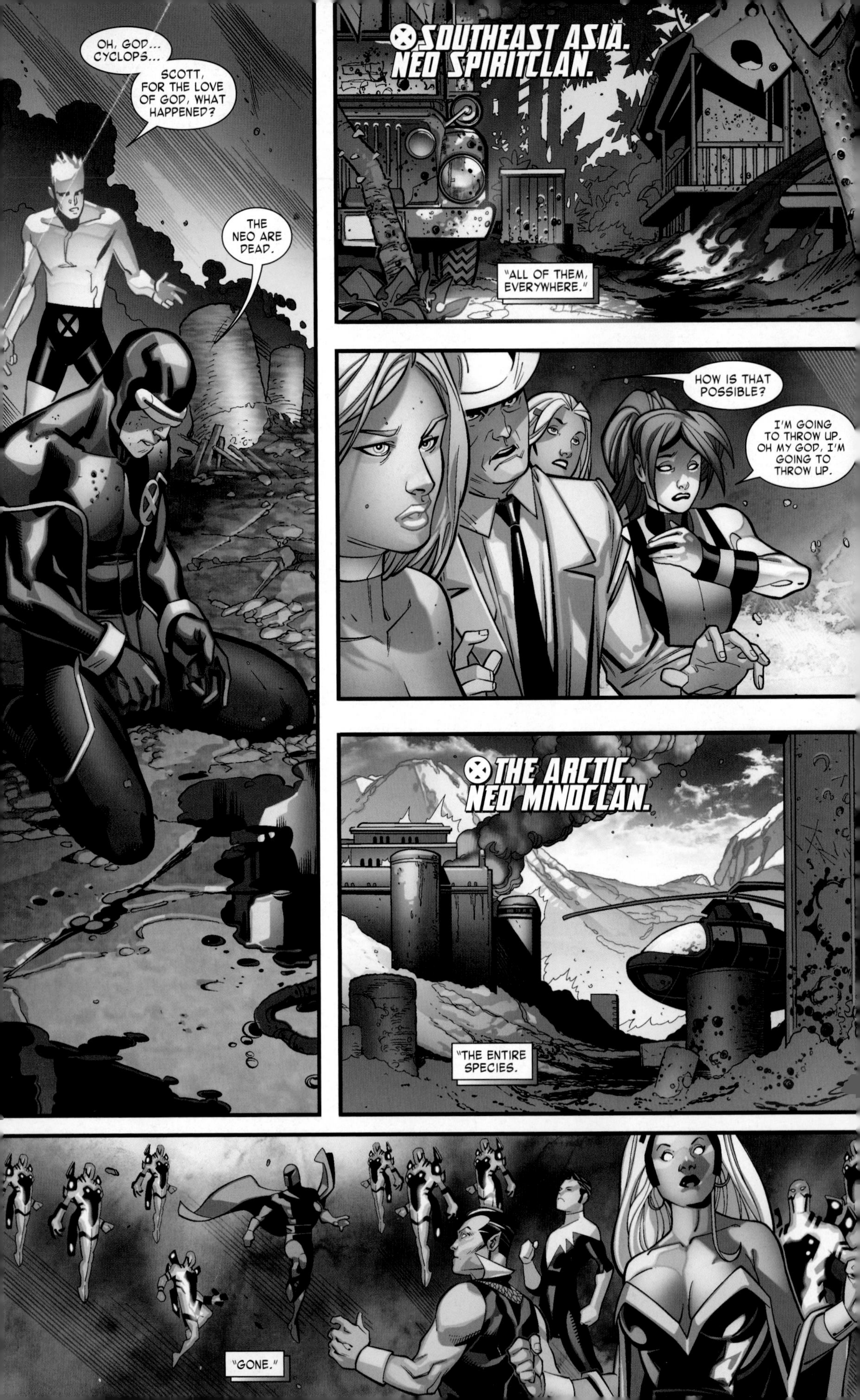
OH, GOD... CYCLOPS...
SCOTT, FOR THE LOVE OF GOD, WHAT HAPPENED?
THE NEO ARE DEAD.
SOUTHEAST ASIA. NEO SPIRITCLAN.
"ALL OF THEM, EVERYWHERE."
HOW IS THAT POSSIBLE?
I'M GOING TO THROW UP. OH MY GOD, I'M GOING TO THROW UP.
THE ARCTIC. NEO MINDCLAN.
"THE ENTIRE SPECIES.
"GONE."

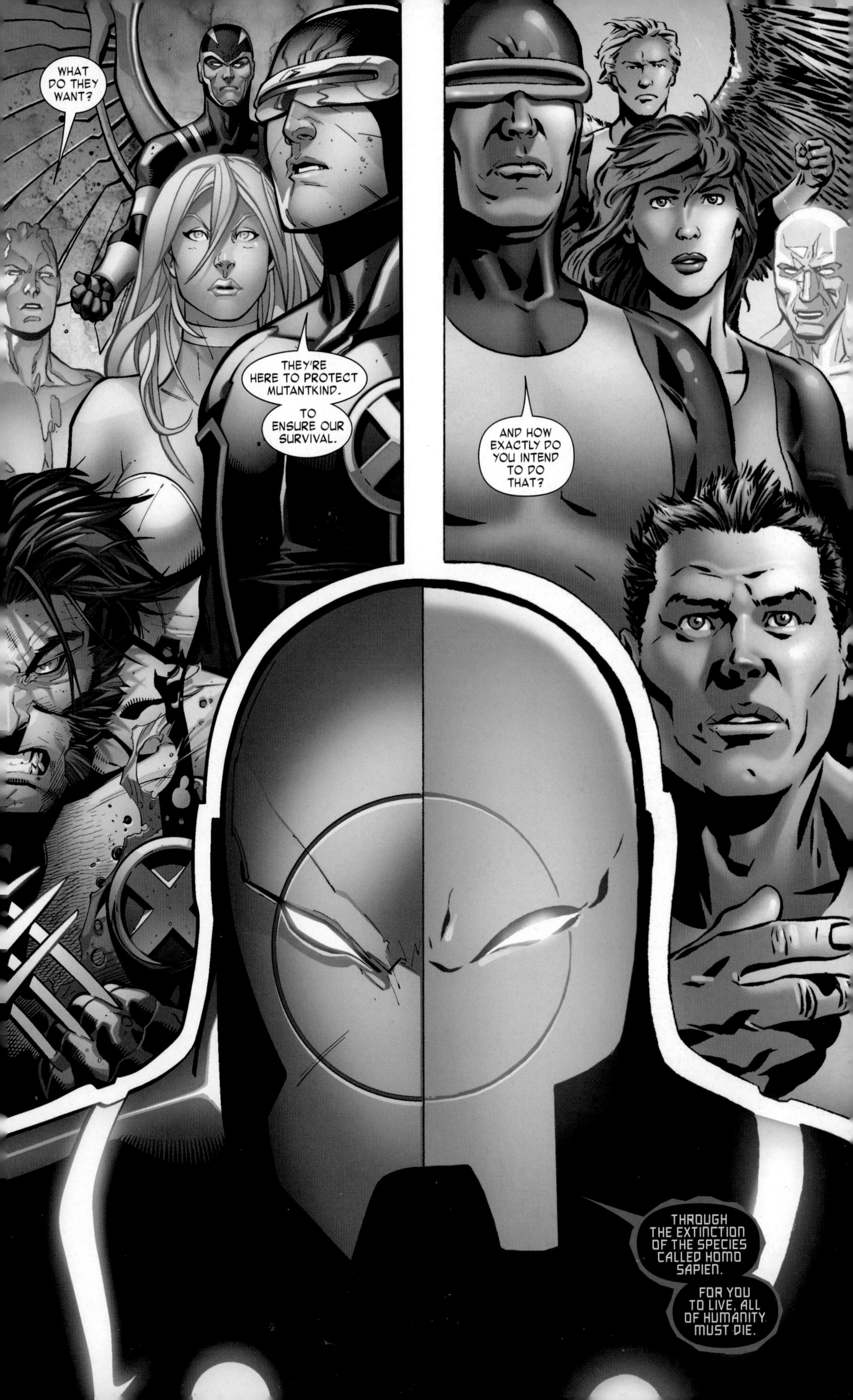
WHAT DO THEY WANT?
THEY'RE HERE TO PROTECT MUTANTKIND.
TO ENSURE OUR SURVIVAL.
AND HOW EXACTLY DO YOU INTEND TO DO THAT?
THROUGH THE EXTINCTION OF THE SPECIES CALLED HOMO SAPIEN.
FOR YOU TO LIVE, ALL OF HUMANITY MUST DIE.

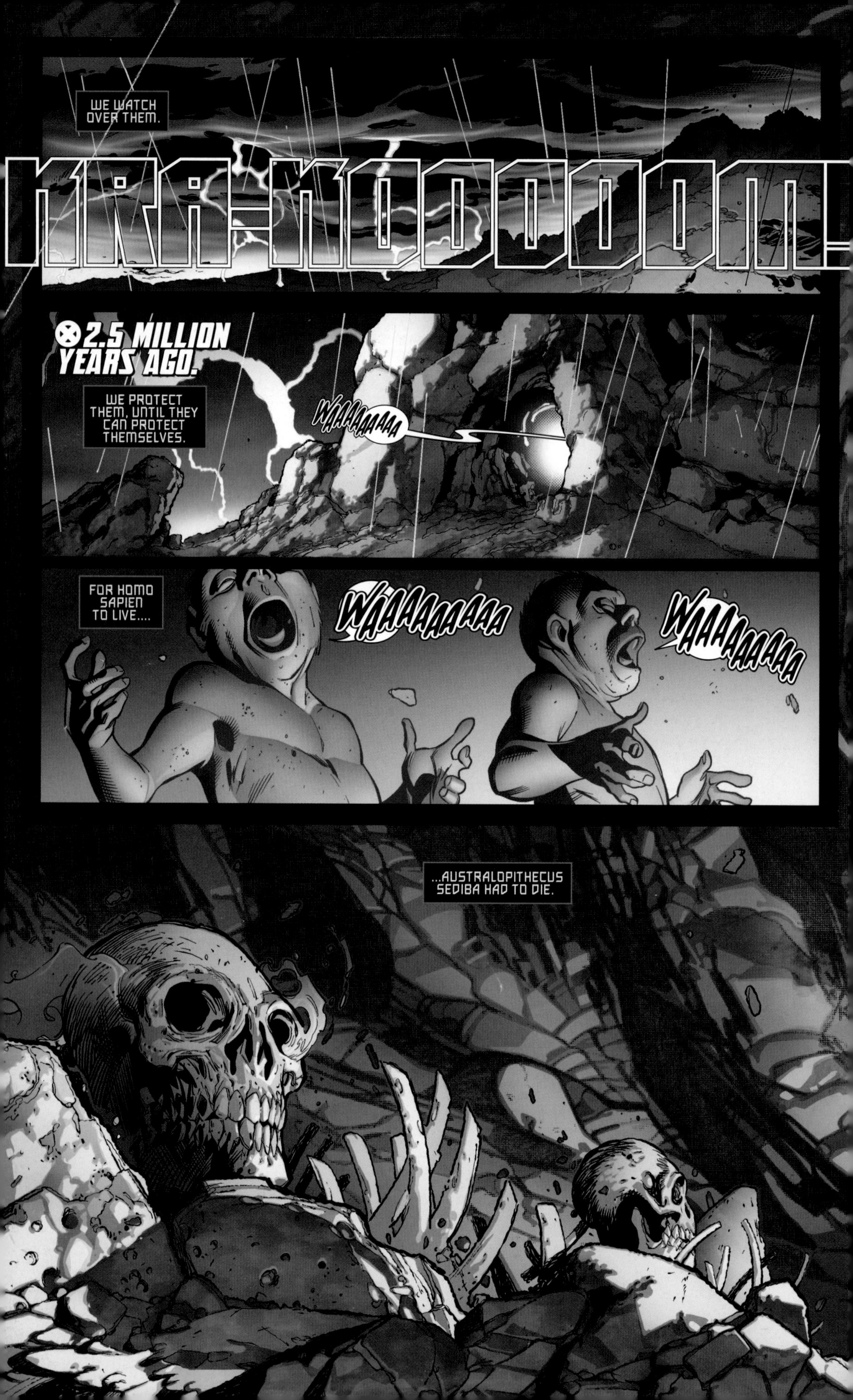
WE WATCH OVER THEM.
KRA-KOOOOOM!
2.5 MILLION YEARS AGO.
WE PROTECT THEM, UNTIL THEY CAN PROTECT THEMSELVES.
WAAAAAAAA
FOR HOMO SAPIEN TO LIVE....
WAAAAAAAAA
WAAAAAAAAA
...AUSTRALOPITHECUS SEDIBA HAD TO DIE.

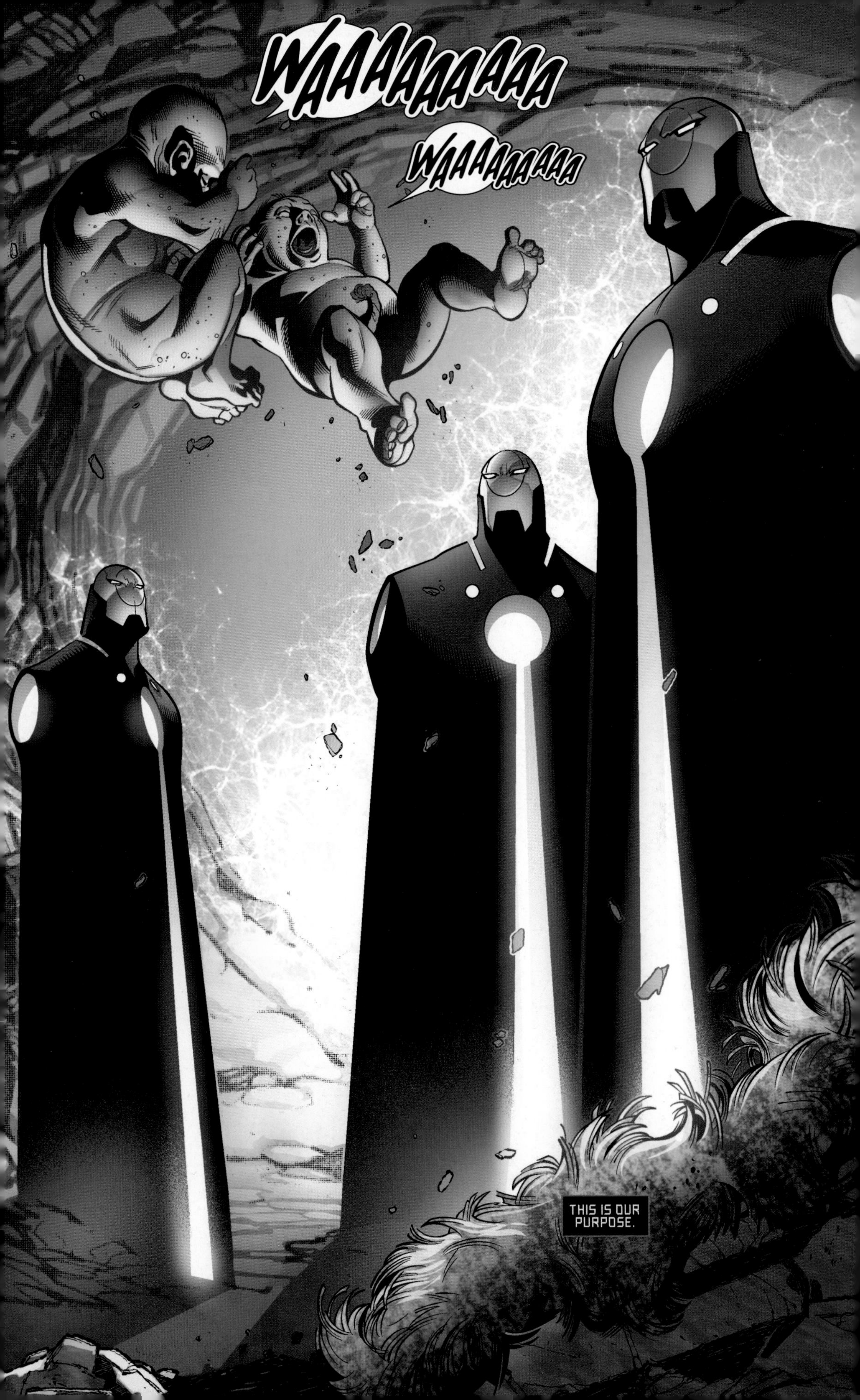
WAAAAAAAAA
WAAAAAAAAA
THIS IS OUR PURPOSE.

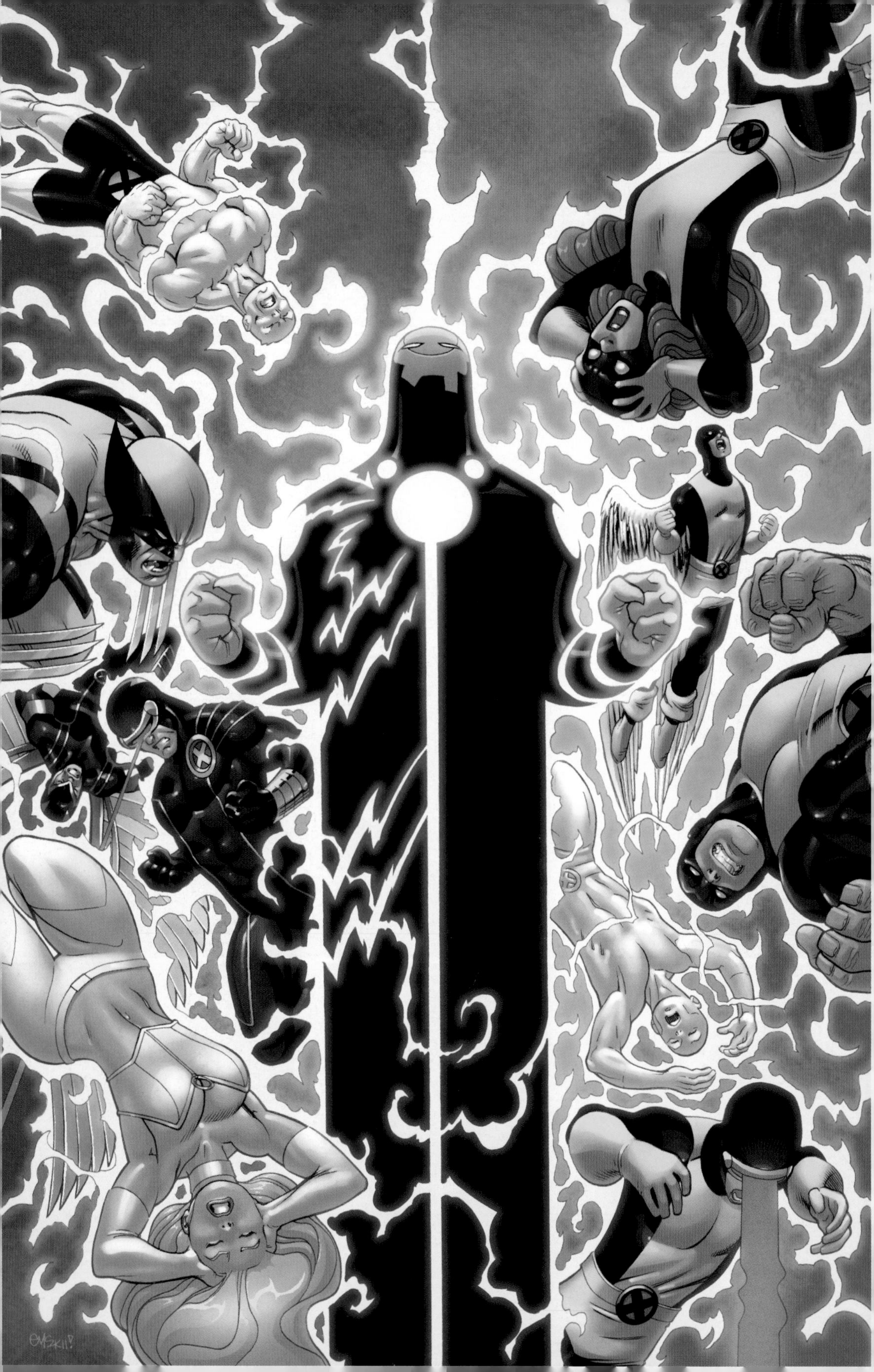

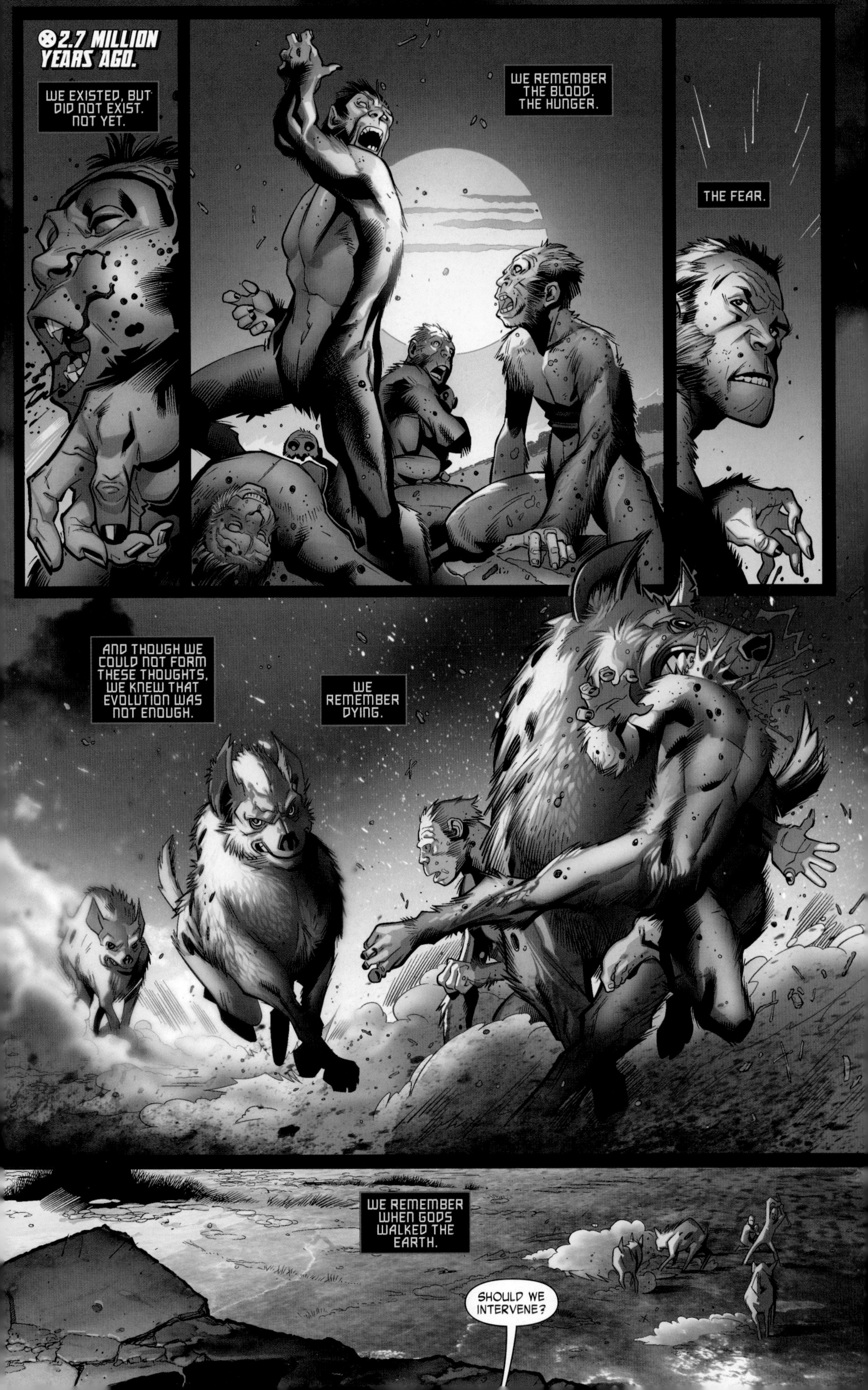
2.7 MILLION YEARS AGO.
WE EXISTED, BUT DID NOT EXIST. NOT YET.
WE REMEMBER THE BLOOD. THE HUNGER.
THE FEAR.
AND THOUGH WE COULD NOT FORM THESE THOUGHTS, WE KNEW THAT EVOLUTION WAS NOT ENOUGH.
WE REMEMBER DYING.
WE REMEMBER WHEN GODS WALKED THE EARTH.
SHOULD WE INTERVENE?

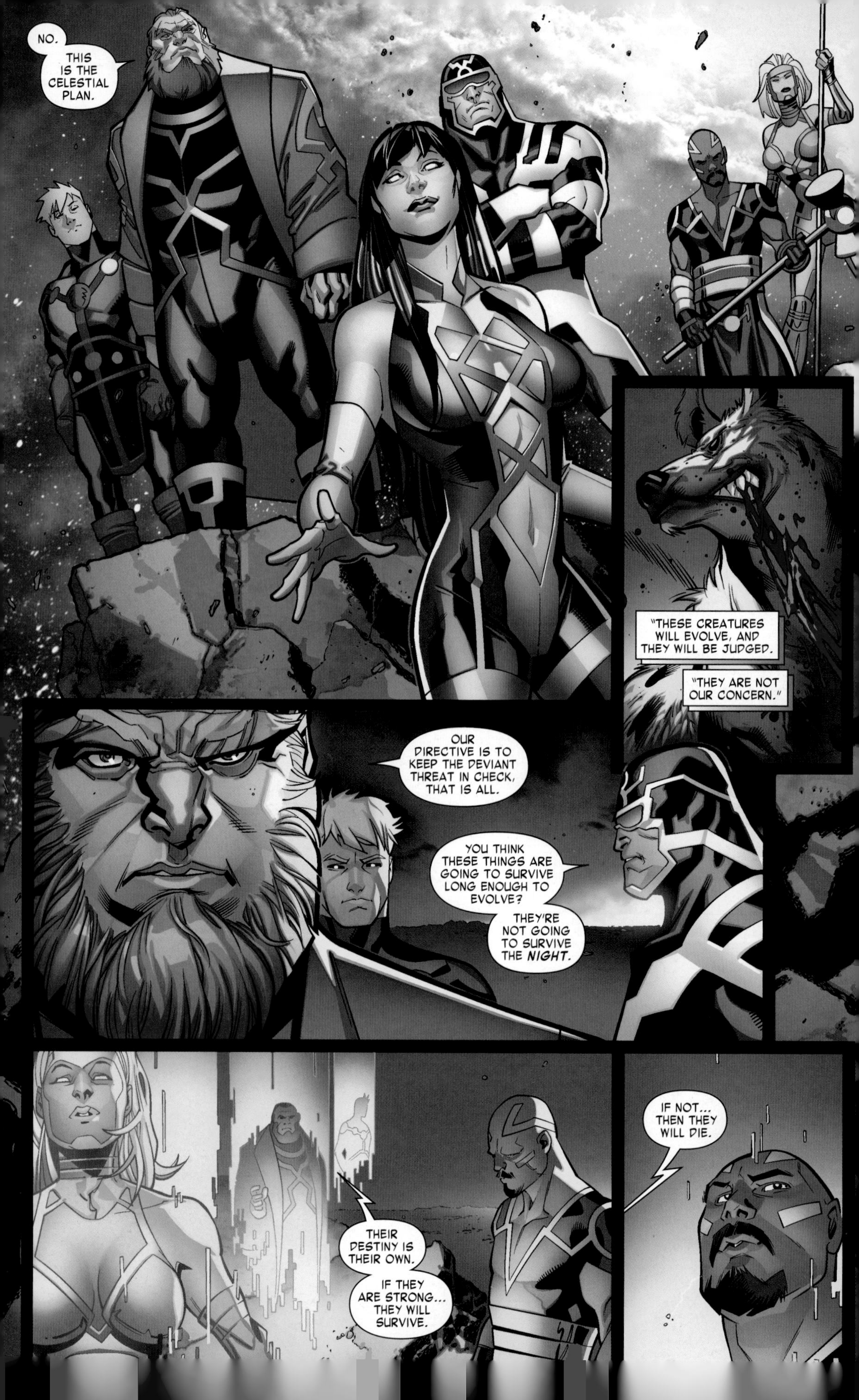
NO.
THIS IS THE CELESTIAL PLAN.
"THESE CREATURES WILL EVOLVE, AND THEY WILL BE JUDGED.
"THEY ARE NOT OUR CONCERN."
OUR DIRECTIVE IS TO KEEP THE DEVIANT THREAT IN CHECK, THAT IS ALL.
YOU THINK THESE THINGS ARE GOING TO SURVIVE LONG ENOUGH TO EVOLVE?
THEY'RE NOT GOING TO SURVIVE THE NIGHT.
THEIR DESTINY IS THEIR OWN.
IF THEY ARE STRONG... THEY WILL SURVIVE.
IF NOT... THEN THEY WILL DIE.

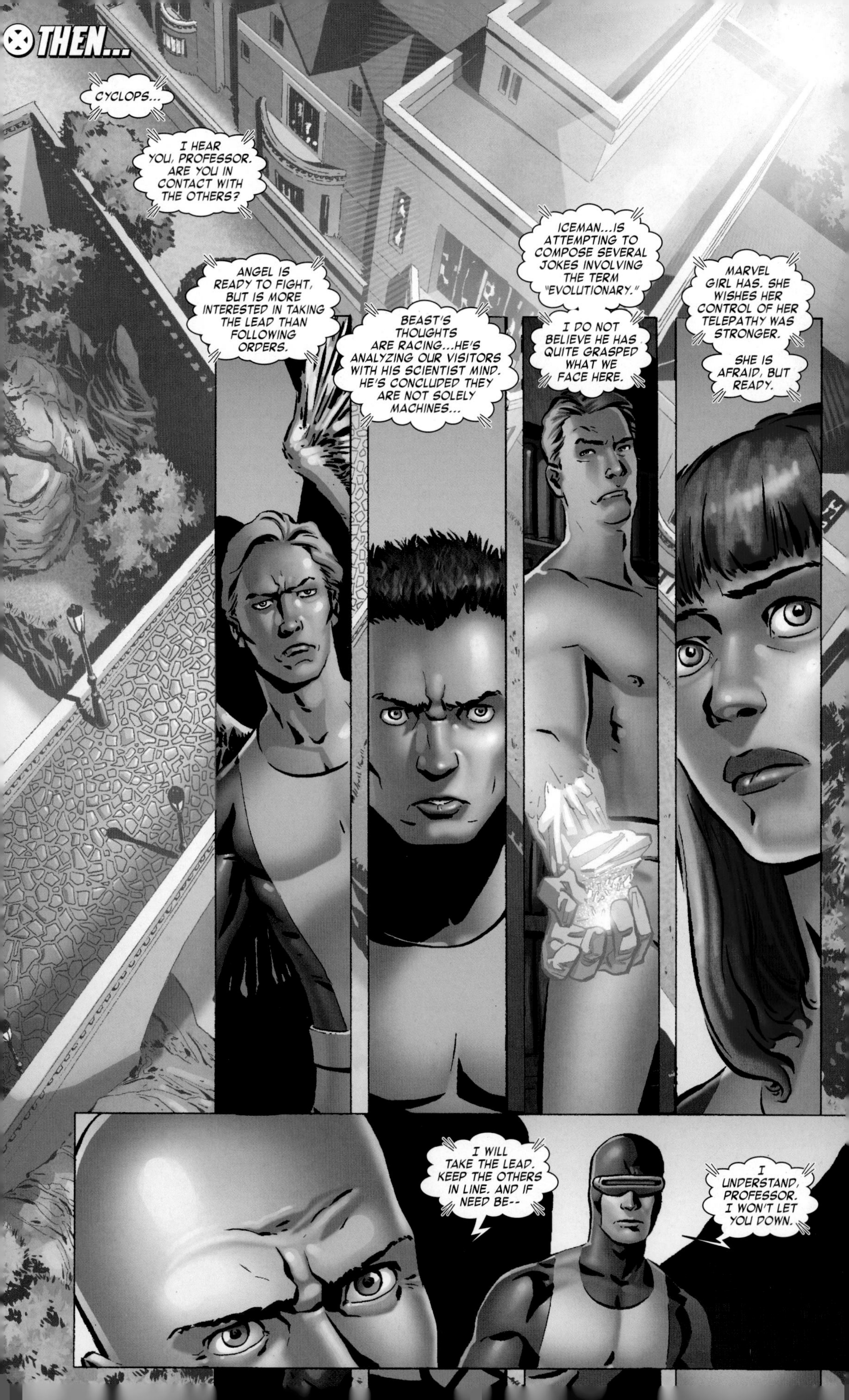
THEN...
CYCLOPS...
I HEAR YOU, PROFESSOR. ARE YOU IN CONTACT WITH THE OTHERS?
ANGEL IS READY TO FIGHT, BUT IS MORE INTERESTED IN TAKING THE LEAD THAN FOLLOWING ORDERS.
BEAST'S THOUGHTS ARE RACING...HE'S ANALYZING OUR VISITORS WITH HIS SCIENTIST MIND. HE'S CONCLUDED THEY ARE NOT SOLELY MACHINES...
ICEMAN...IS ATTEMPTING TO COMPOSE SEVERAL JOKES INVOLVING THE TERM "EVOLUTIONARY."
I DO NOT BELIEVE HE HAS QUITE GRASPED WHAT WE FACE HERE.
MARVEL GIRL HAS. SHE WISHES HER CONTROL OF HER TELEPATHY WAS STRONGER.
SHE IS AFRAID, BUT READY.
I WILL TAKE THE LEAD. KEEP THE OTHERS IN LINE. AND IF NEED BE--
I UNDERSTAND, PROFESSOR. I WON'T LET YOU DOWN.

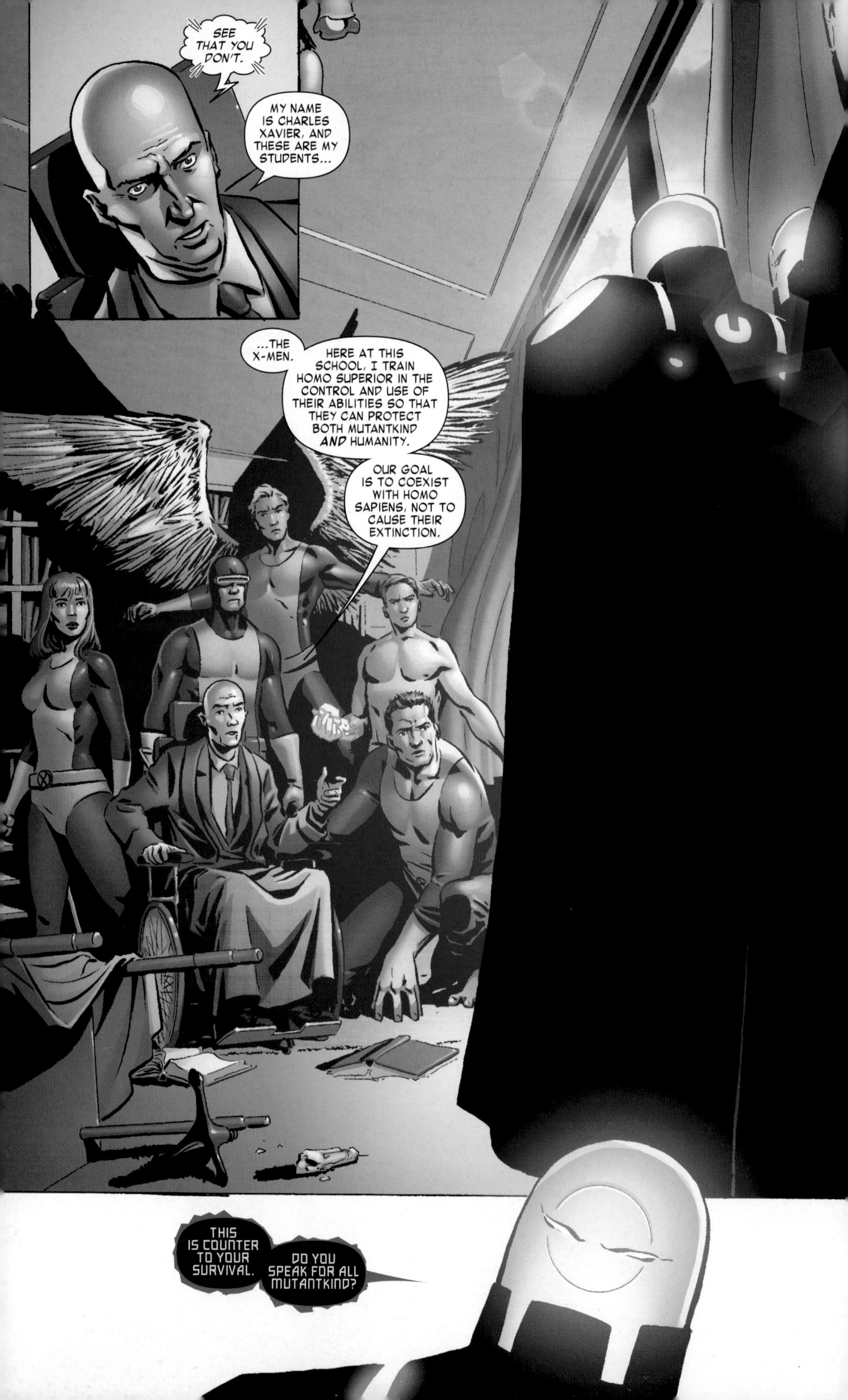
SEE THAT YOU DON'T.
MY NAME IS CHARLES XAVIER, AND THESE ARE MY STUDENTS...
...THE X-MEN.
HERE AT THIS SCHOOL, I TRAIN HOMO SUPERIOR IN THE CONTROL AND USE OF THEIR ABILITIES SO THAT THEY CAN PROTECT BOTH MUTANTKIND AND HUMANITY.
OUR GOAL IS TO COEXIST WITH HOMO SAPIENS, NOT TO CAUSE THEIR EXTINCTION.
THIS IS COUNTER TO YOUR SURVIVAL.
DO YOU SPEAK FOR ALL MUTANTKIND?

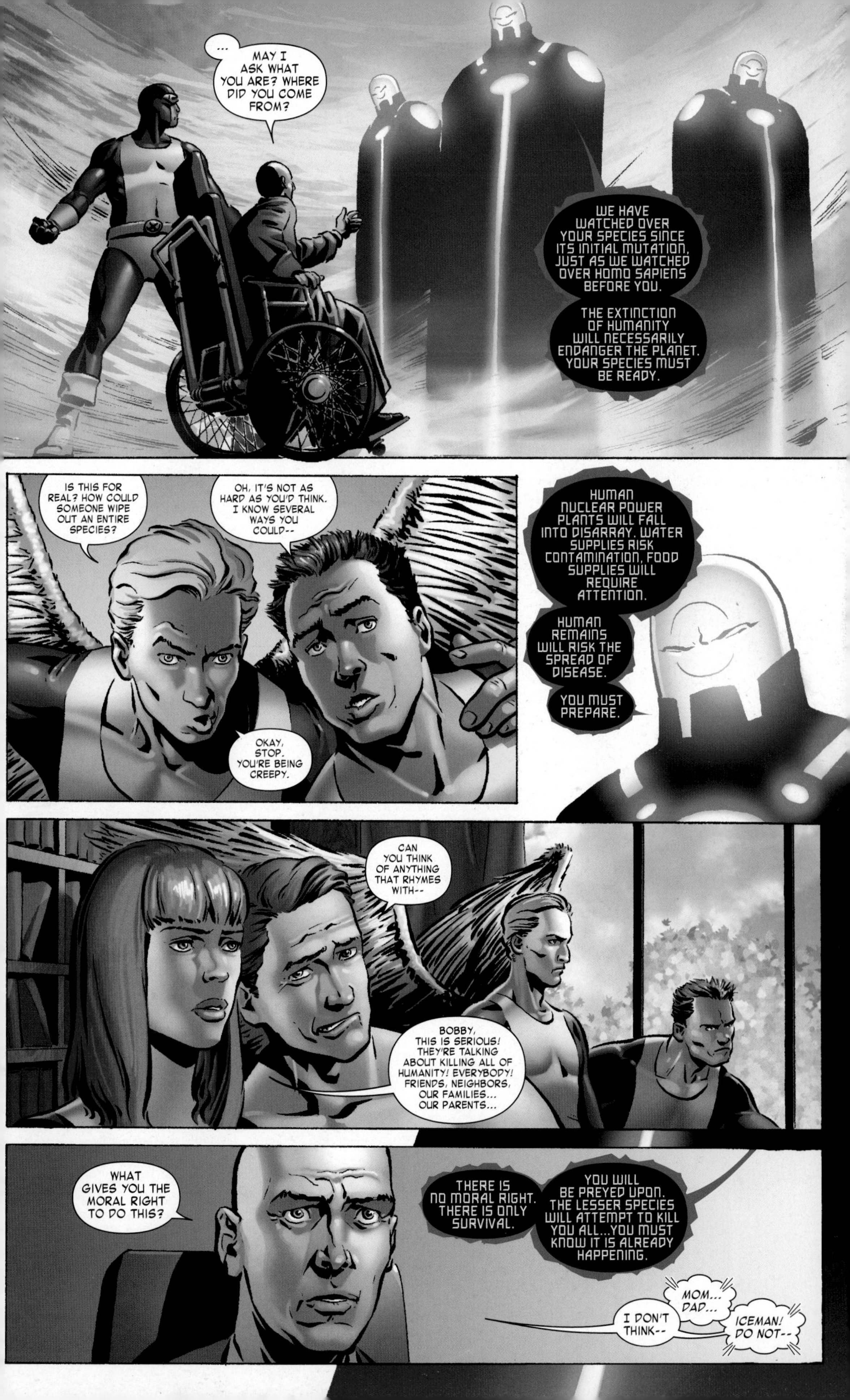
...
MAY I ASK WHAT YOU ARE? WHERE DID YOU COME FROM?
WE HAVE WATCHED OVER YOUR SPECIES SINCE ITS INITIAL MUTATION, JUST AS WE WATCHED OVER HOMO SAPIENS BEFORE YOU.
THE EXTINCTION OF HUMANITY WILL NECESSARILY ENDANGER THE PLANET. YOUR SPECIES MUST BE READY.
IS THIS FOR REAL? HOW COULD SOMEONE WIPE OUT AN ENTIRE SPECIES?
OH, IT'S NOT AS HARD AS YOU'D THINK. I KNOW SEVERAL WAYS YOU COULD--
OKAY, STOP. YOU'RE BEING CREEPY.
HUMAN NUCLEAR POWER PLANTS WILL FALL INTO DISARRAY. WATER SUPPLIES RISK CONTAMINATION, FOOD SUPPLIES WILL REQUIRE ATTENTION.
HUMAN REMAINS WILL RISK THE SPREAD OF DISEASE.
YOU MUST PREPARE.
CAN YOU THINK OF ANYTHING THAT RHYMES WITH--
BOBBY, THIS IS SERIOUS! THEY'RE TALKING ABOUT KILLING ALL OF HUMANITY! EVERYBODY! FRIENDS, NEIGHBORS, OUR FAMILIES... OUR PARENTS...
WHAT GIVES YOU THE MORAL RIGHT TO DO THIS?
THERE IS NO MORAL RIGHT. THERE IS ONLY SURVIVAL.
YOU WILL BE PREYED UPON. THE LESSER SPECIES WILL ATTEMPT TO KILL YOU ALL...YOU MUST KNOW IT IS ALREADY HAPPENING.
MOM... DAD...
I DON'T THINK--
ICEMAN! DO NOT--

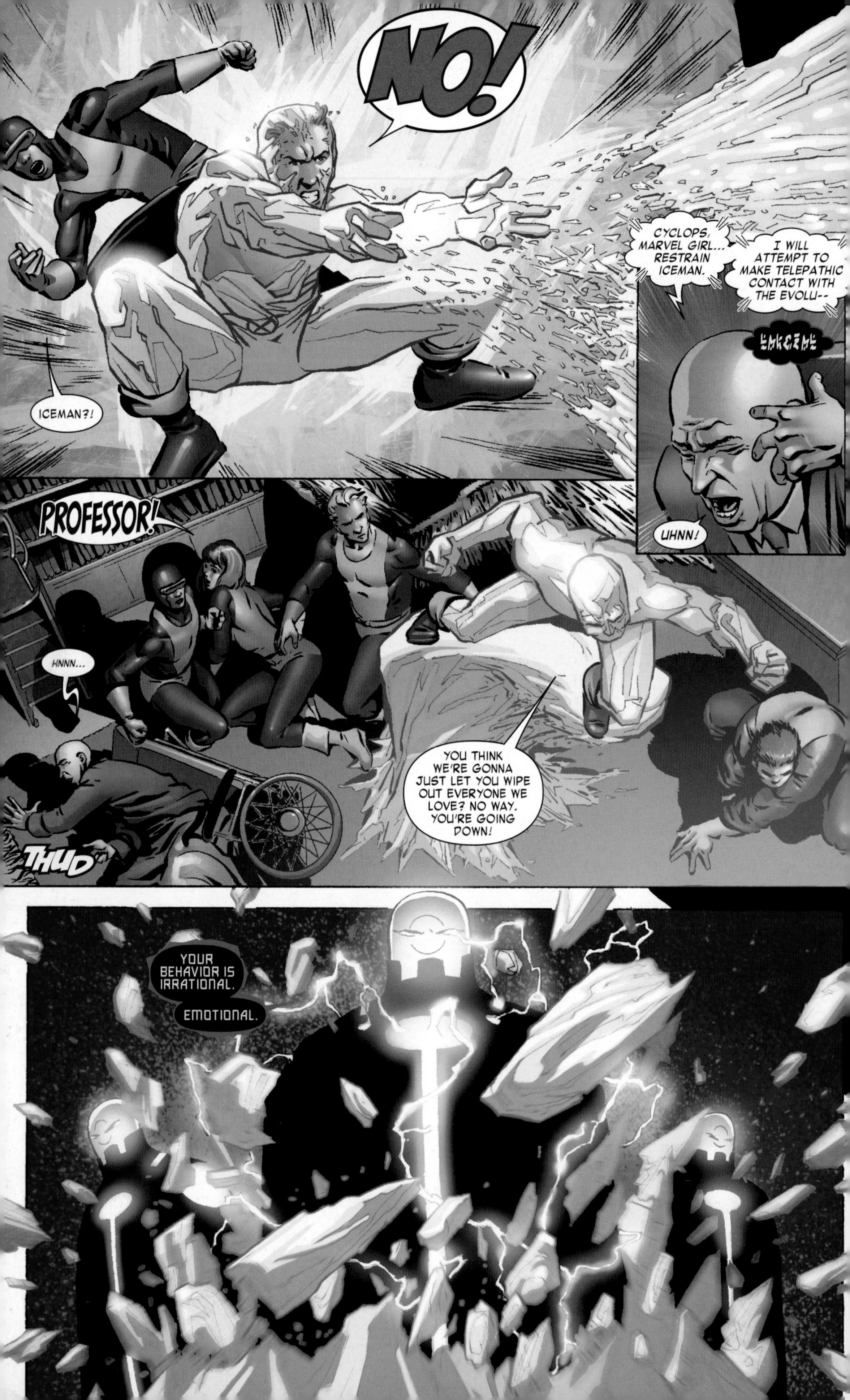
NO!
ICEMAN?!
CYCLOPS, MARVEL GIRL... RESTRAIN ICEMAN.
I WILL ATTEMPT TO MAKE TELEPATHIC CONTACT WITH THE EVOLU--
UHNN!
PROFESSOR!
HNNN...
THUD
YOU THINK WE'RE GONNA JUST LET YOU WIPE OUT EVERYONE WE LOVE? NO WAY. YOU'RE GOING DOWN!
YOUR BEHAVIOR IS IRRATIONAL.
EMOTIONAL.

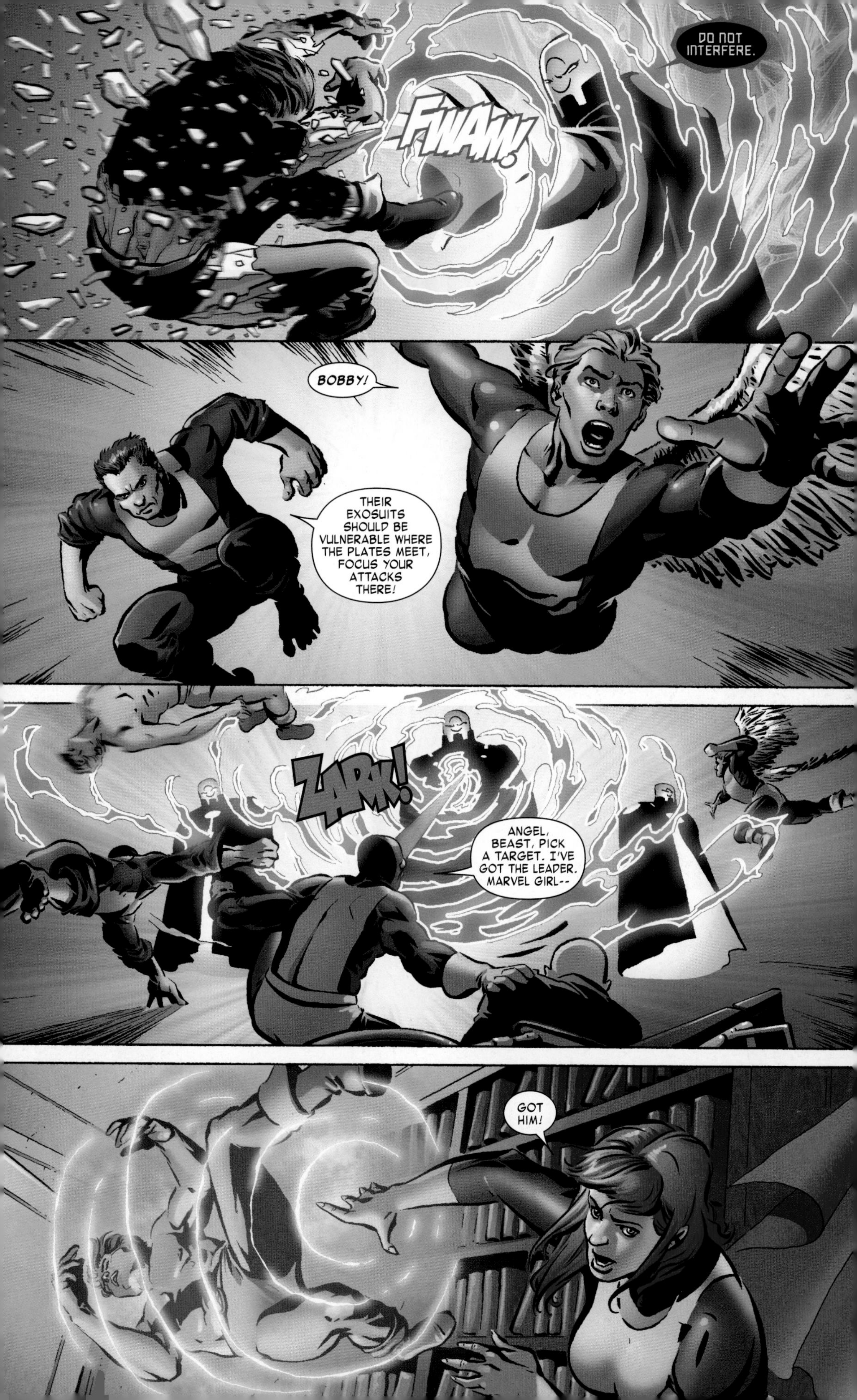
DO NOT INTERFERE.
FWAM!
BOBBY!
THEIR EXOSUITS SHOULD BE VULNERABLE WHERE THE PLATES MEET, FOCUS YOUR ATTACKS THERE!
ZARK!
ANGEL, BEAST, PICK A TARGET. I'VE GOT THE LEADER. MARVEL GIRL--
GOT HIM!

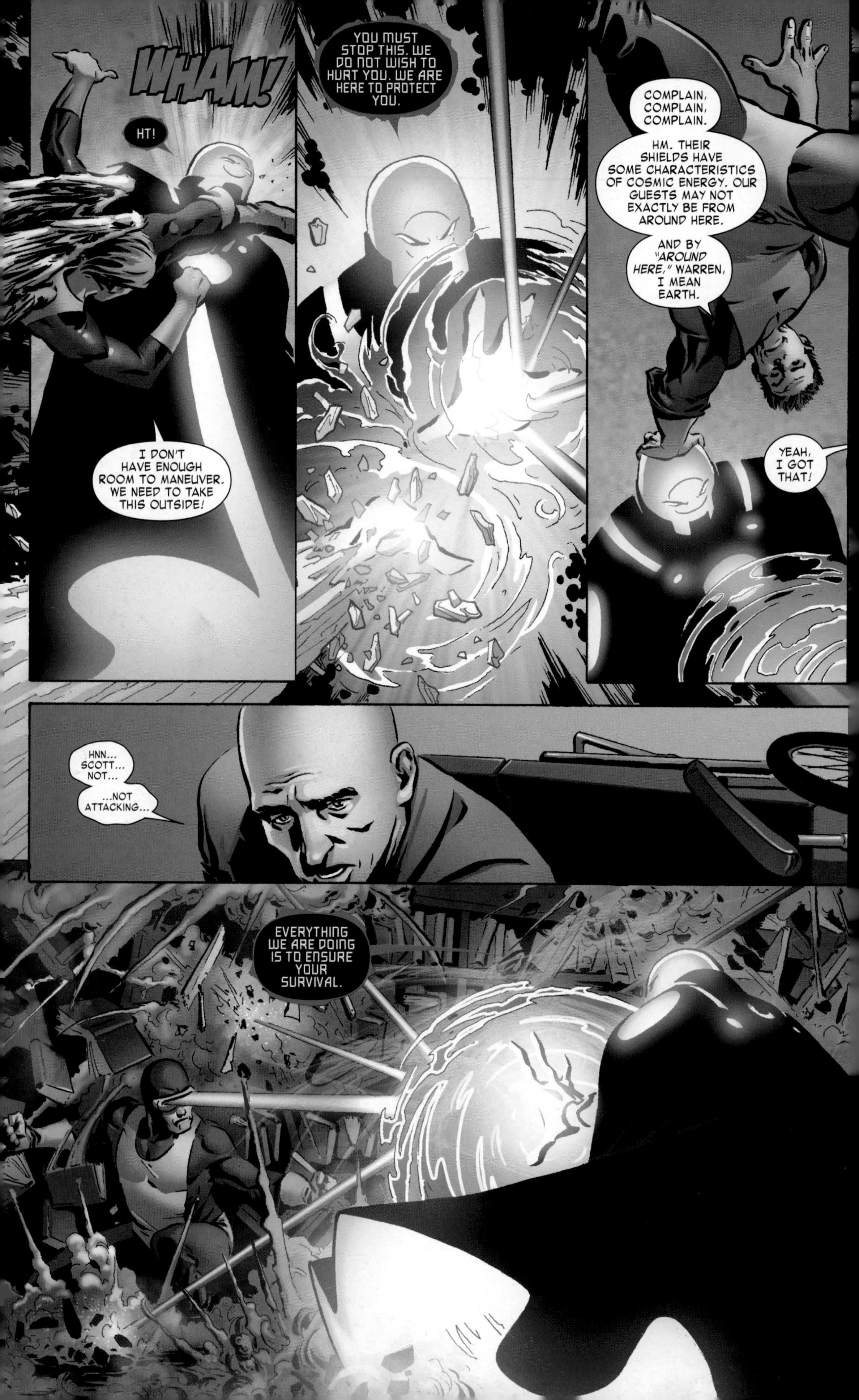
WHAM!
HT!
I DON'T HAVE ENOUGH ROOM TO MANEUVER. WE NEED TO TAKE THIS OUTSIDE!
YOU MUST STOP THIS. WE DO NOT WISH TO HURT YOU. WE ARE HERE TO PROTECT YOU.
COMPLAIN, COMPLAIN, COMPLAIN.
HM. THEIR SHIELDS HAVE SOME CHARACTERISTICS OF COSMIC ENERGY. OUR GUESTS MAY NOT EXACTLY BE FROM AROUND HERE.
AND BY "AROUND HERE," WARREN, I MEAN EARTH.
YEAH, I GOT THAT!
HNN... SCOTT... NOT...
...NOT ATTACKING...
EVERYTHING WE ARE DOING IS TO ENSURE YOUR SURVIVAL.

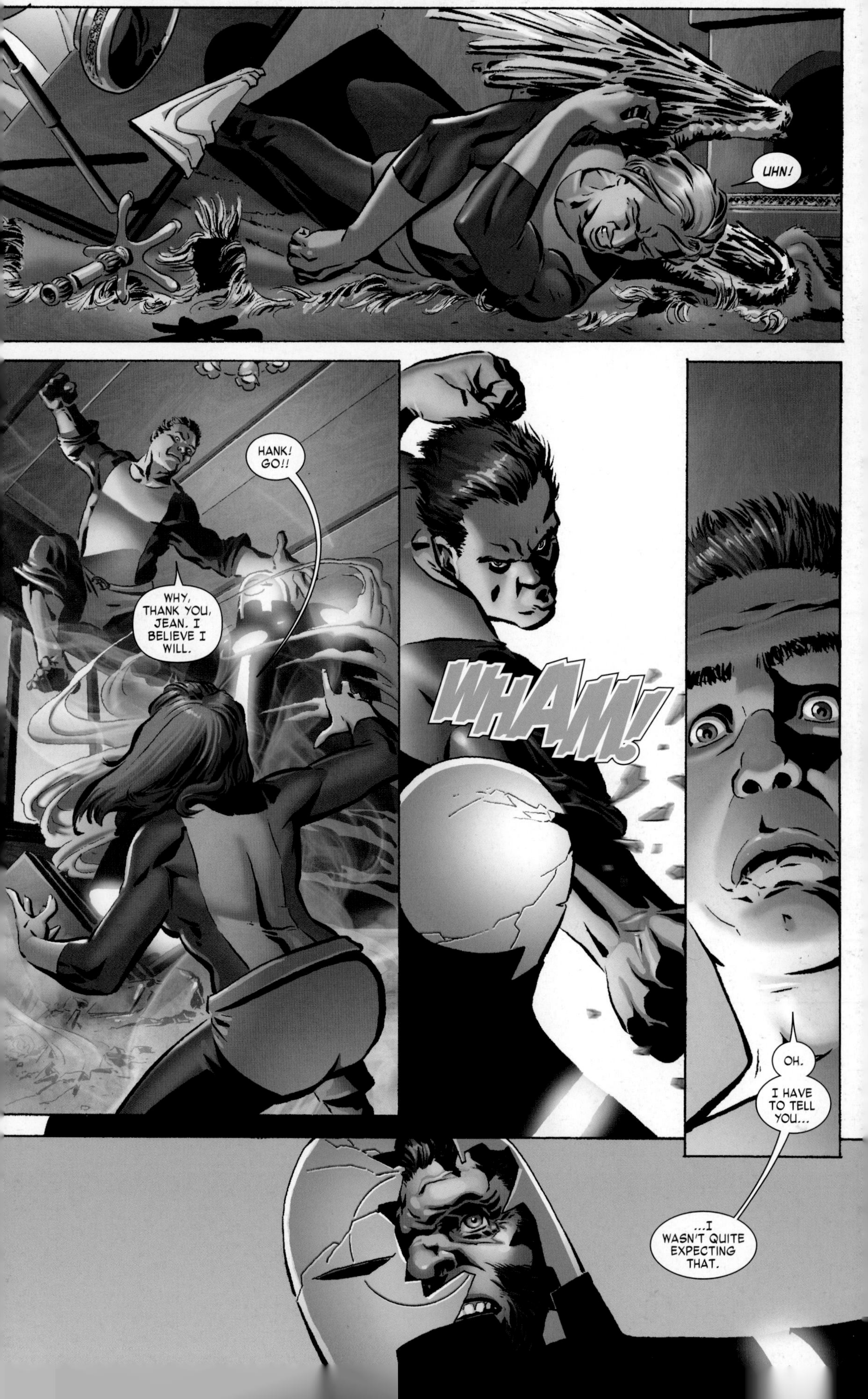
UHN!
HANK! GO!!
WHY, THANK YOU, JEAN. I BELIEVE I WILL.
WHAM!
OH.
I HAVE TO TELL YOU...
...I WASN'T QUITE EXPECTING THAT.

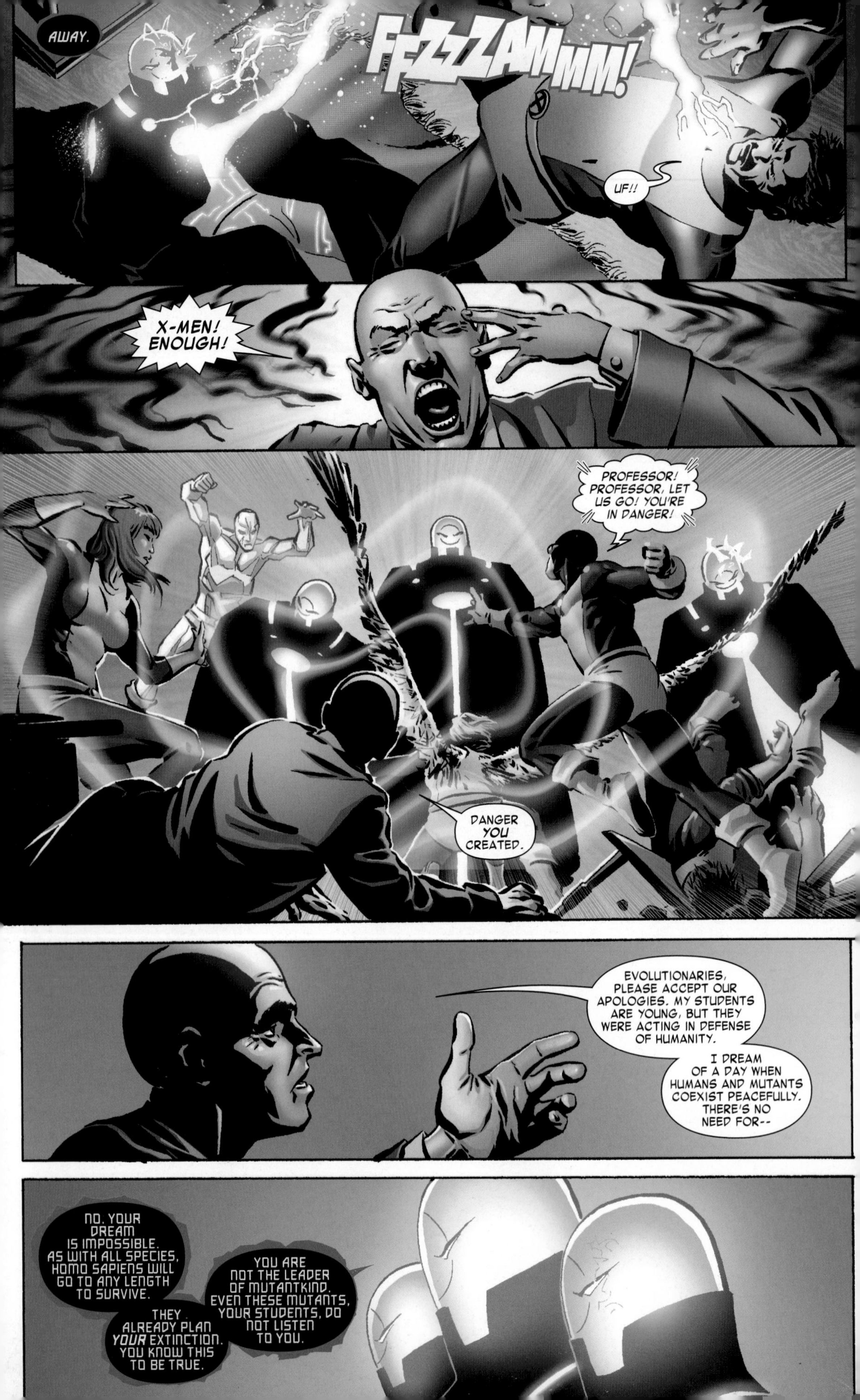
AWAY.
FFZZZAMMMM!
UF!!
X-MEN! ENOUGH!
PROFESSOR! PROFESSOR, LET US GO! YOU'RE IN DANGER!
DANGER YOU CREATED.
EVOLUTIONARIES, PLEASE ACCEPT OUR APOLOGIES. MY STUDENTS ARE YOUNG, BUT THEY WERE ACTING IN DEFENSE OF HUMANITY.
I DREAM OF A DAY WHEN HUMANS AND MUTANTS COEXIST PEACEFULLY. THERE'S NO NEED FOR--
NO. YOUR DREAM IS IMPOSSIBLE. AS WITH ALL SPECIES, HOMO SAPIENS WILL GO TO ANY LENGTH TO SURVIVE.
THEY ALREADY PLAN YOUR EXTINCTION. YOU KNOW THIS TO BE TRUE.
YOU ARE NOT THE LEADER OF MUTANTKIND. EVEN THESE MUTANTS, YOUR STUDENTS, DO NOT LISTEN TO YOU.

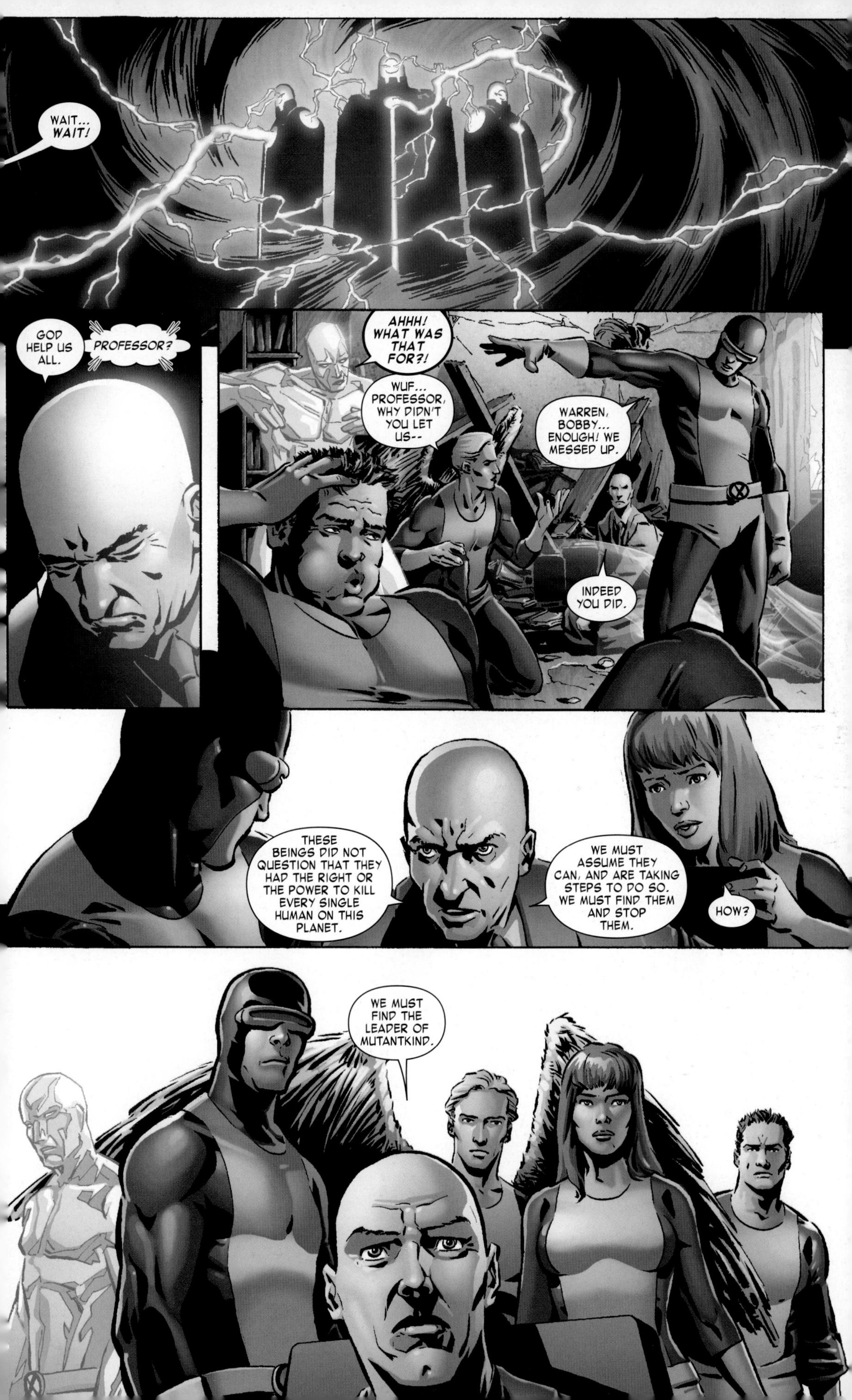
WAIT... WAIT!
GOD HELP US ALL.
PROFESSOR?
AHHH! WHAT WAS THAT FOR?!
WUF... PROFESSOR, WHY DIDN'T YOU LET US--
WARREN, BOBBY... ENOUGH! WE MESSED UP.
INDEED YOU DID.
THESE BEINGS DID NOT QUESTION THAT THEY HAD THE RIGHT OR THE POWER TO KILL EVERY SINGLE HUMAN ON THIS PLANET.
WE MUST ASSUME THEY CAN, AND ARE TAKING STEPS TO DO SO. WE MUST FIND THEM AND STOP THEM.
HOW?
WE MUST FIND THE LEADER OF MUTANTKIND.

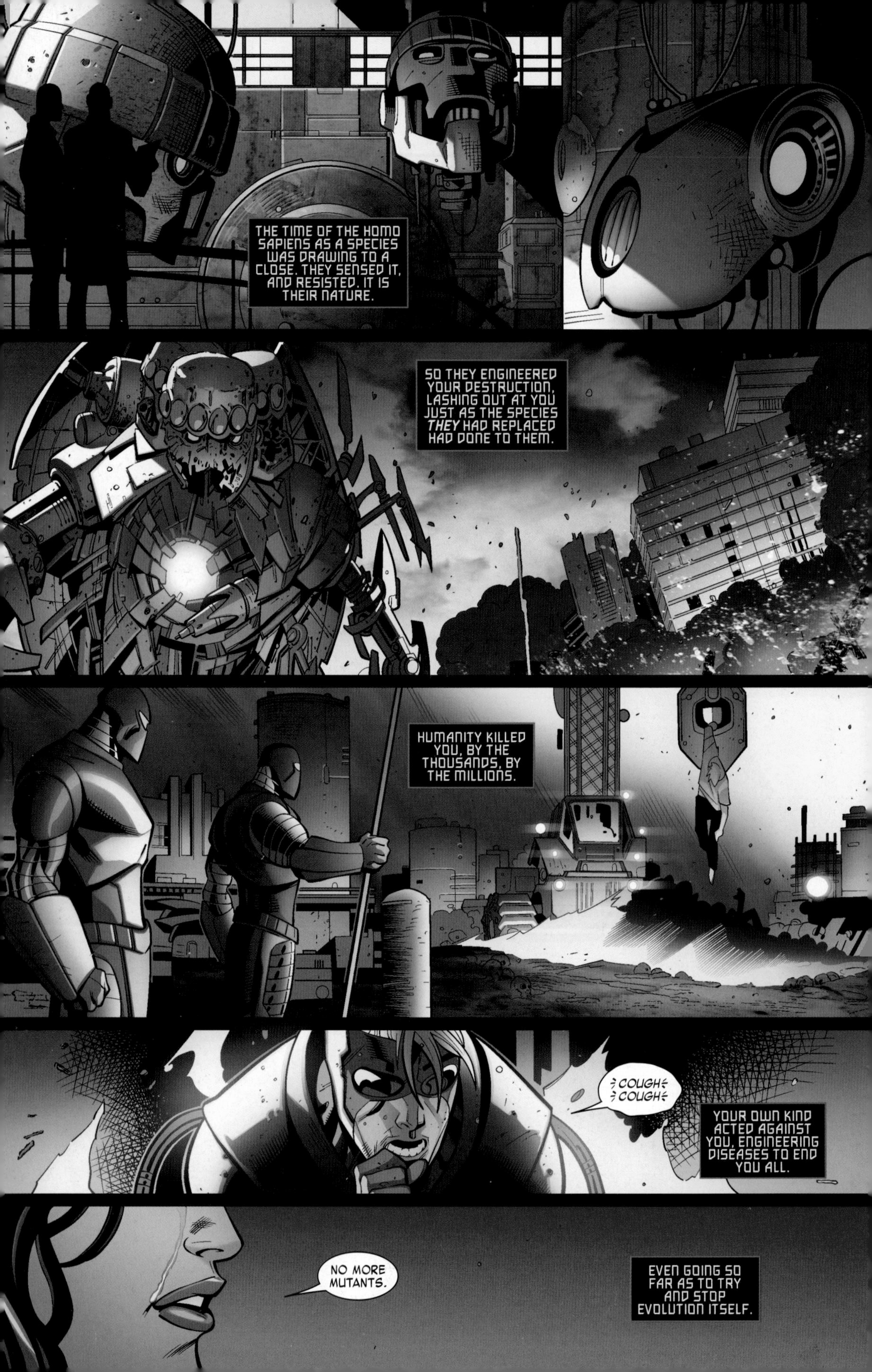
THE TIME OF THE HOMO SAPIENS AS A SPECIES WAS DRAWING TO A CLOSE. THEY SENSED IT, AND RESISTED. IT IS THEIR NATURE.
SO THEY ENGINEERED YOUR DESTRUCTION, LASHING OUT AT YOU JUST AS THE SPECIES *THEY* HAD REPLACED HAD DONE TO THEM.
HUMANITY KILLED YOU, BY THE THOUSANDS, BY THE MILLIONS.
COUGH COUGH
YOUR OWN KIND ACTED AGAINST YOU, ENGINEERING DISEASES TO END YOU ALL.
NO MORE MUTANTS.
EVEN GOING SO FAR AS TO TRY AND STOP EVOLUTION ITSELF.

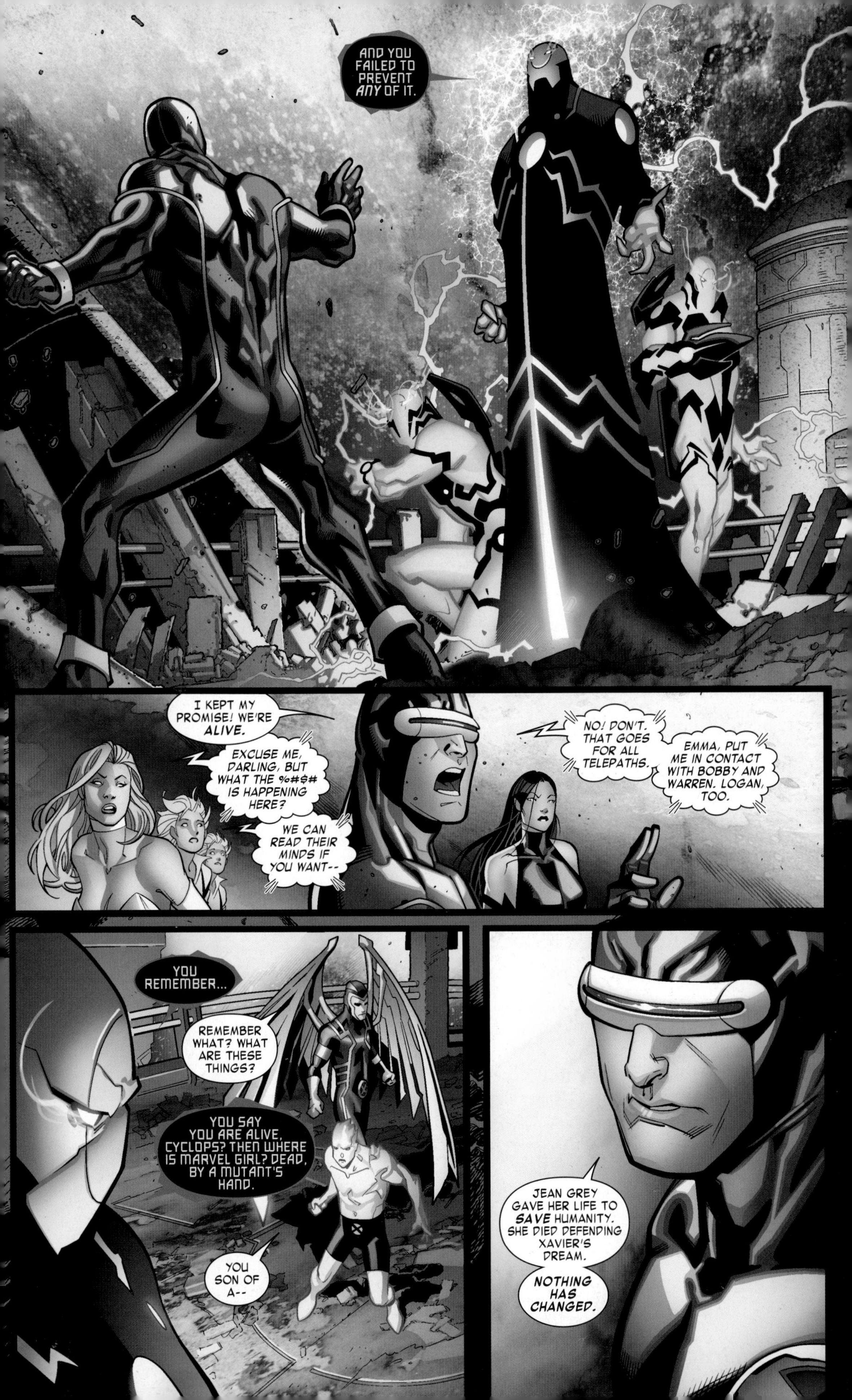
AND YOU FAILED TO PREVENT *ANY* OF IT.
I KEPT MY PROMISE! WE'RE *ALIVE.*
EXCUSE ME, DARLING, BUT WHAT THE %#$# IS HAPPENING HERE?
WE CAN READ THEIR MINDS IF YOU WANT--
NO! DON'T. THAT GOES FOR ALL TELEPATHS.
EMMA, PUT ME IN CONTACT WITH BOBBY AND WARREN. LOGAN, TOO.
YOU REMEMBER...
REMEMBER WHAT? WHAT ARE THESE THINGS?
YOU SAY YOU ARE ALIVE, CYCLOPS? THEN WHERE IS MARVEL GIRL? DEAD, BY A MUTANT'S HAND.
YOU SON OF A--
JEAN GREY GAVE HER LIFE TO *SAVE* HUMANITY. SHE DIED DEFENDING XAVIER'S DREAM.
NOTHING HAS CHANGED.

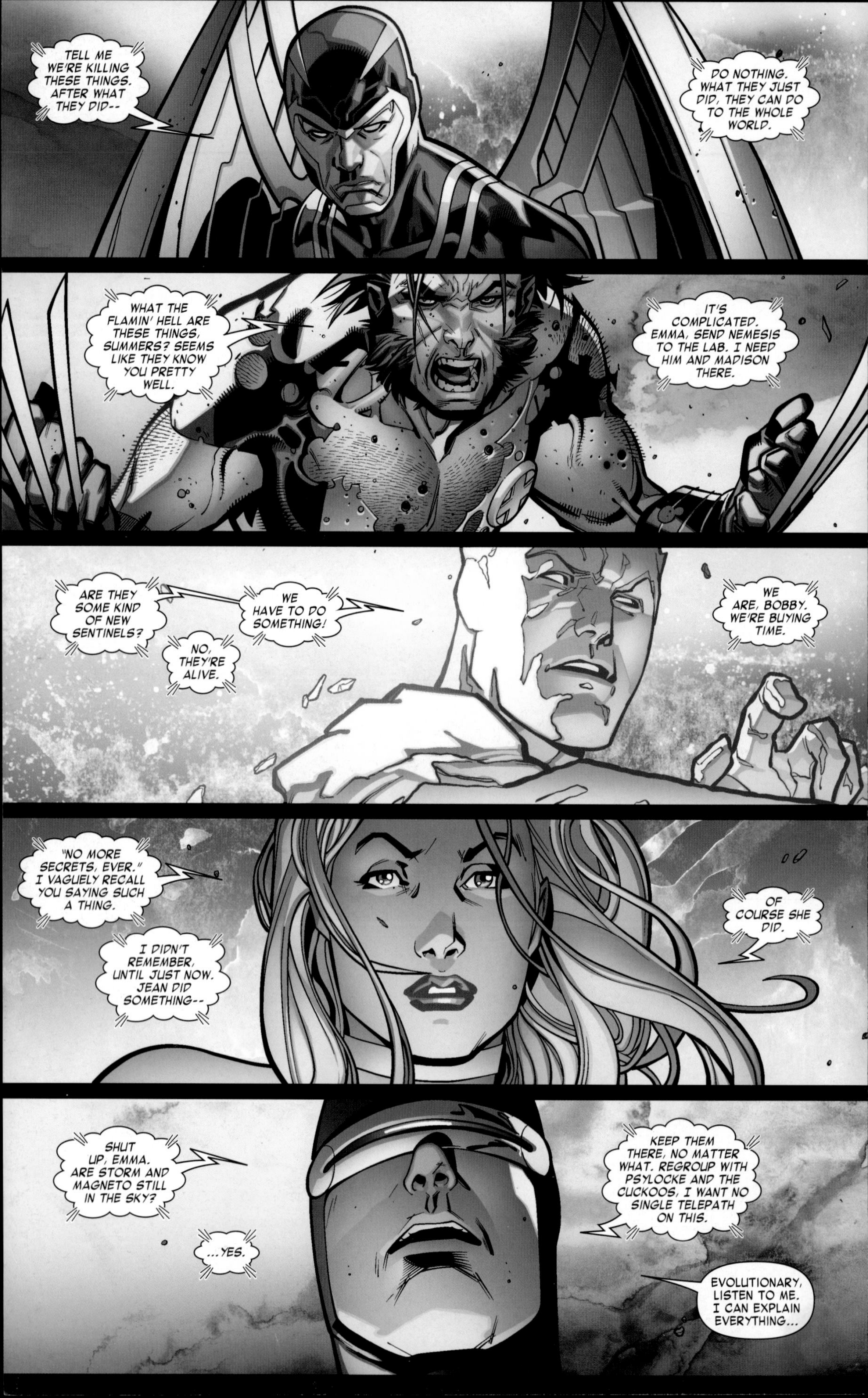
TELL ME WE'RE KILLING THESE THINGS. AFTER WHAT THEY DID--
DO NOTHING. WHAT THEY JUST DID, THEY CAN DO TO THE WHOLE WORLD.
WHAT THE FLAMIN' HELL ARE THESE THINGS, SUMMERS? SEEMS LIKE THEY KNOW YOU PRETTY WELL.
IT'S COMPLICATED. EMMA, SEND NEMESIS TO THE LAB. I NEED HIM AND MADISON THERE.
ARE THEY SOME KIND OF NEW SENTINELS?
NO, THEY'RE ALIVE.
WE HAVE TO DO SOMETHING!
WE ARE, BOBBY. WE'RE BUYING TIME.
"NO MORE SECRETS, EVER." I VAGUELY RECALL YOU SAYING SUCH A THING.
I DIDN'T REMEMBER, UNTIL JUST NOW. JEAN DID SOMETHING--
OF COURSE SHE DID.
SHUT UP, EMMA. ARE STORM AND MAGNETO STILL IN THE SKY?
...YES.
KEEP THEM THERE, NO MATTER WHAT. REGROUP WITH PSYLOCKE AND THE CUCKOOS, I WANT NO SINGLE TELEPATH ON THIS.
EVOLUTIONARY, LISTEN TO ME. I CAN EXPLAIN EVERYTHING...

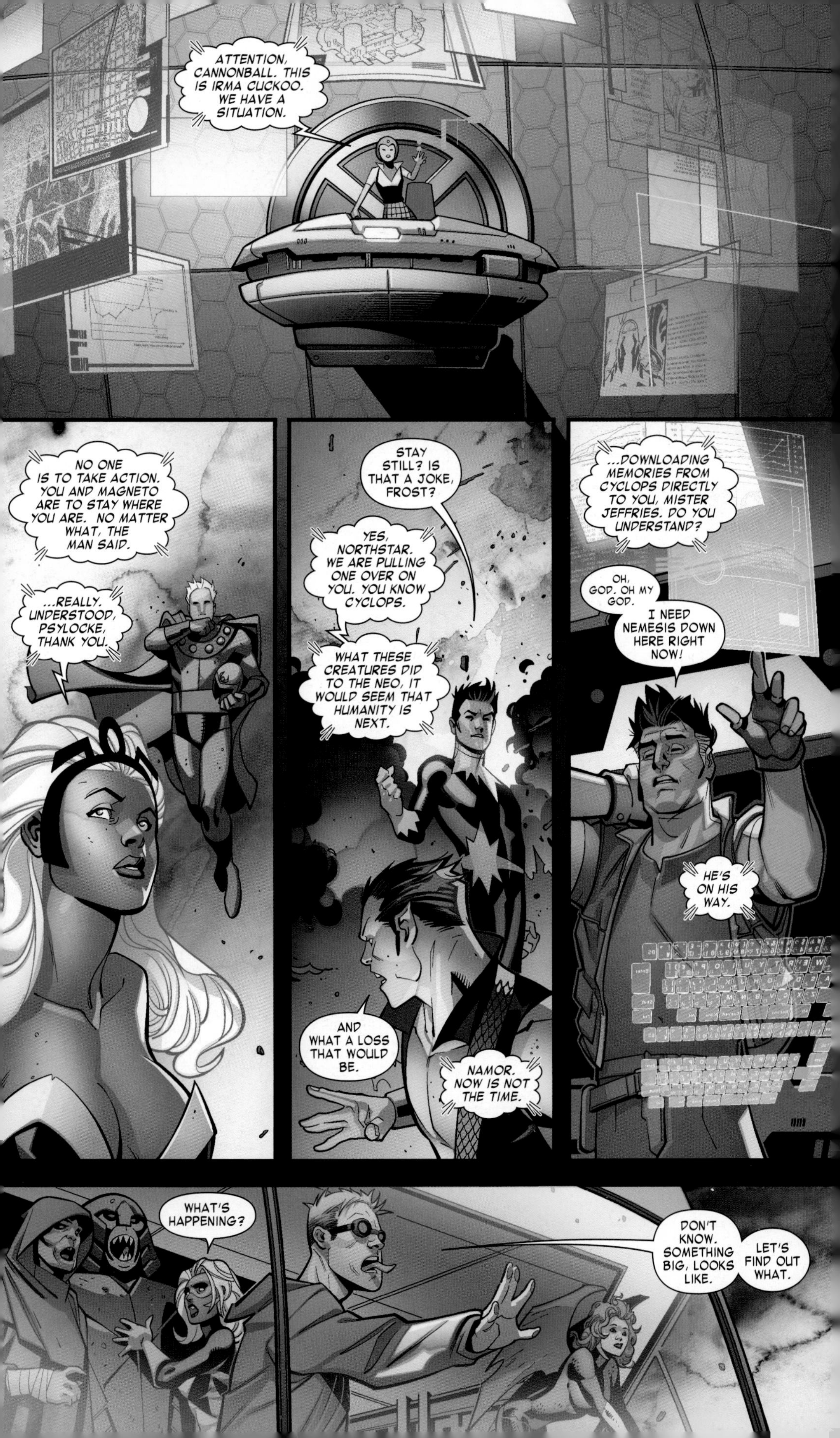
ATTENTION, CANNONBALL. THIS IS IRMA CUCKOO. WE HAVE A SITUATION.
NO ONE IS TO TAKE ACTION. YOU AND MAGNETO ARE TO STAY WHERE YOU ARE. NO MATTER WHAT, THE MAN SAID.
...REALLY. UNDERSTOOD, PSYLOCKE, THANK YOU.
STAY STILL? IS THAT A JOKE, FROST?
YES, NORTHSTAR. WE ARE PULLING ONE OVER ON YOU. YOU KNOW CYCLOPS.
WHAT THESE CREATURES DID TO THE NEO, IT WOULD SEEM THAT HUMANITY IS NEXT.
AND WHAT A LOSS THAT WOULD BE.
NAMOR. NOW IS NOT THE TIME.
...DOWNLOADING MEMORIES FROM CYCLOPS DIRECTLY TO YOU, MISTER JEFFRIES. DO YOU UNDERSTAND?
OH, GOD. OH MY GOD.
I NEED NEMESIS DOWN HERE RIGHT NOW!
HE'S ON HIS WAY.
WHAT'S HAPPENING?
DON'T KNOW. SOMETHING BIG, LOOKS LIKE.
LET'S FIND OUT WHAT.

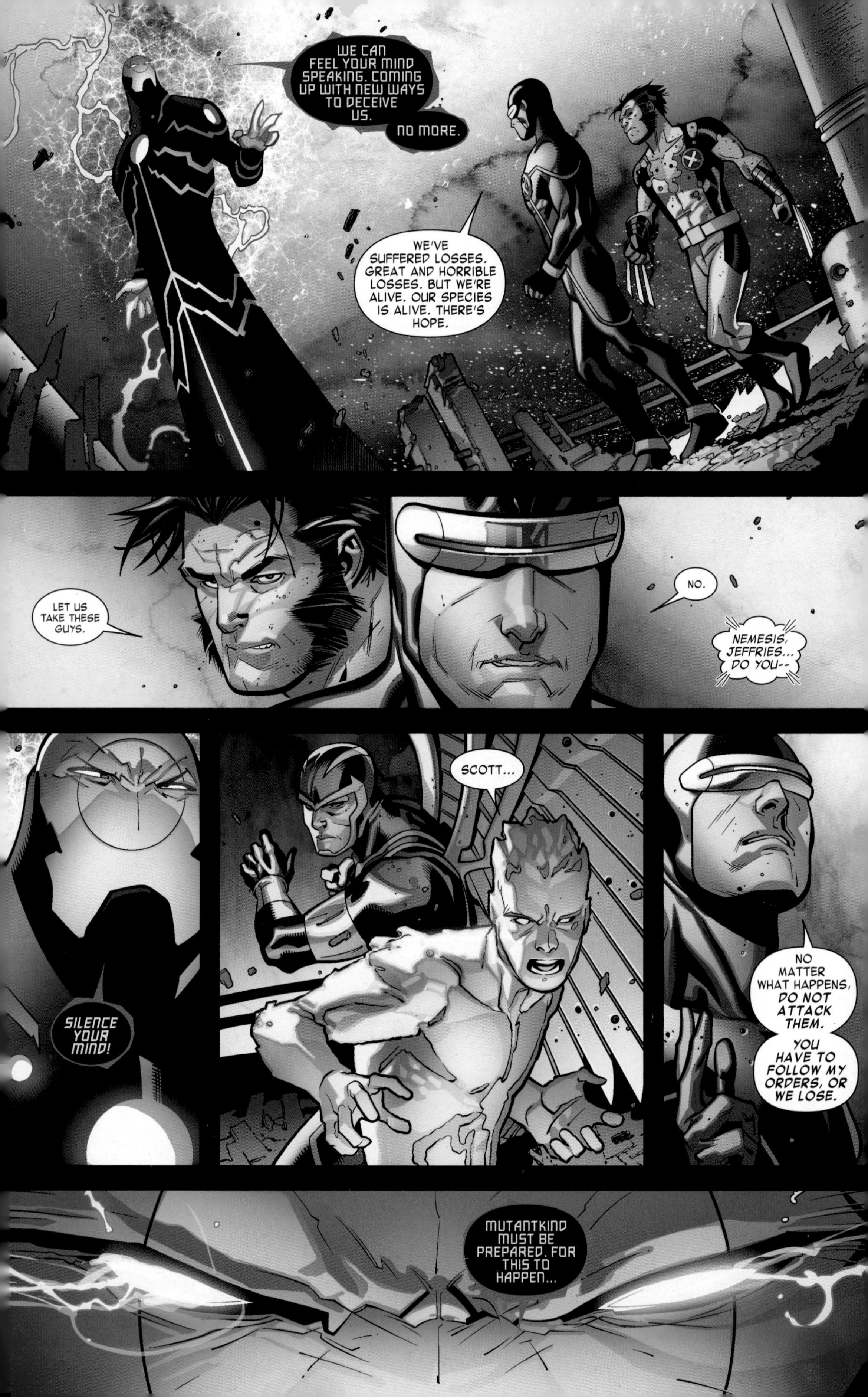
WE CAN FEEL YOUR MIND SPEAKING. COMING UP WITH NEW WAYS TO DECEIVE US.
NO MORE.
WE'VE SUFFERED LOSSES. GREAT AND HORRIBLE LOSSES. BUT WE'RE ALIVE. OUR SPECIES IS ALIVE. THERE'S HOPE.
LET US TAKE THESE GUYS.
NO.
NEMESIS, JEFFRIES... DO YOU--
SILENCE YOUR MIND!
SCOTT...
NO MATTER WHAT HAPPENS, DO NOT ATTACK THEM.
YOU HAVE TO FOLLOW MY ORDERS, OR WE LOSE.
MUTANTKIND MUST BE PREPARED. FOR THIS TO HAPPEN...

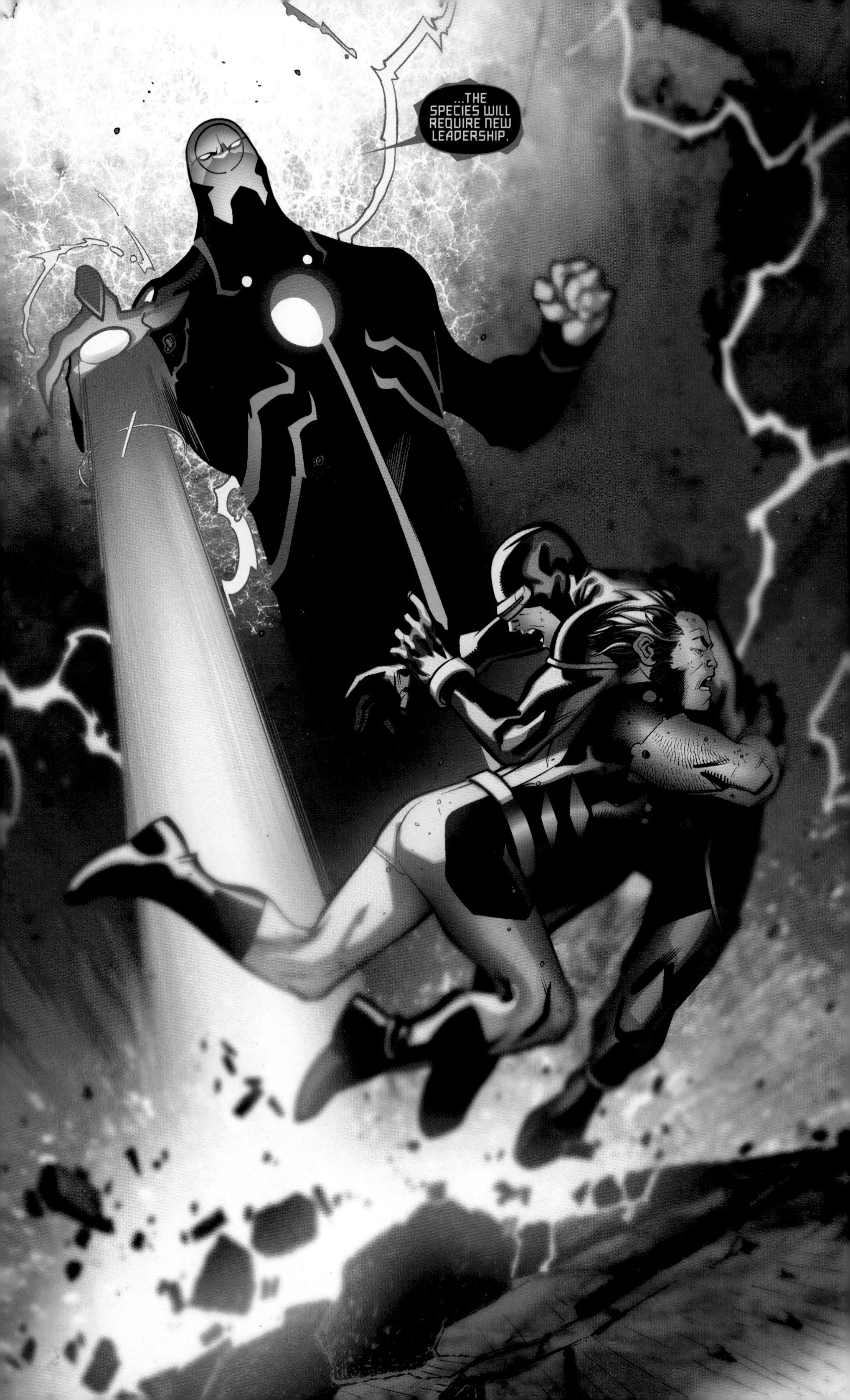
...THE SPECIES WILL REQUIRE NEW LEADERSHIP.

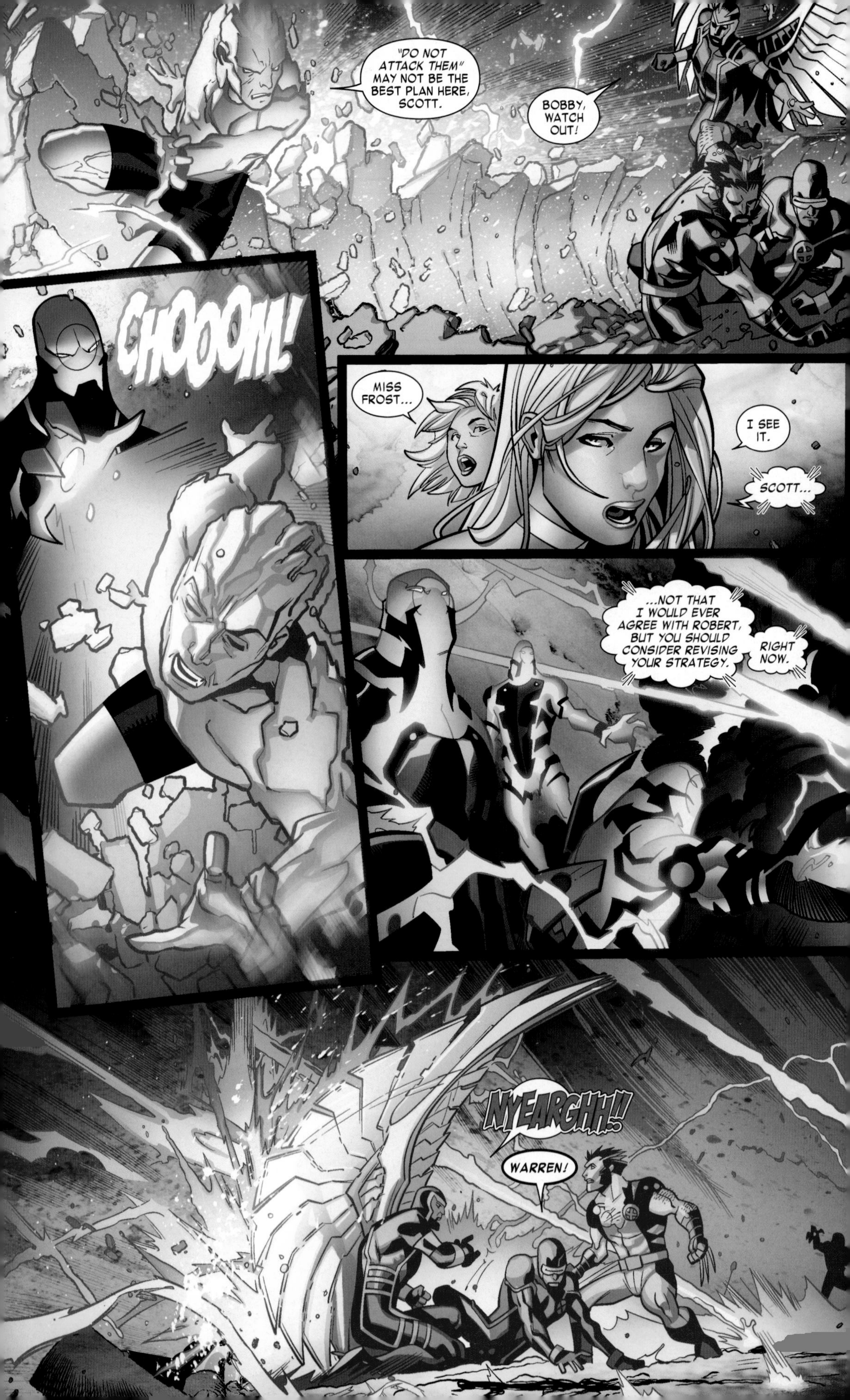
"DO NOT ATTACK THEM" MAY NOT BE THE BEST PLAN HERE, SCOTT.
BOBBY, WATCH OUT!
CHOOOM!
MISS FROST...
I SEE IT.
SCOTT...
...NOT THAT I WOULD EVER AGREE WITH ROBERT, BUT YOU SHOULD CONSIDER REVISING YOUR STRATEGY.
RIGHT NOW.
NYEARGHH!!
WARREN!

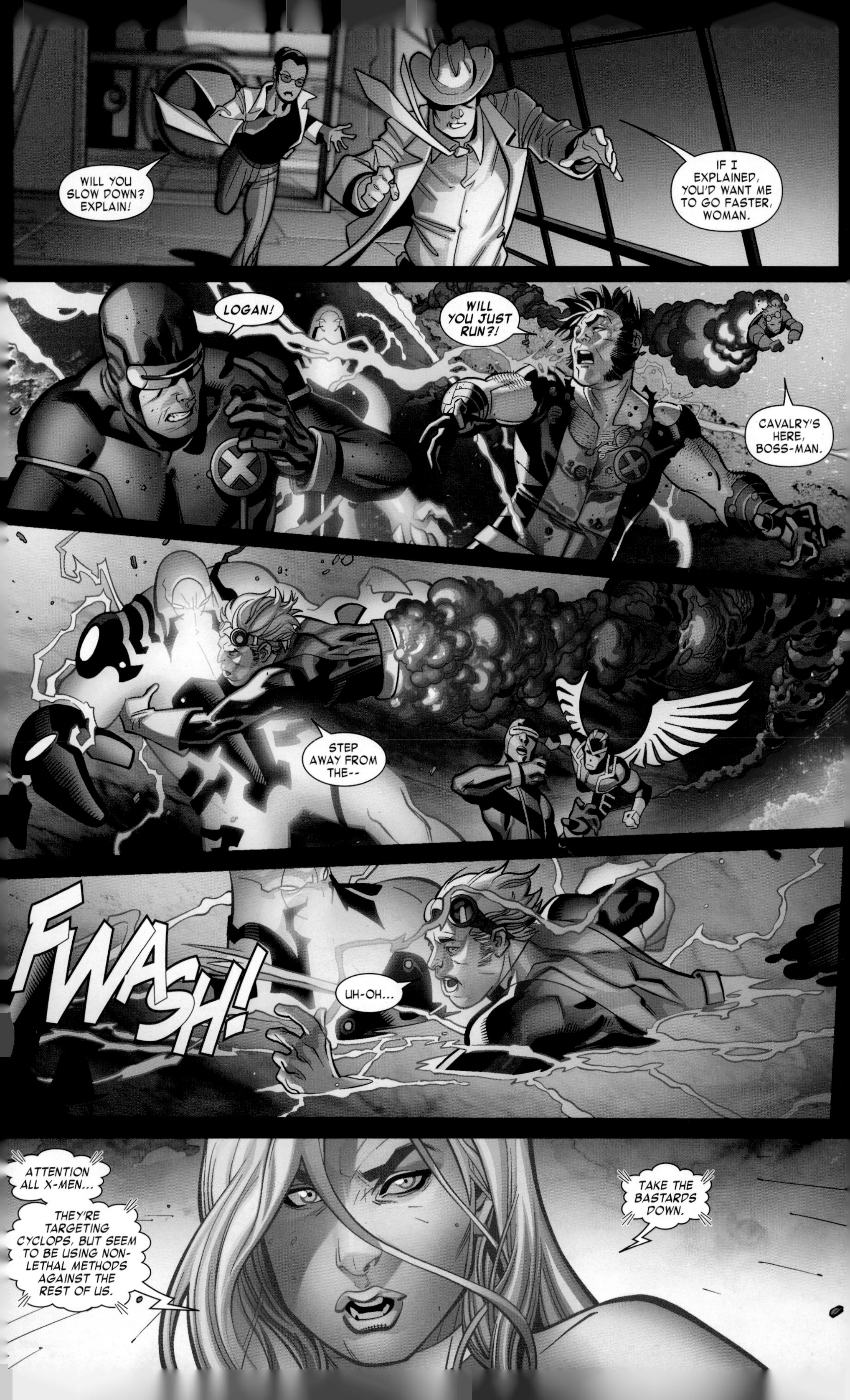
WILL YOU SLOW DOWN? EXPLAIN!
IF I EXPLAINED, YOU'D WANT ME TO GO FASTER, WOMAN.
LOGAN!
WILL YOU JUST RUN?!
CAVALRY'S HERE, BOSS-MAN.
STEP AWAY FROM THE--
FWASH!
UH-OH...
ATTENTION ALL X-MEN...
THEY'RE TARGETING CYCLOPS, BUT SEEM TO BE USING NON-LETHAL METHODS AGAINST THE REST OF US.
TAKE THE BASTARDS DOWN.

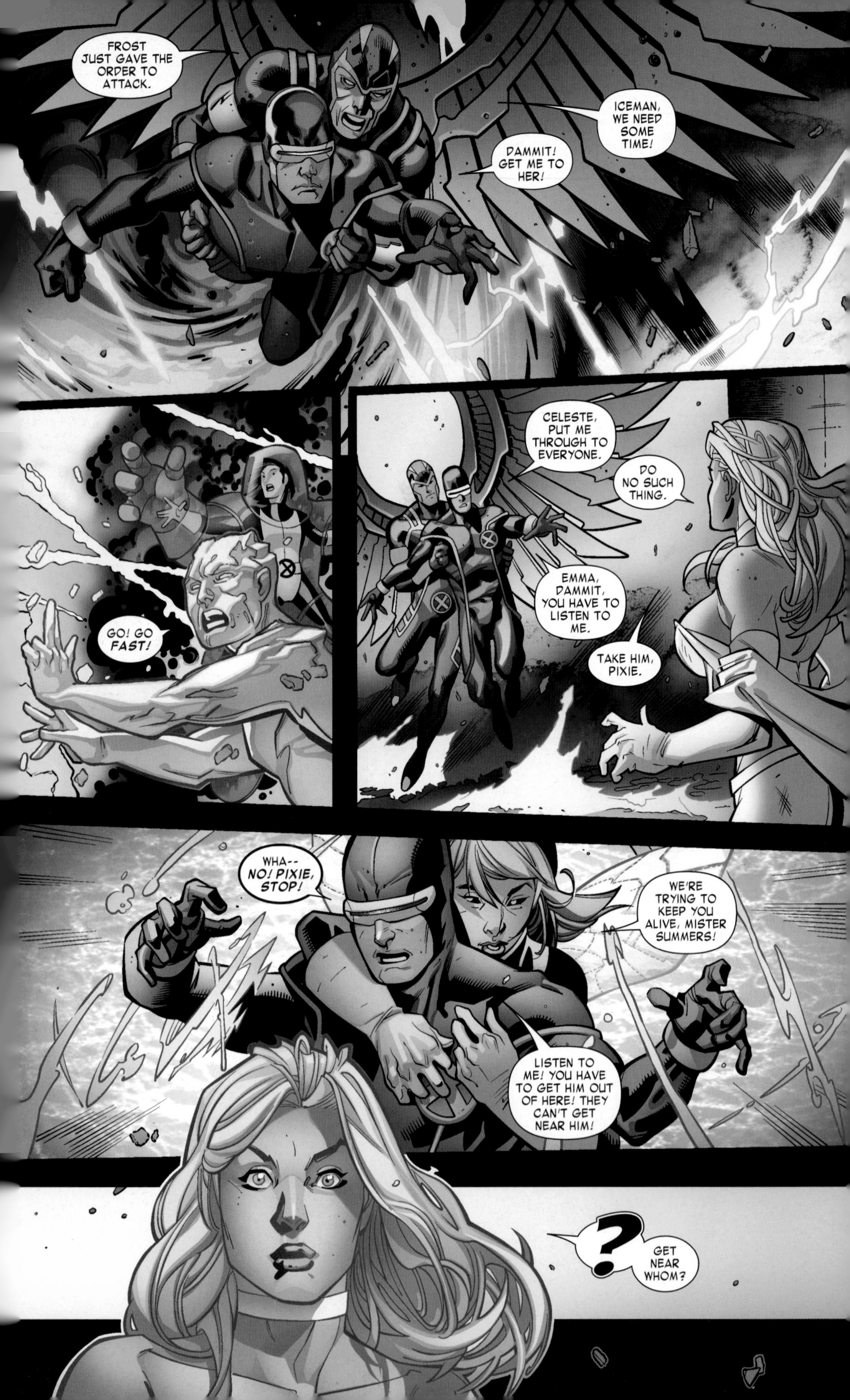
FROST JUST GAVE THE ORDER TO ATTACK.
DAMMIT! GET ME TO HER!
ICEMAN, WE NEED SOME TIME!
GO! GO FAST!
CELESTE, PUT ME THROUGH TO EVERYONE.
DO NO SUCH THING.
EMMA, DAMMIT, YOU HAVE TO LISTEN TO ME.
TAKE HIM, PIXIE.
WHA-- NO! PIXIE, STOP!
WE'RE TRYING TO KEEP YOU ALIVE, MISTER SUMMERS!
LISTEN TO ME! YOU HAVE TO GET HIM OUT OF HERE! THEY CAN'T GET NEAR HIM!
?
GET NEAR WHOM?

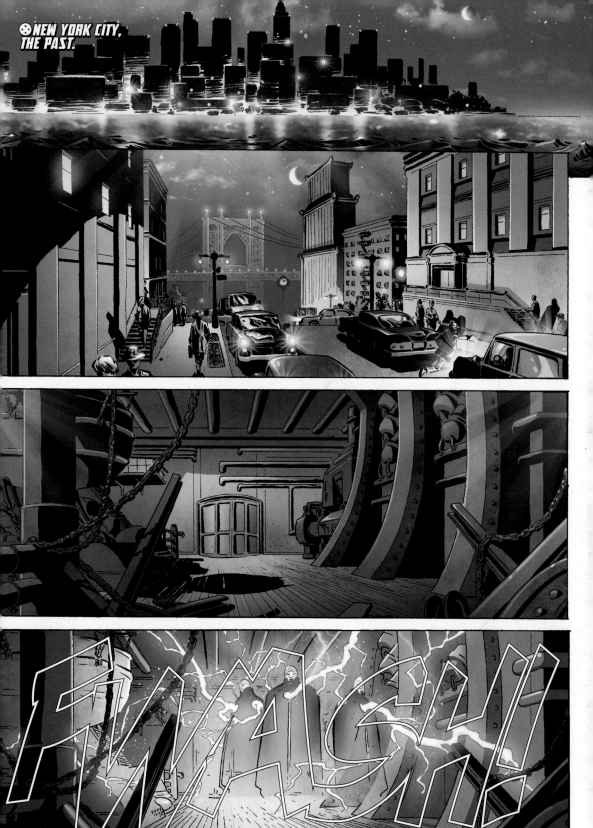

FWASH!

WE COULD FEEL YOU. YOUR POWER.

TELL ME. DO YOU SPEAK FOR MUTANTKIND?

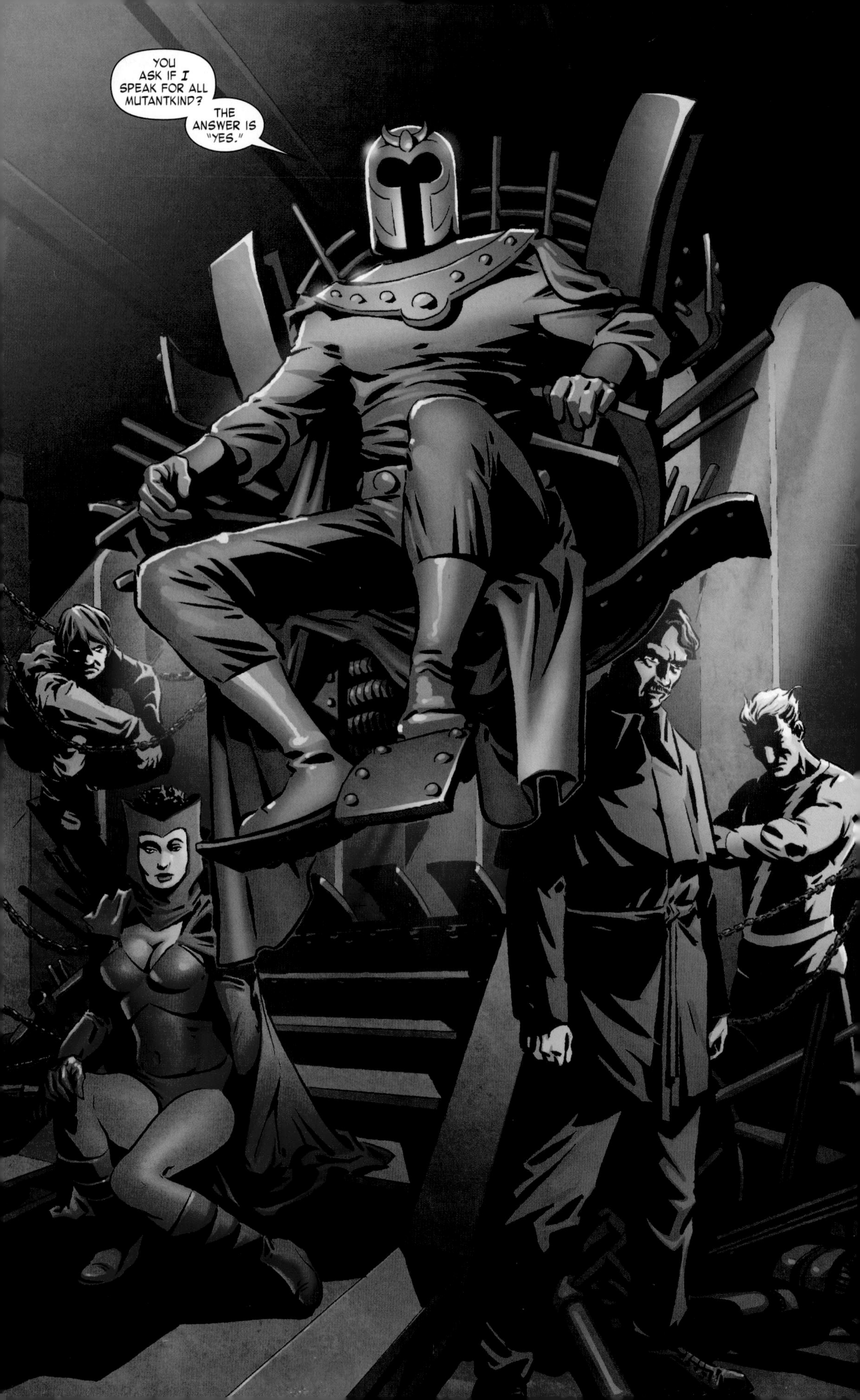
YOU ASK IF *I* SPEAK FOR ALL MUTANTKIND? THE ANSWER IS "YES."

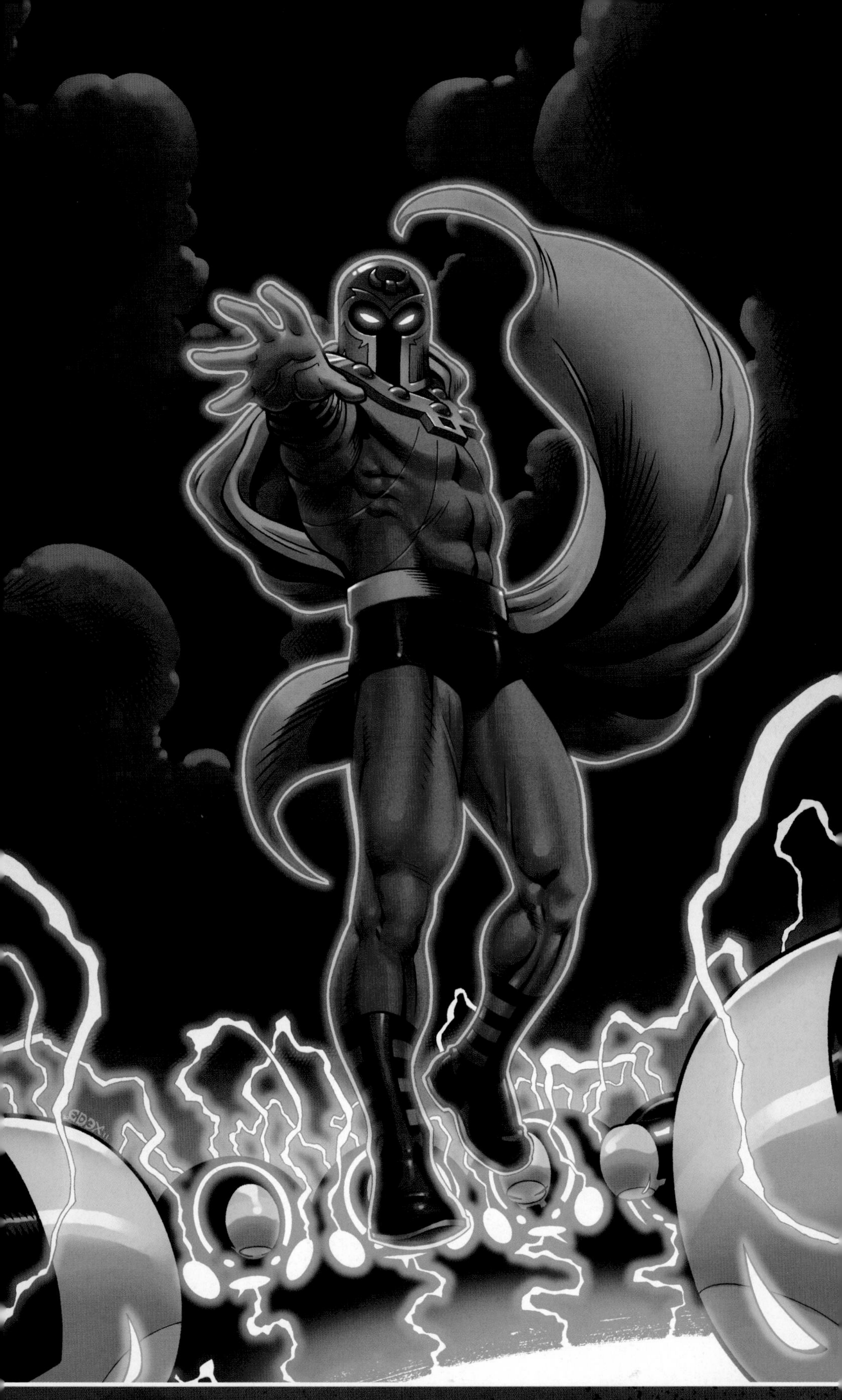

THIRTEEN

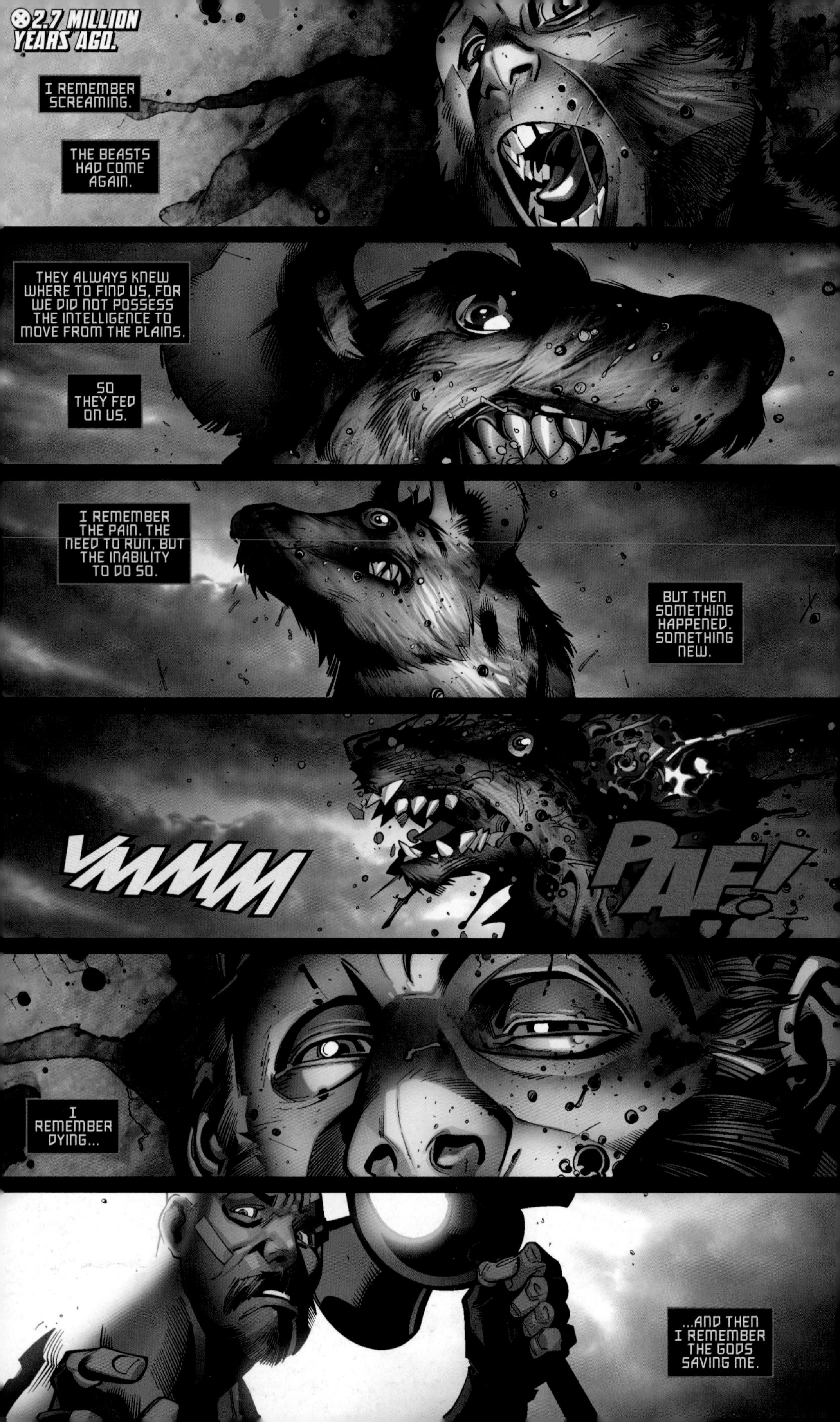
2.7 MILLION YEARS AGO.
I REMEMBER SCREAMING.
THE BEASTS HAD COME AGAIN.
THEY ALWAYS KNEW WHERE TO FIND US, FOR WE DID NOT POSSESS THE INTELLIGENCE TO MOVE FROM THE PLAINS.
SO THEY FED ON US.
I REMEMBER THE PAIN. THE NEED TO RUN, BUT THE INABILITY TO DO SO.
BUT THEN SOMETHING HAPPENED. SOMETHING NEW.
VMMM
PAF!
I REMEMBER DYING...
...AND THEN I REMEMBER THE GODS SAVING ME.

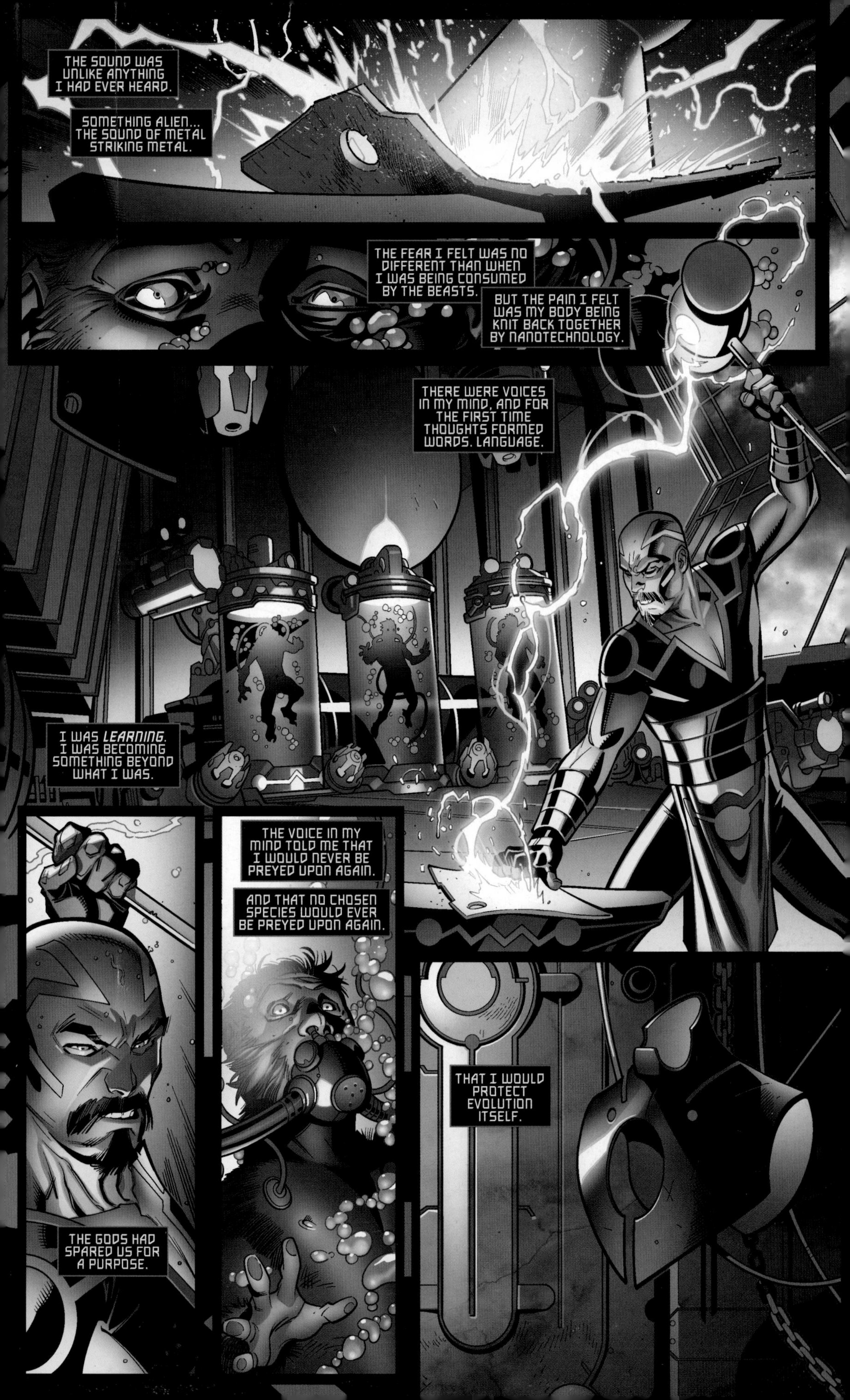
THE SOUND WAS UNLIKE ANYTHING I HAD EVER HEARD.
SOMETHING ALIEN... THE SOUND OF METAL STRIKING METAL.
THE FEAR I FELT WAS NO DIFFERENT THAN WHEN I WAS BEING CONSUMED BY THE BEASTS.
BUT THE PAIN I FELT WAS MY BODY BEING KNIT BACK TOGETHER BY NANOTECHNOLOGY.
THERE WERE VOICES IN MY MIND, AND FOR THE FIRST TIME THOUGHTS FORMED WORDS. LANGUAGE.
I WAS *LEARNING*. I WAS BECOMING SOMETHING BEYOND WHAT I WAS.
THE GODS HAD SPARED US FOR A PURPOSE.
THE VOICE IN MY MIND TOLD ME THAT I WOULD NEVER BE PREYED UPON AGAIN.
AND THAT NO CHOSEN SPECIES WOULD EVER BE PREYED UPON AGAIN.
THAT I WOULD PROTECT EVOLUTION ITSELF.

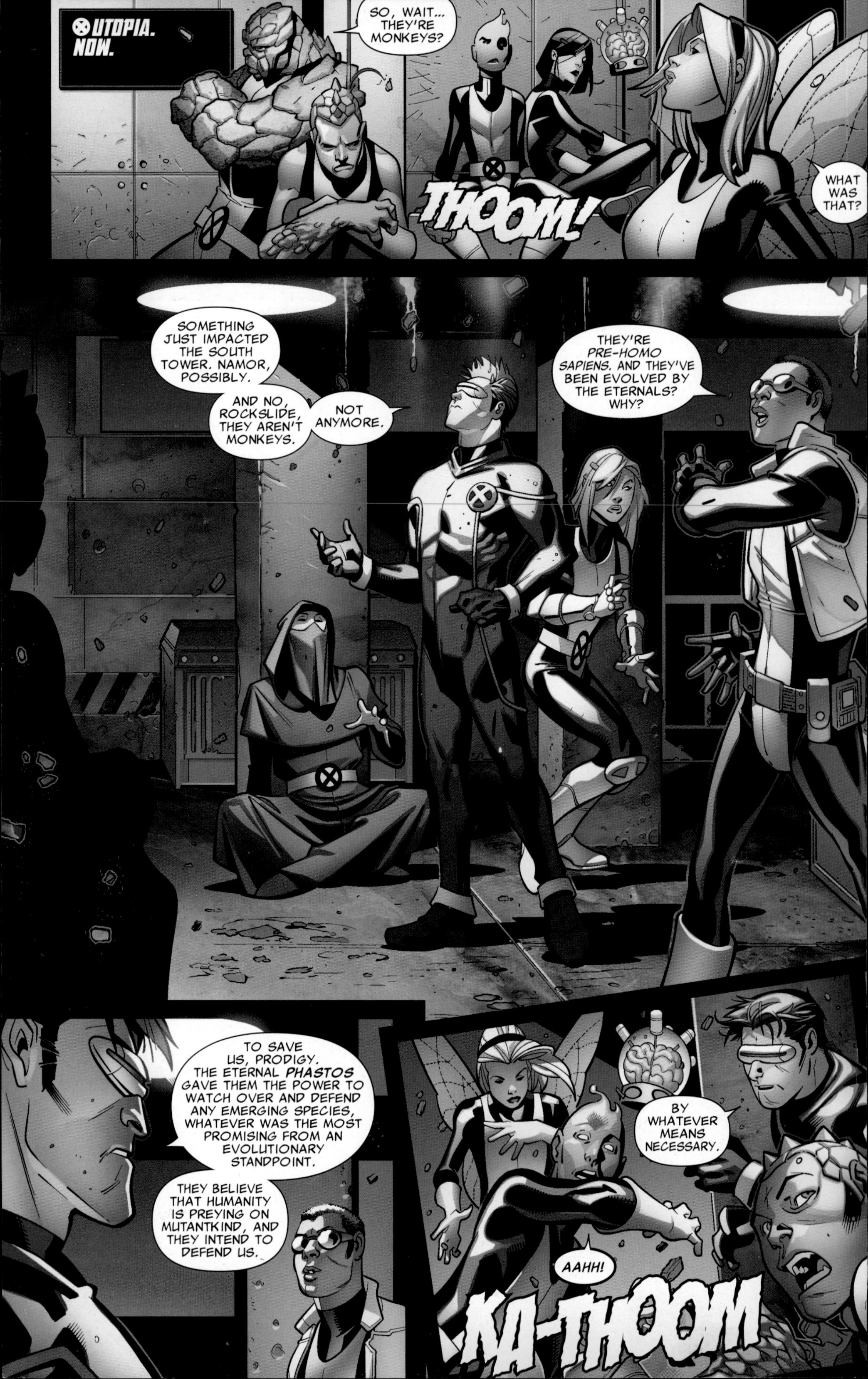
UTOPIA. NOW.
SO, WAIT... THEY'RE MONKEYS?
THOOM!
WHAT WAS THAT?
SOMETHING JUST IMPACTED THE SOUTH TOWER. NAMOR, POSSIBLY.
AND NO, ROCKSLIDE, THEY AREN'T MONKEYS.
NOT ANYMORE.
THEY'RE PRE-HOMO SAPIENS. AND THEY'VE BEEN EVOLVED BY THE ETERNALS? WHY?
TO SAVE US, PRODIGY. THE ETERNAL PHASTOS GAVE THEM THE POWER TO WATCH OVER AND DEFEND ANY EMERGING SPECIES, WHATEVER WAS THE MOST PROMISING FROM AN EVOLUTIONARY STANDPOINT.
THEY BELIEVE THAT HUMANITY IS PREYING ON MUTANTKIND, AND THEY INTEND TO DEFEND US.
BY WHATEVER MEANS NECESSARY.
AAHH!
KA-THOOM

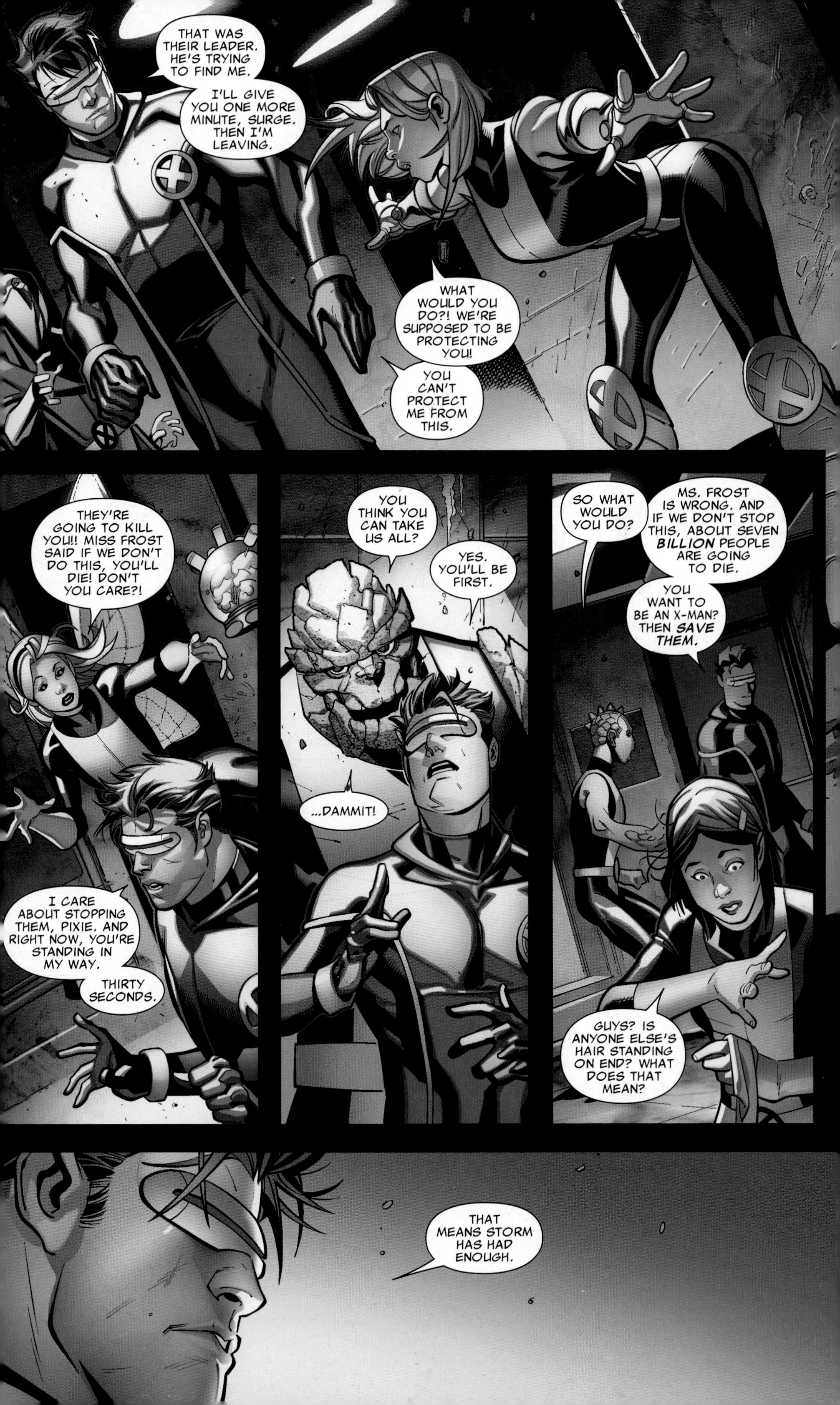
THAT WAS THEIR LEADER. HE'S TRYING TO FIND ME.
I'LL GIVE YOU ONE MORE MINUTE, SURGE. THEN I'M LEAVING.
WHAT WOULD YOU DO?! WE'RE SUPPOSED TO BE PROTECTING YOU!
YOU CAN'T PROTECT ME FROM THIS.
THEY'RE GOING TO KILL YOU!! MISS FROST SAID IF WE DON'T DO THIS, YOU'LL DIE! DON'T YOU CARE?!
I CARE ABOUT STOPPING THEM, PIXIE. AND RIGHT NOW, YOU'RE STANDING IN MY WAY.
THIRTY SECONDS.
YOU THINK YOU CAN TAKE US ALL?
YES. YOU'LL BE FIRST.
...DAMMIT!
SO WHAT WOULD YOU DO?
MS. FROST IS WRONG. AND IF WE DON'T STOP THIS, ABOUT SEVEN BILLION PEOPLE ARE GOING TO DIE.
YOU WANT TO BE AN X-MAN? THEN SAVE THEM.
GUYS? IS ANYONE ELSE'S HAIR STANDING ON END? WHAT DOES THAT MEAN?
THAT MEANS STORM HAS HAD ENOUGH.

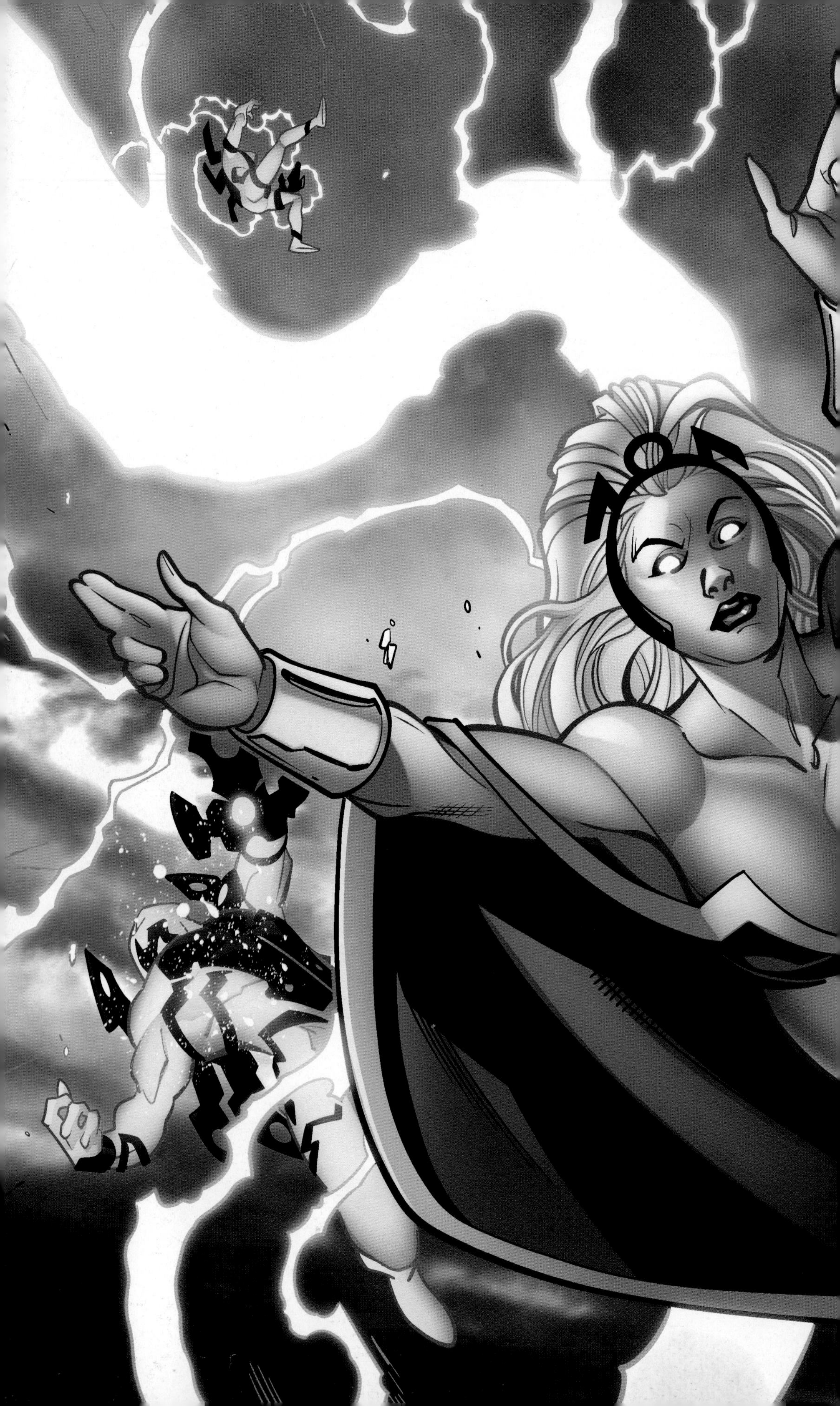

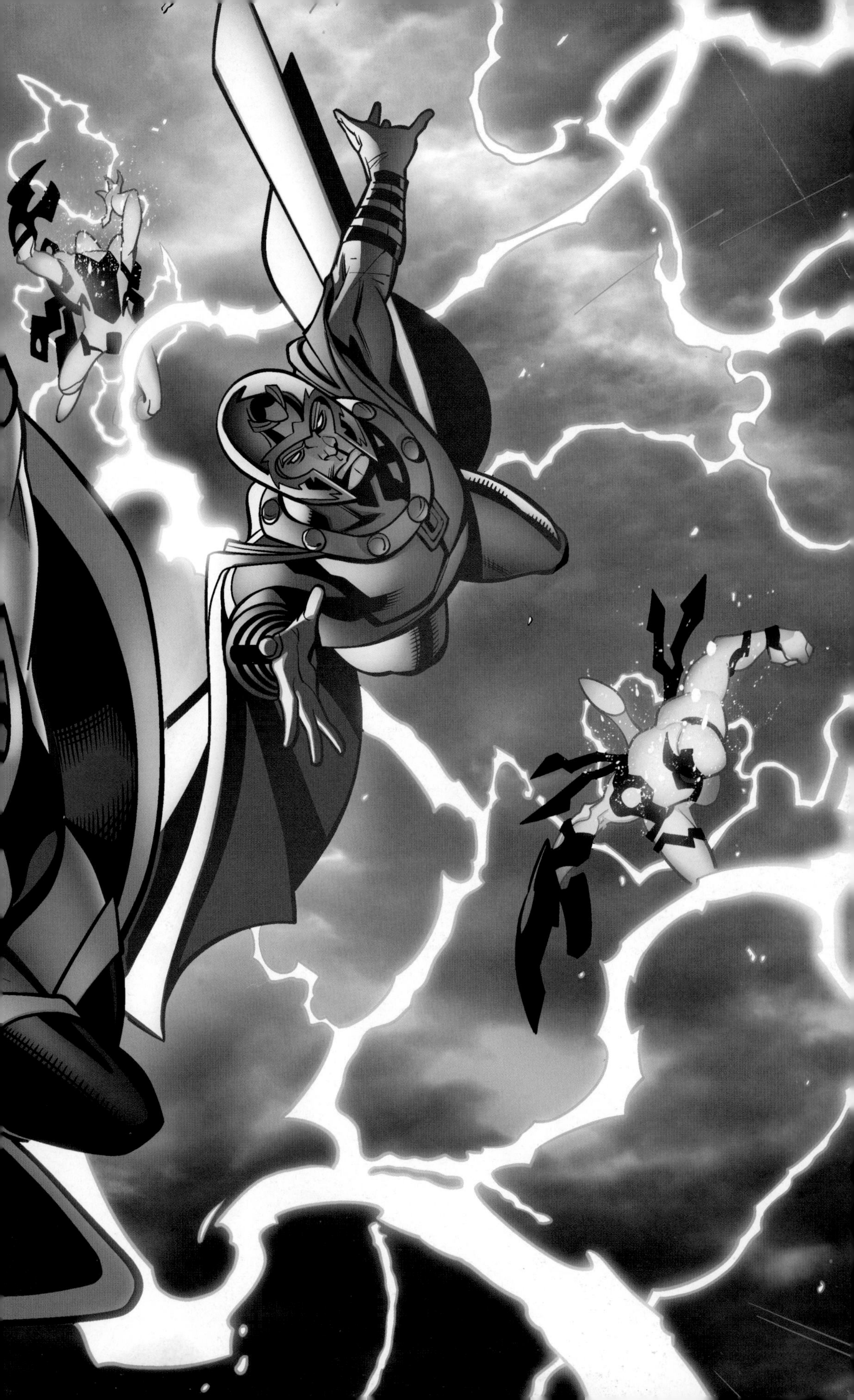

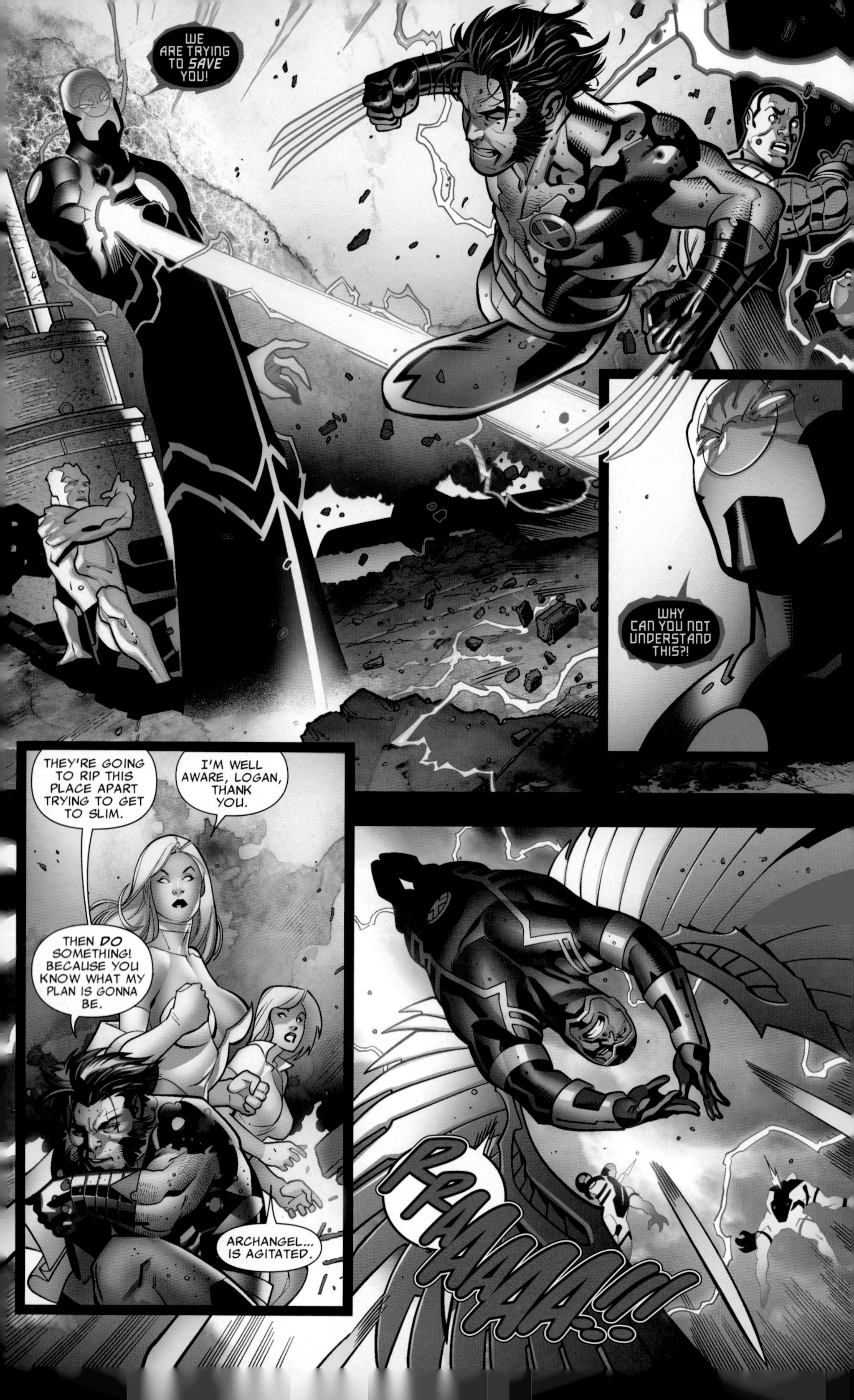
WE ARE TRYING TO SAVE YOU!
WHY CAN YOU NOT UNDERSTAND THIS?!
THEY'RE GOING TO RIP THIS PLACE APART TRYING TO GET TO SLIM.
I'M WELL AWARE, LOGAN, THANK YOU.
THEN DO SOMETHING! BECAUSE YOU KNOW WHAT MY PLAN IS GONNA BE.
ARCHANGEL... IS AGITATED.
RRAAAAA!!!

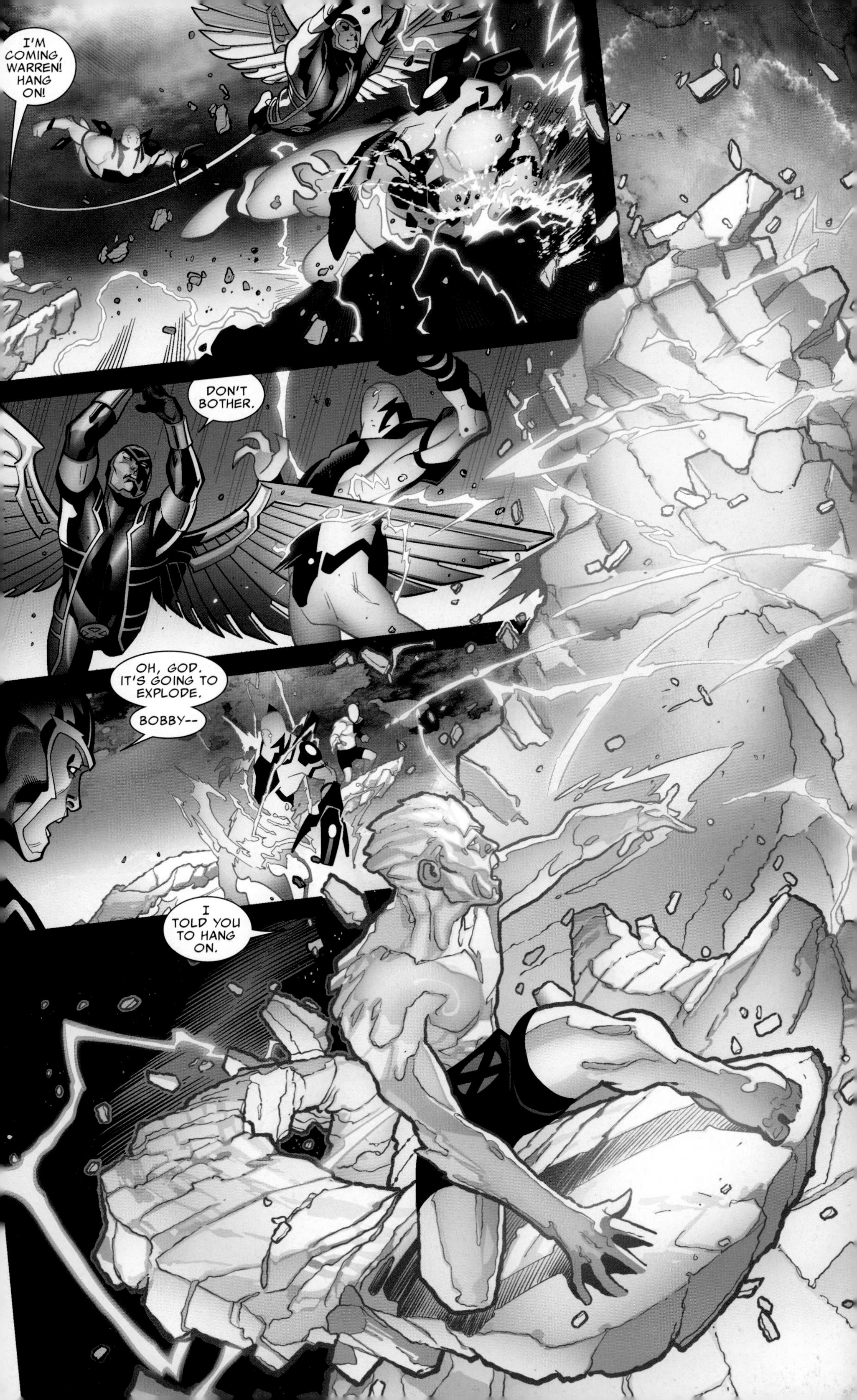
I'M COMING, WARREN! HANG ON!
DON'T BOTHER.
OH, GOD. IT'S GOING TO EXPLODE.
BOBBY--
I TOLD YOU TO HANG ON.

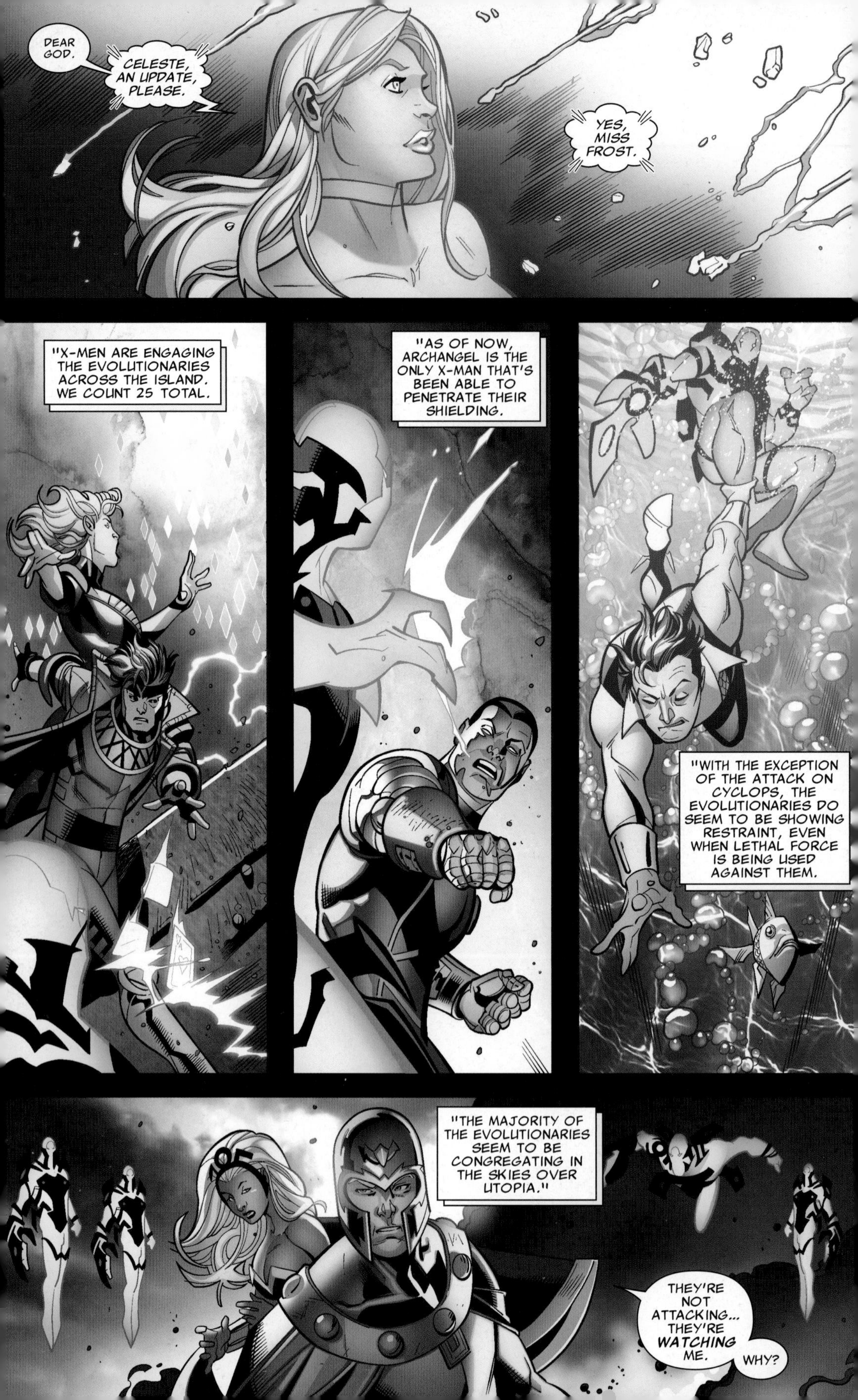
DEAR GOD.
CELESTE, AN UPDATE, PLEASE.
YES, MISS FROST.
"X-MEN ARE ENGAGING THE EVOLUTIONARIES ACROSS THE ISLAND. WE COUNT 25 TOTAL.
"AS OF NOW, ARCHANGEL IS THE ONLY X-MAN THAT'S BEEN ABLE TO PENETRATE THEIR SHIELDING.
"WITH THE EXCEPTION OF THE ATTACK ON CYCLOPS, THE EVOLUTIONARIES DO SEEM TO BE SHOWING RESTRAINT, EVEN WHEN LETHAL FORCE IS BEING USED AGAINST THEM.
"THE MAJORITY OF THE EVOLUTIONARIES SEEM TO BE CONGREGATING IN THE SKIES OVER UTOPIA."
THEY'RE NOT ATTACKING... THEY'RE WATCHING ME.
WHY?

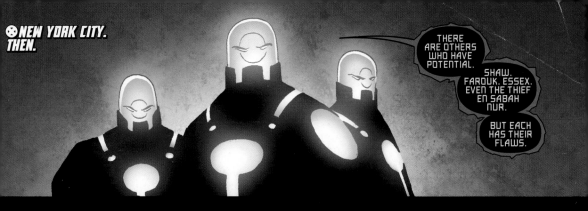

THERE ARE OTHERS WHO HAVE POTENTIAL.

SHAW. FAROUK. ESSEX. EVEN THE THIEF EN SABAH NUR.

BUT EACH HAS THEIR FLAWS.

FLAWS ARE FOR LESSER BEINGS. I AM MAGNETO.

YOU MAY CONTINUE.

HOMO SUPERIOR IS BEING PREYED UPON BY HOMO SAPIEN, AN EVOLUTIONARY DEAD-END SPECIES. THIS IS NOT ACCEPTABLE.

OUR EXISTENCE IS TO PROTECT GENETICALLY SUPERIOR SPECIES. HOMO SAPIENS MUST BE ELIMINATED. WE INTEND TO DO THIS.

BUT MUTANTKIND REQUIRES LEADERSHIP, THEY MUST BE PREPARED FOR THE VACUUM LEFT BY HUMANITY'S END.

AND HOW DO YOU PLAN TO ACCOMPLISH THIS EXTINCTION OF MAN?

THEIR DNA WILL BE TARGETED. IT WILL BE INSTANTANEOUS, PLANET-WIDE. IT WILL BE WHAT THEY THEMSELVES ARE NOT... MERCIFUL.

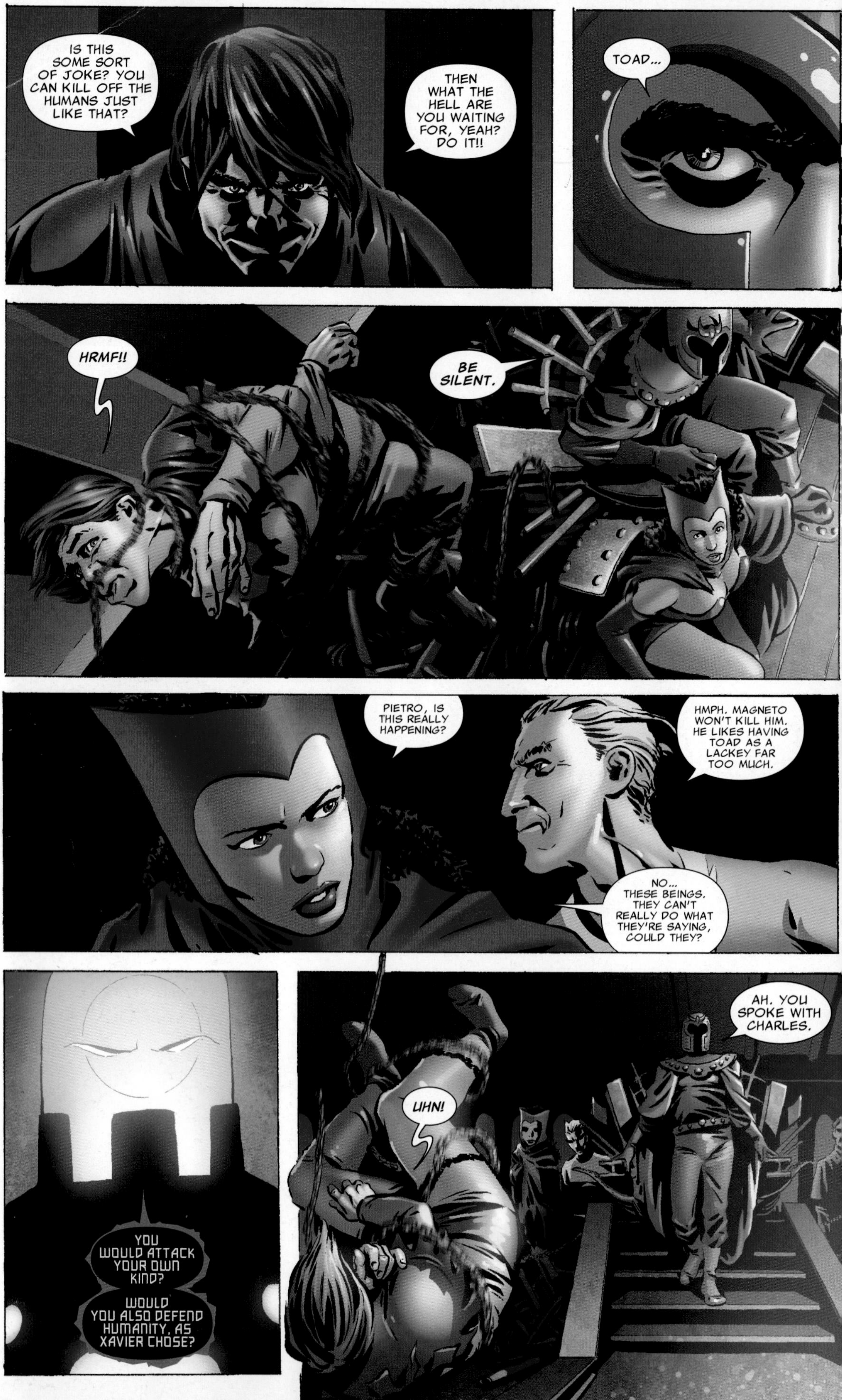
IS THIS SOME SORT OF JOKE? YOU CAN KILL OFF THE HUMANS JUST LIKE THAT?
THEN WHAT THE HELL ARE YOU WAITING FOR, YEAH? DO IT!!
TOAD...
HRMF!!
BE SILENT.
PIETRO, IS THIS REALLY HAPPENING?
HMPH. MAGNETO WON'T KILL HIM. HE LIKES HAVING TOAD AS A LACKEY FAR TOO MUCH.
NO... THESE BEINGS. THEY CAN'T REALLY DO WHAT THEY'RE SAYING, COULD THEY?
YOU WOULD ATTACK YOUR OWN KIND?
WOULD YOU ALSO DEFEND HUMANITY, AS XAVIER CHOSE?
UHN!
AH. YOU SPOKE WITH CHARLES.

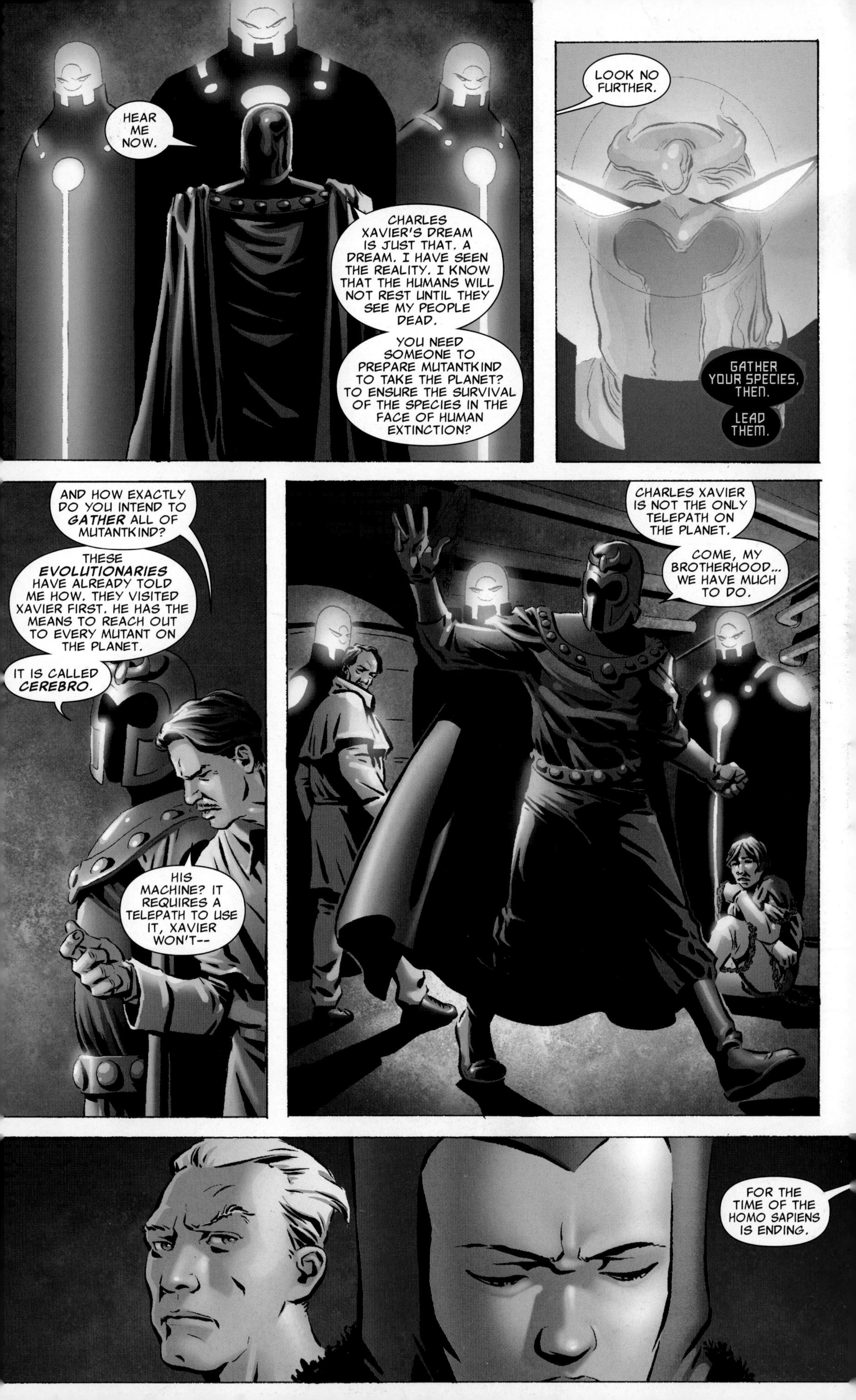
HEAR ME NOW.
CHARLES XAVIER'S DREAM IS JUST THAT. A DREAM. I HAVE SEEN THE REALITY. I KNOW THAT THE HUMANS WILL NOT REST UNTIL THEY SEE MY PEOPLE DEAD.
YOU NEED SOMEONE TO PREPARE MUTANTKIND TO TAKE THE PLANET? TO ENSURE THE SURVIVAL OF THE SPECIES IN THE FACE OF HUMAN EXTINCTION?
LOOK NO FURTHER.
GATHER YOUR SPECIES, THEN.
LEAD THEM.
AND HOW EXACTLY DO YOU INTEND TO *GATHER* ALL OF MUTANTKIND?
THESE *EVOLUTIONARIES* HAVE ALREADY TOLD ME HOW. THEY VISITED XAVIER FIRST. HE HAS THE MEANS TO REACH OUT TO EVERY MUTANT ON THE PLANET.
IT IS CALLED *CEREBRO*.
HIS MACHINE? IT REQUIRES A TELEPATH TO USE IT, XAVIER WON'T--
CHARLES XAVIER IS NOT THE ONLY TELEPATH ON THE PLANET.
COME, MY BROTHERHOOD... WE HAVE MUCH TO DO.
FOR THE TIME OF THE HOMO SAPIENS IS ENDING.

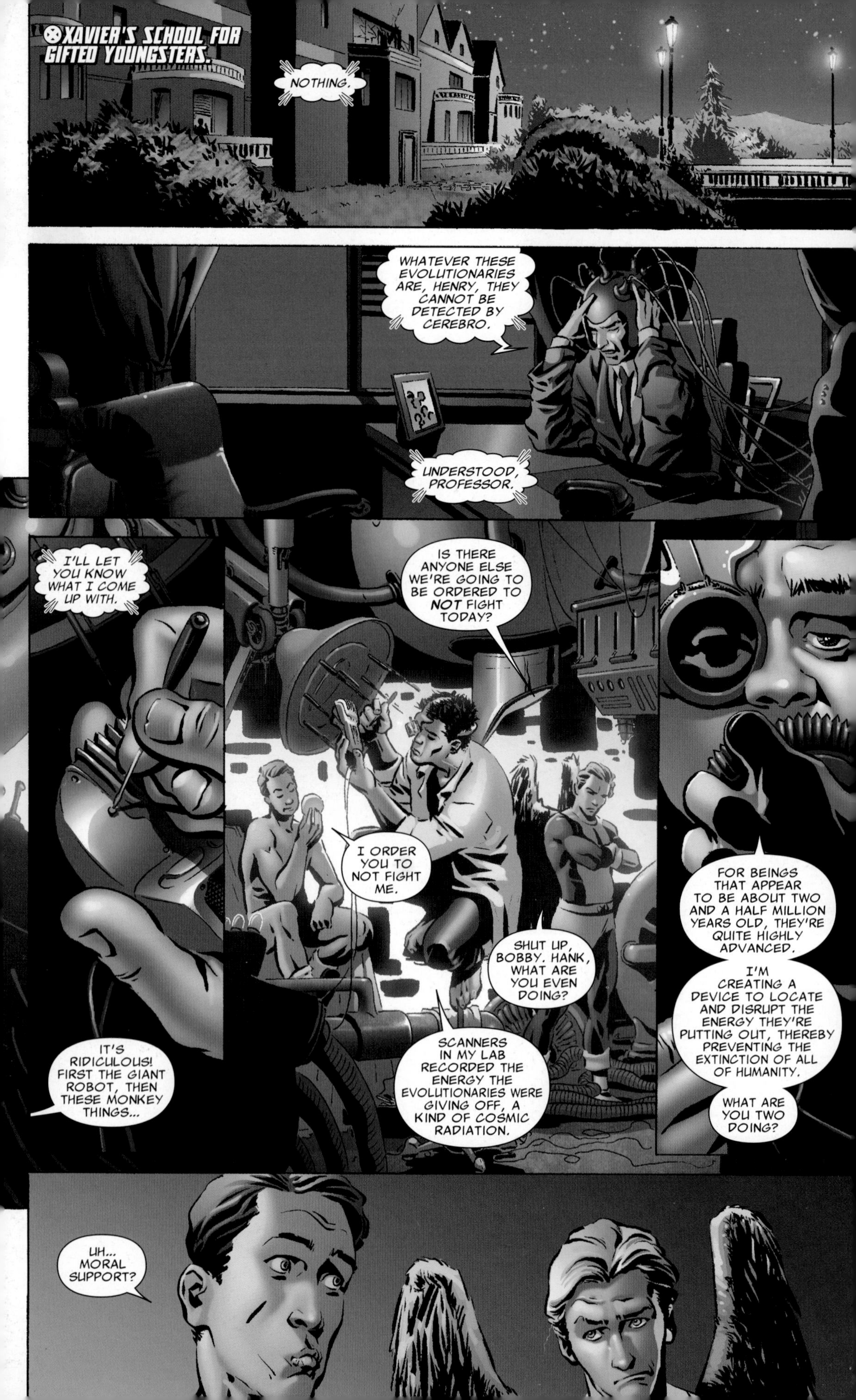
XAVIER'S SCHOOL FOR GIFTED YOUNGSTERS.
NOTHING.
WHATEVER THESE EVOLUTIONARIES ARE, HENRY, THEY CANNOT BE DETECTED BY CEREBRO.
UNDERSTOOD, PROFESSOR.
I'LL LET YOU KNOW WHAT I COME UP WITH.
IT'S RIDICULOUS! FIRST THE GIANT ROBOT, THEN THESE MONKEY THINGS...
IS THERE ANYONE ELSE WE'RE GOING TO BE ORDERED TO NOT FIGHT TODAY?
I ORDER YOU TO NOT FIGHT ME.
SHUT UP, BOBBY. HANK, WHAT ARE YOU EVEN DOING?
SCANNERS IN MY LAB RECORDED THE ENERGY THE EVOLUTIONARIES WERE GIVING OFF, A KIND OF COSMIC RADIATION.
FOR BEINGS THAT APPEAR TO BE ABOUT TWO AND A HALF MILLION YEARS OLD, THEY'RE QUITE HIGHLY ADVANCED.
I'M CREATING A DEVICE TO LOCATE AND DISRUPT THE ENERGY THEY'RE PUTTING OUT, THEREBY PREVENTING THE EXTINCTION OF ALL OF HUMANITY.
WHAT ARE YOU TWO DOING?
UH... MORAL SUPPORT?

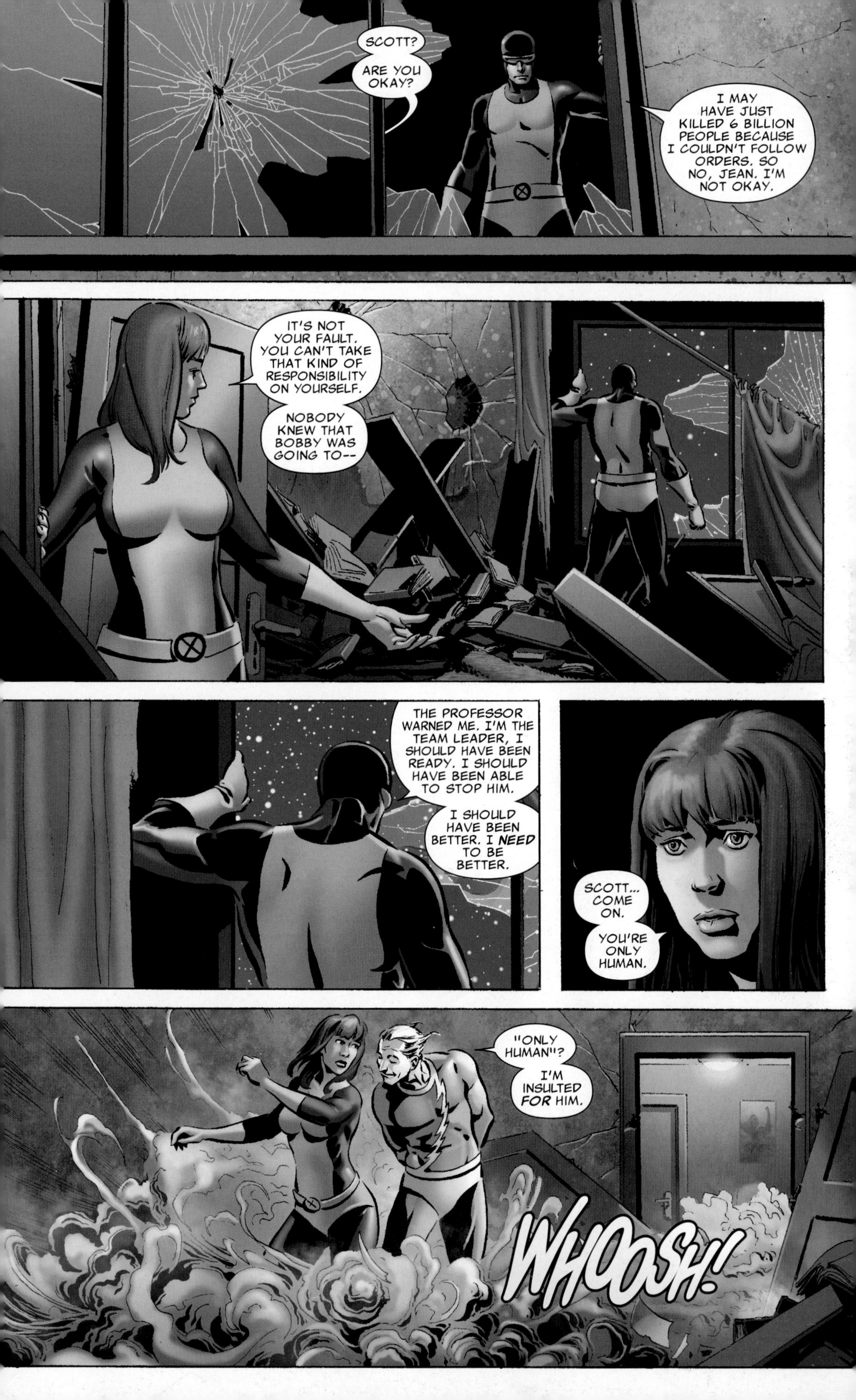
SCOTT?
ARE YOU OKAY?
I MAY HAVE JUST KILLED 6 BILLION PEOPLE BECAUSE I COULDN'T FOLLOW ORDERS. SO NO, JEAN. I'M NOT OKAY.
IT'S NOT YOUR FAULT. YOU CAN'T TAKE THAT KIND OF RESPONSIBILITY ON YOURSELF.
NOBODY KNEW THAT BOBBY WAS GOING TO--
THE PROFESSOR WARNED ME. I'M THE TEAM LEADER, I SHOULD HAVE BEEN READY. I SHOULD HAVE BEEN ABLE TO STOP HIM.
I SHOULD HAVE BEEN BETTER. I *NEED* TO BE BETTER.
SCOTT... COME ON.
YOU'RE ONLY HUMAN.
"ONLY HUMAN"?
I'M INSULTED *FOR* HIM.
WHOOSH!

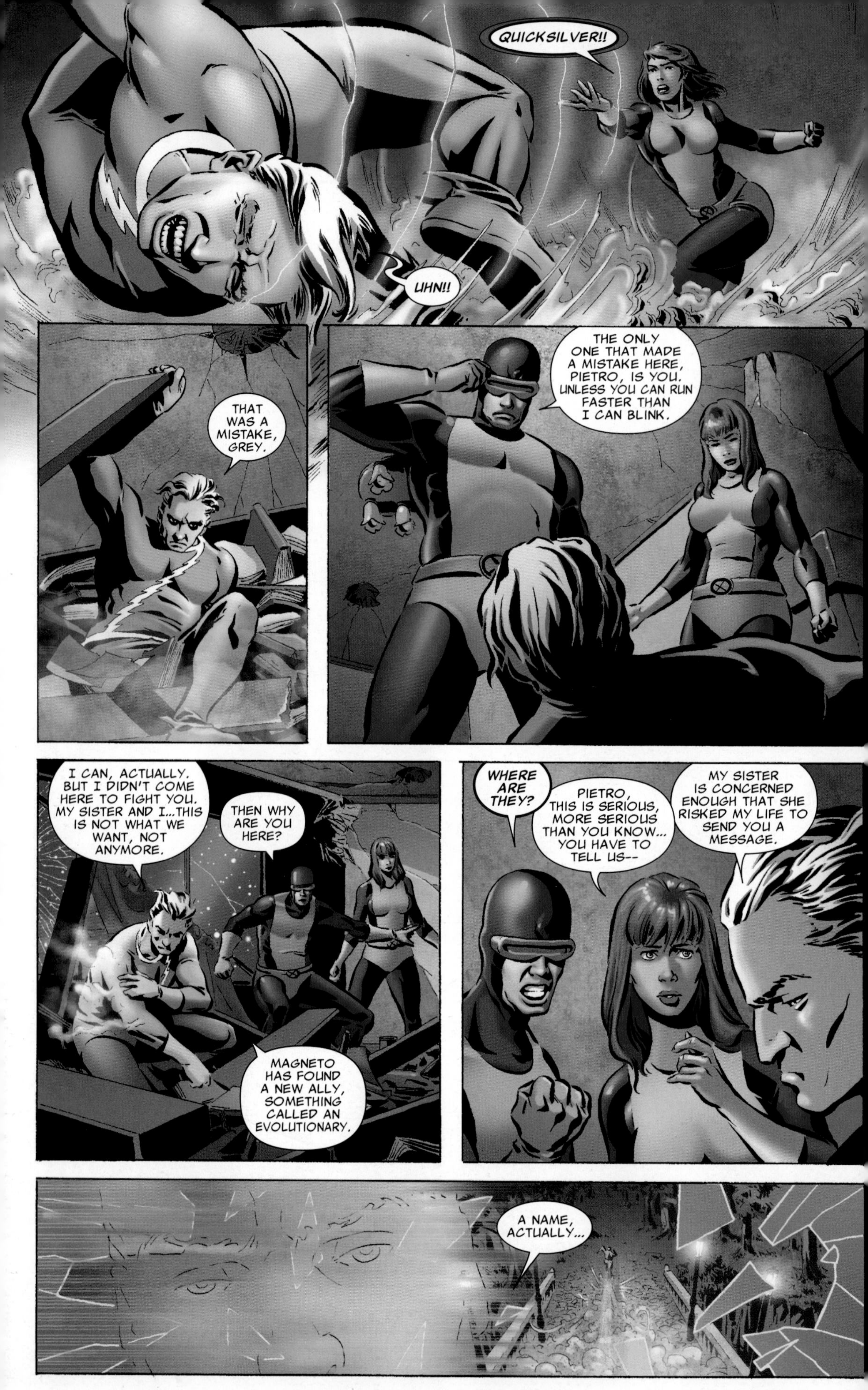
QUICKSILVER!!
UHN!!
THAT WAS A MISTAKE, GREY.
THE ONLY ONE THAT MADE A MISTAKE HERE, PIETRO, IS YOU. UNLESS YOU CAN RUN FASTER THAN I CAN BLINK.
I CAN, ACTUALLY. BUT I DIDN'T COME HERE TO FIGHT YOU. MY SISTER AND I...THIS IS NOT WHAT WE WANT, NOT ANYMORE.
THEN WHY ARE YOU HERE?
MAGNETO HAS FOUND A NEW ALLY, SOMETHING CALLED AN EVOLUTIONARY.
WHERE ARE THEY?
PIETRO, THIS IS SERIOUS, MORE SERIOUS THAN YOU KNOW... YOU HAVE TO TELL US--
MY SISTER IS CONCERNED ENOUGH THAT SHE RISKED MY LIFE TO SEND YOU A MESSAGE.
A NAME, ACTUALLY...

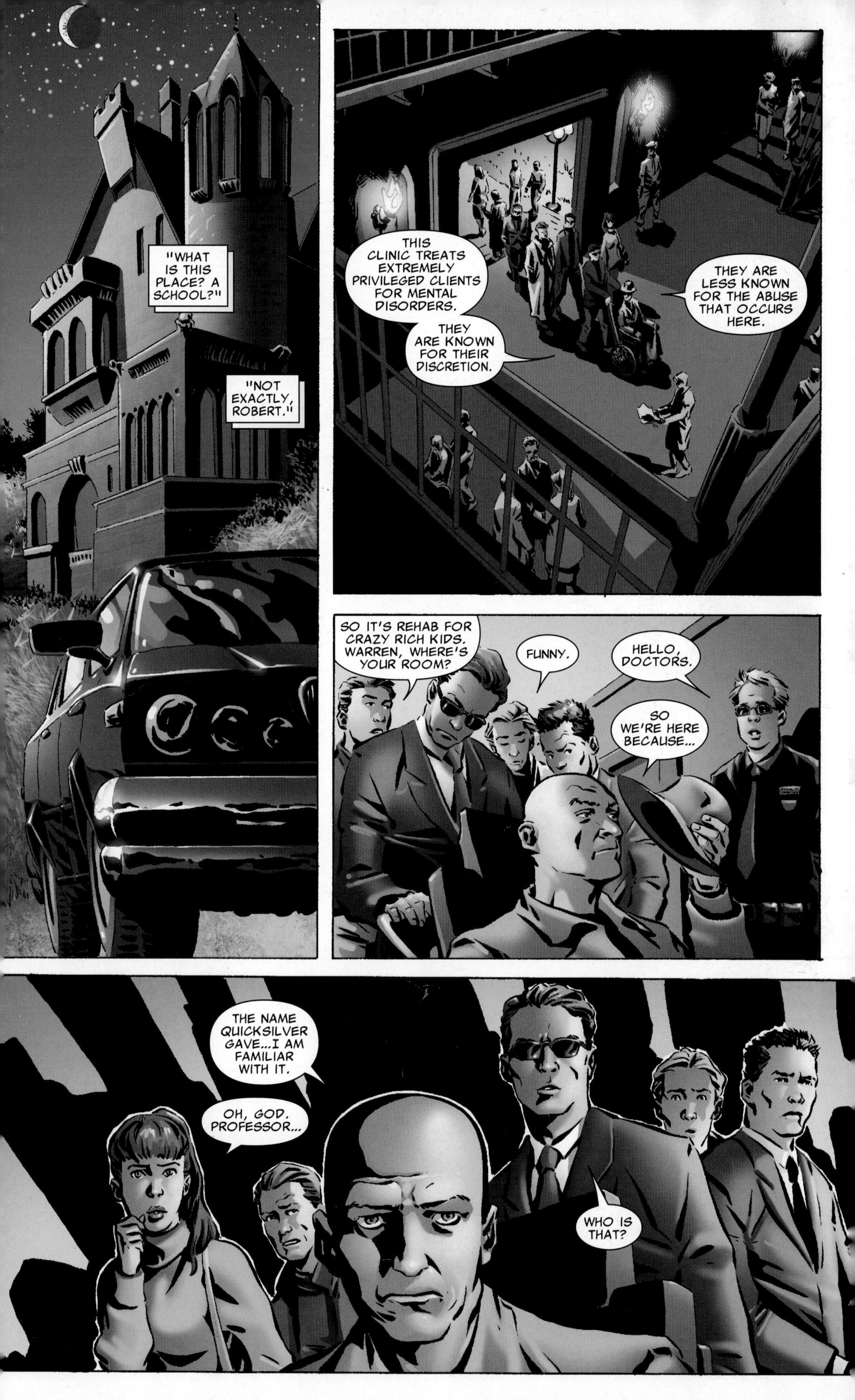
"WHAT IS THIS PLACE? A SCHOOL?"
"NOT EXACTLY, ROBERT."
THIS CLINIC TREATS EXTREMELY PRIVILEGED CLIENTS FOR MENTAL DISORDERS.
THEY ARE KNOWN FOR THEIR DISCRETION.
THEY ARE LESS KNOWN FOR THE ABUSE THAT OCCURS HERE.
SO IT'S REHAB FOR CRAZY RICH KIDS. WARREN, WHERE'S YOUR ROOM?
FUNNY.
HELLO, DOCTORS.
SO WE'RE HERE BECAUSE...
THE NAME QUICKSILVER GAVE...I AM FAMILIAR WITH IT.
OH, GOD. PROFESSOR...
WHO IS THAT?

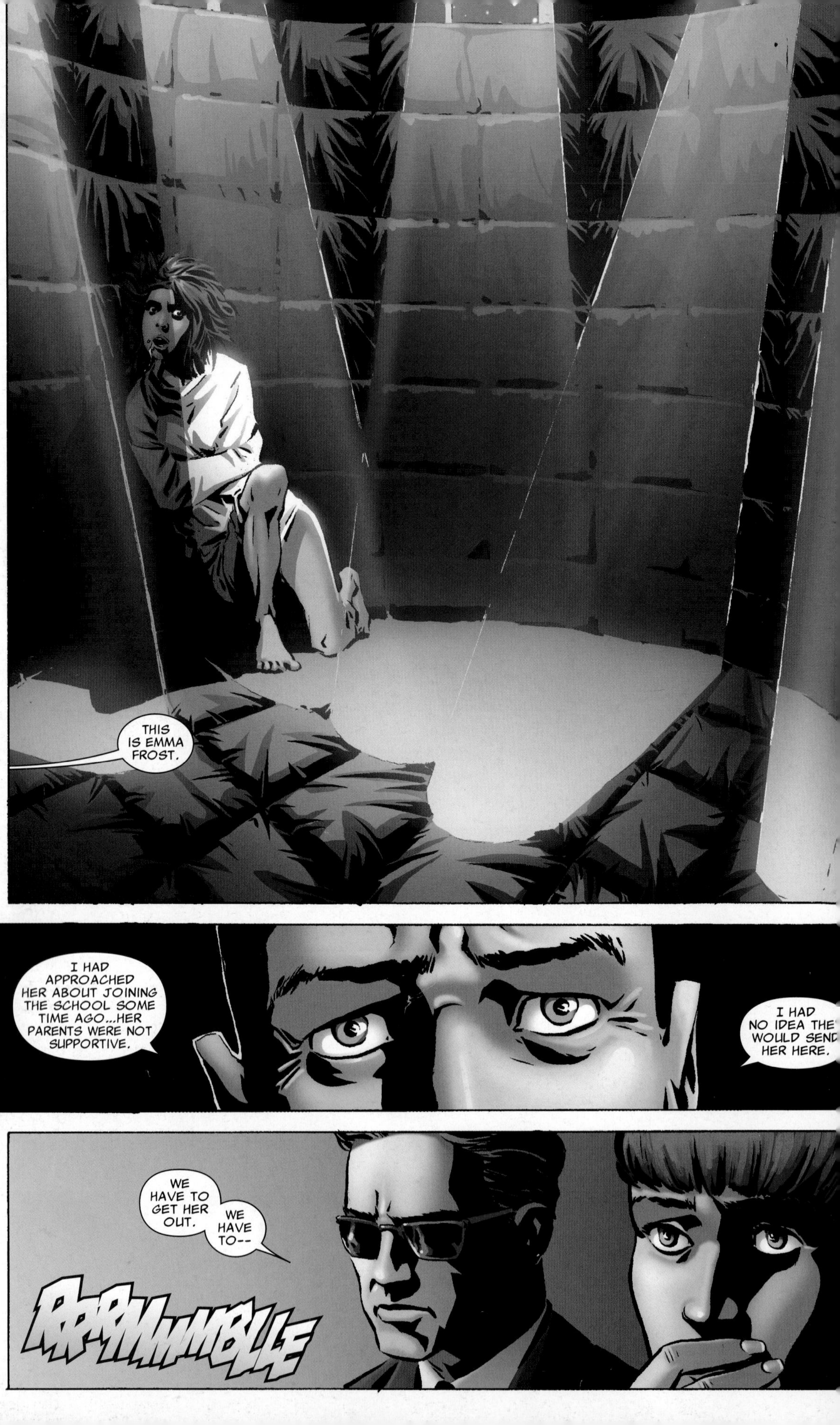
THIS IS EMMA FROST.
I HAD APPROACHED HER ABOUT JOINING THE SCHOOL SOME TIME AGO...HER PARENTS WERE NOT SUPPORTIVE.
I HAD NO IDEA THEY WOULD SEND HER HERE.
WE HAVE TO GET HER OUT.
WE HAVE TO--
RRRRMMMMBLLE

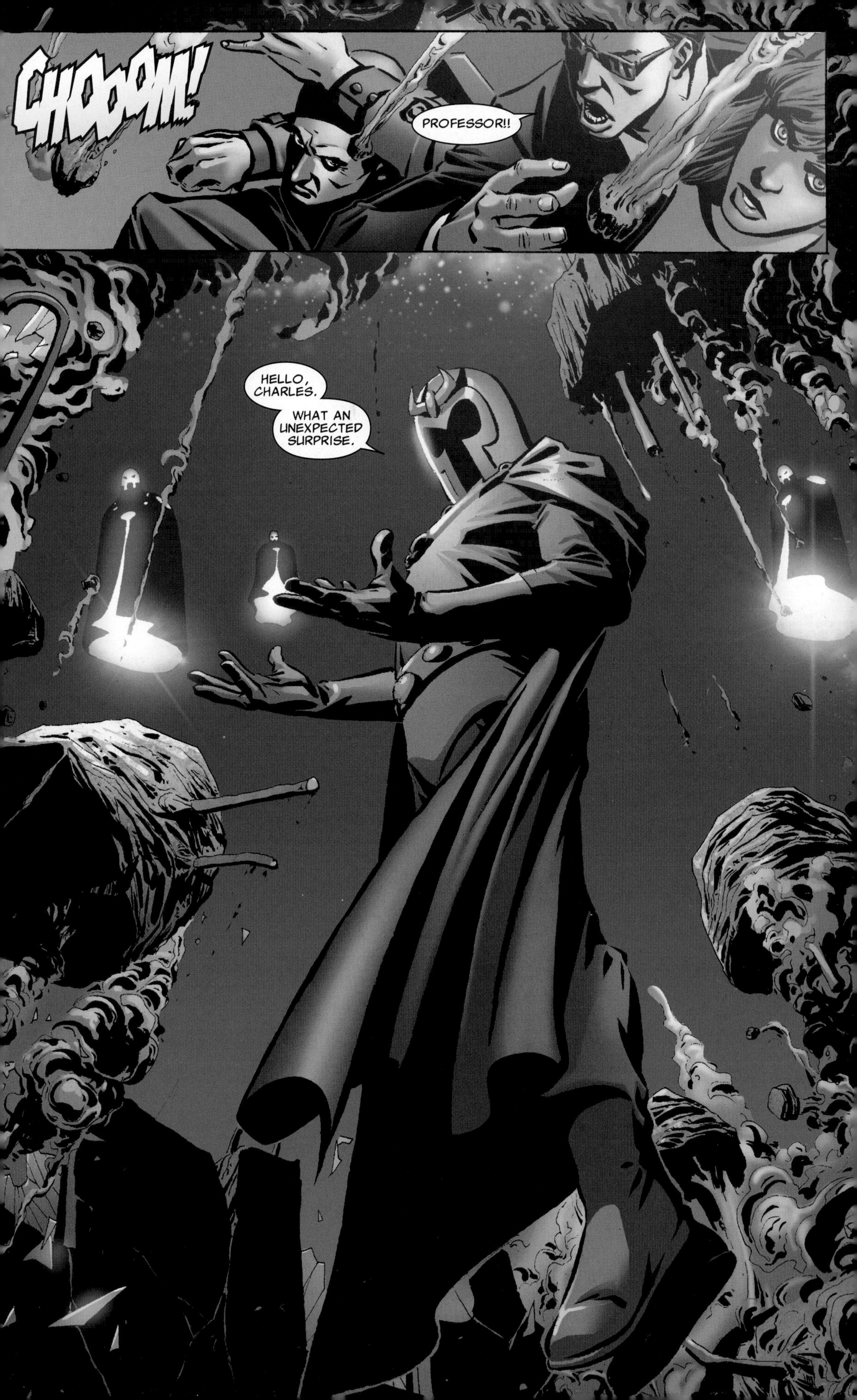
CHOOOM!
PROFESSOR!!
HELLO, CHARLES.
WHAT AN UNEXPECTED SURPRISE.

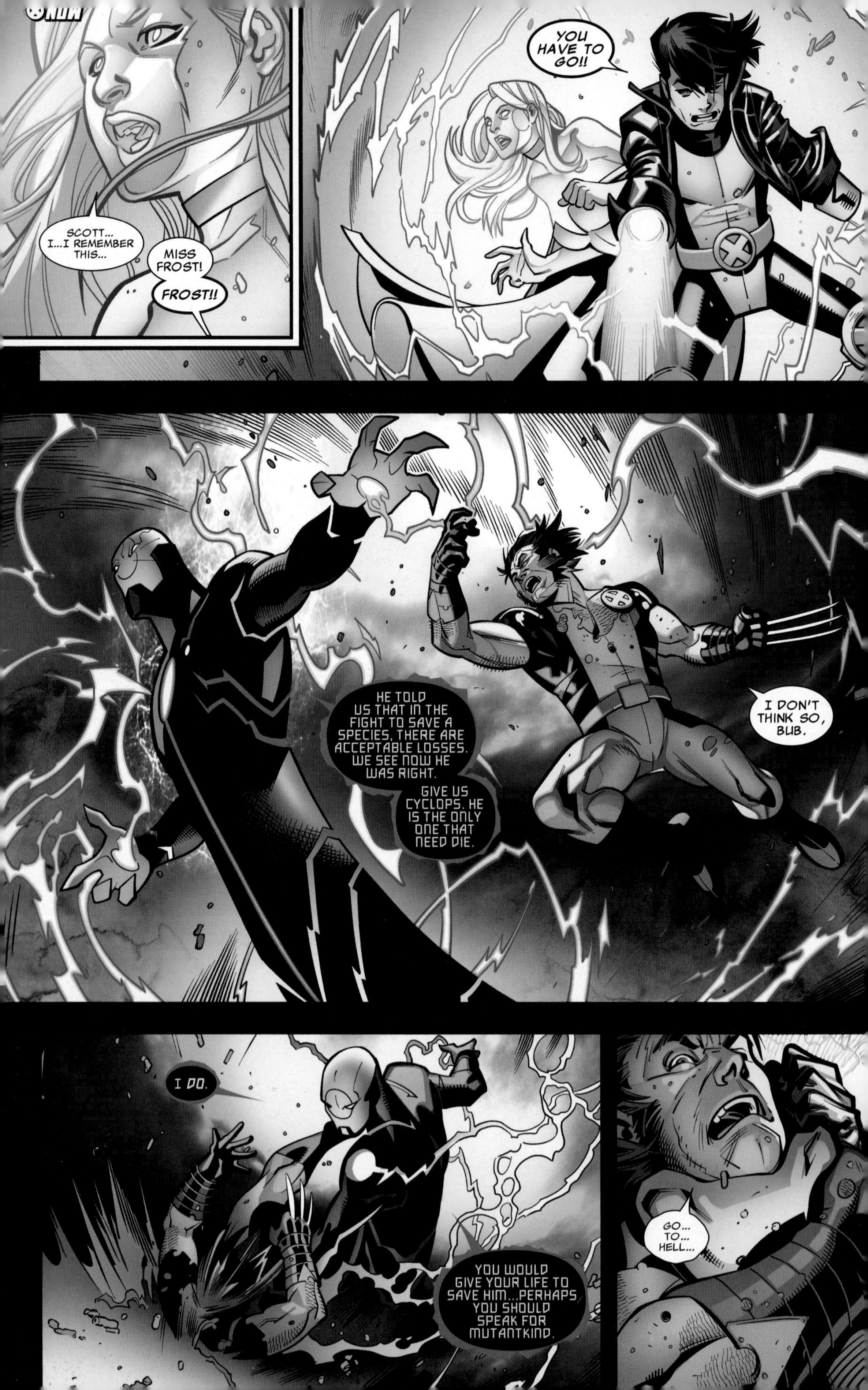

NOW
SCOTT... I...I REMEMBER THIS...
MISS FROST!
FROST!!
YOU HAVE TO GO!!
HE TOLD US THAT IN THE FIGHT TO SAVE A SPECIES, THERE ARE ACCEPTABLE LOSSES. WE SEE NOW HE WAS RIGHT.
GIVE US CYCLOPS. HE IS THE ONLY ONE THAT NEED DIE.
I DON'T THINK SO, BUB.
I DO.
YOU WOULD GIVE YOUR LIFE TO SAVE HIM...PERHAPS YOU SHOULD SPEAK FOR MUTANTKIND.
GO... TO... HELL...

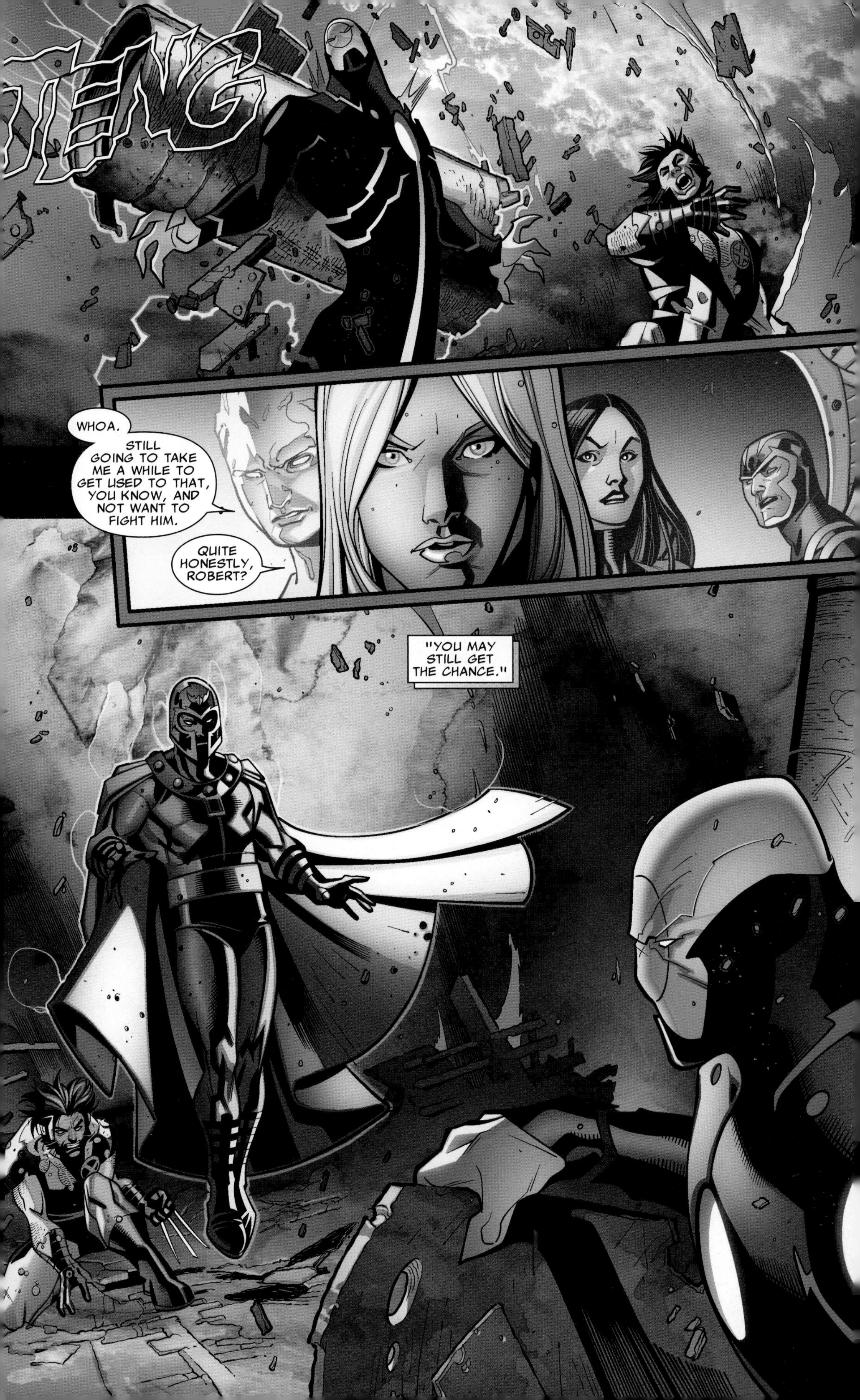
TLENG
WHOA.
STILL GOING TO TAKE ME A WHILE TO GET USED TO THAT, YOU KNOW, AND NOT WANT TO FIGHT HIM.
QUITE HONESTLY, ROBERT?
"YOU MAY STILL GET THE CHANCE."

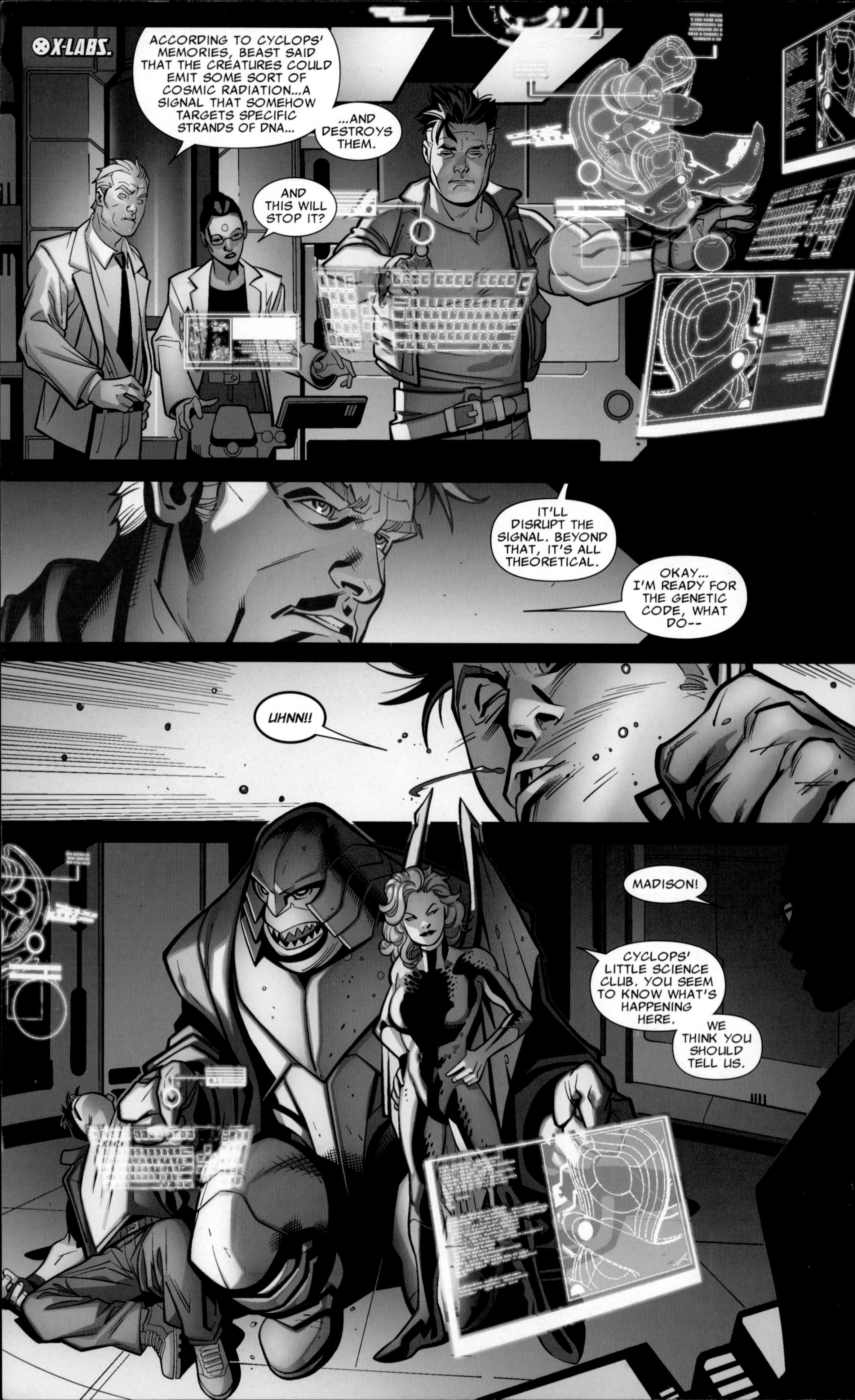
X-LABS.
ACCORDING TO CYCLOPS' MEMORIES, BEAST SAID THAT THE CREATURES COULD EMIT SOME SORT OF COSMIC RADIATION...A SIGNAL THAT SOMEHOW TARGETS SPECIFIC STRANDS OF DNA...
...AND DESTROYS THEM.
AND THIS WILL STOP IT?
IT'LL DISRUPT THE SIGNAL. BEYOND THAT, IT'S ALL THEORETICAL.
OKAY... I'M READY FOR THE GENETIC CODE, WHAT DO--
UHNN!!
MADISON!
CYCLOPS' LITTLE SCIENCE CLUB. YOU SEEM TO KNOW WHAT'S HAPPENING HERE.
WE THINK YOU SHOULD TELL US.

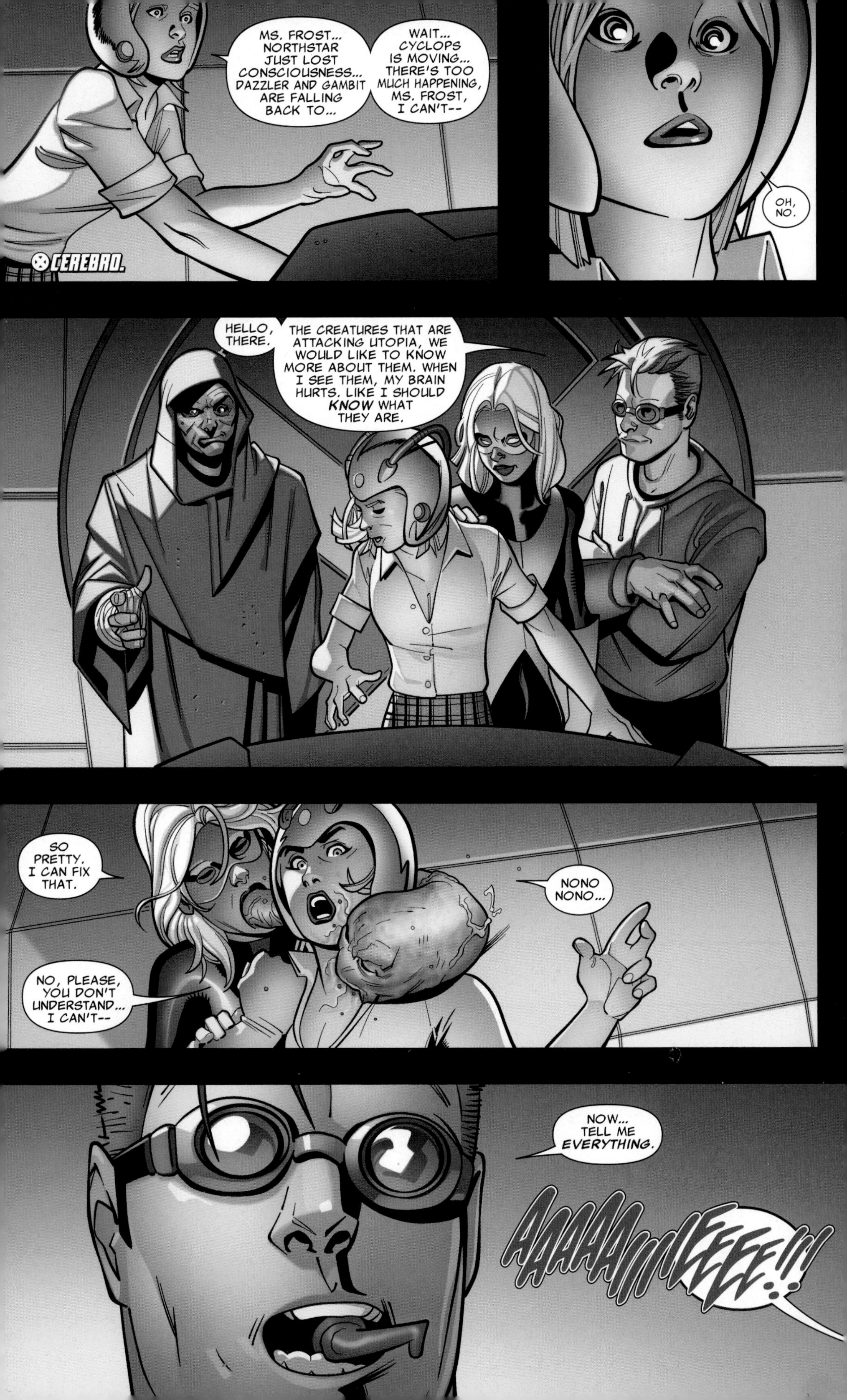
MS. FROST... NORTHSTAR JUST LOST CONSCIOUSNESS... DAZZLER AND GAMBIT ARE FALLING BACK TO...
WAIT... CYCLOPS IS MOVING... THERE'S TOO MUCH HAPPENING, MS. FROST, I CAN'T--
CEREBRO.
OH, NO.
HELLO, THERE.
THE CREATURES THAT ARE ATTACKING UTOPIA, WE WOULD LIKE TO KNOW MORE ABOUT THEM. WHEN I SEE THEM, MY BRAIN HURTS. LIKE I SHOULD KNOW WHAT THEY ARE.
SO PRETTY. I CAN FIX THAT.
NO, PLEASE, YOU DON'T UNDERSTAND... I CAN'T--
NONO NONO...
NOW... TELL ME EVERYTHING.
AAAAAIIIIEEEE!!!

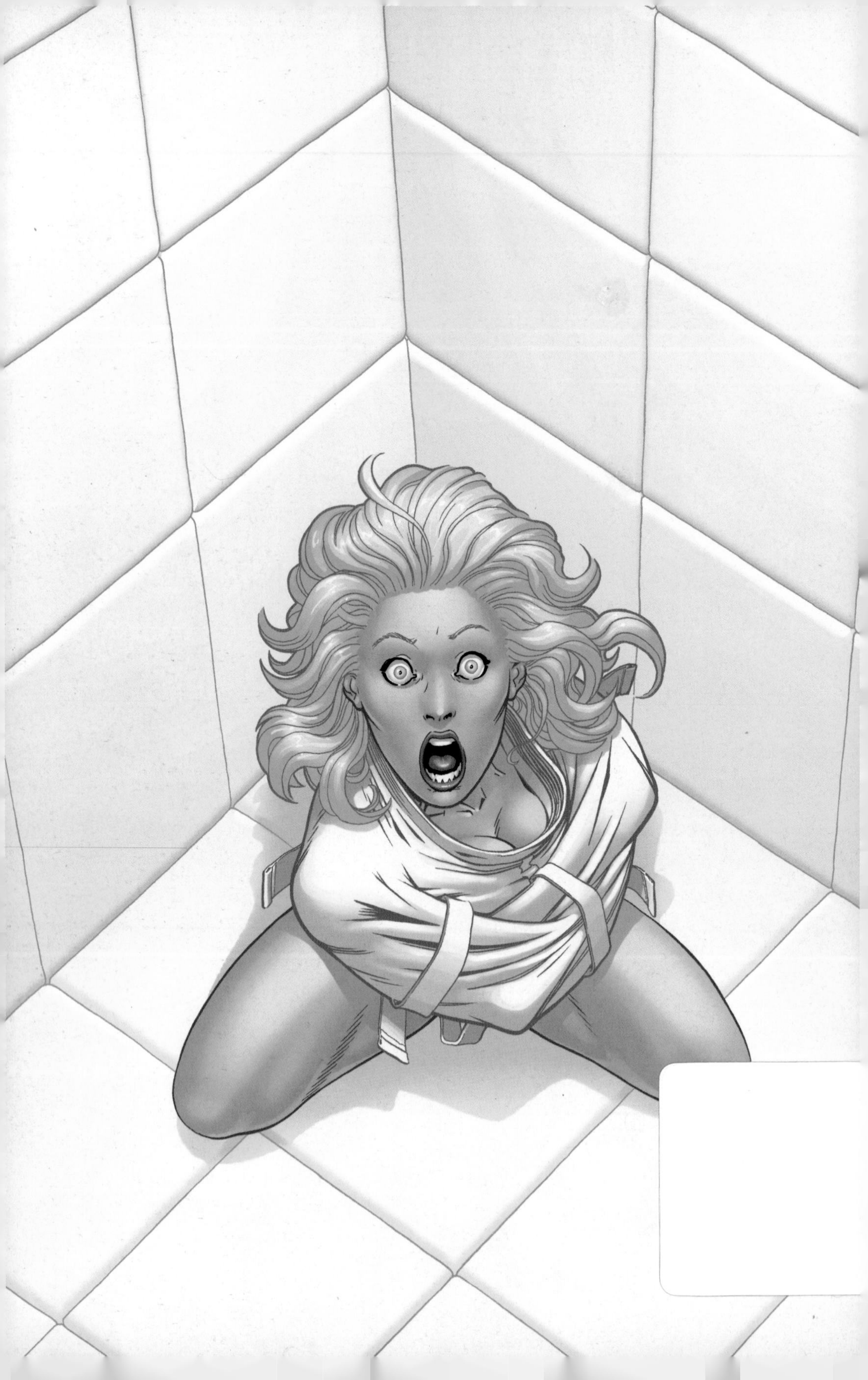

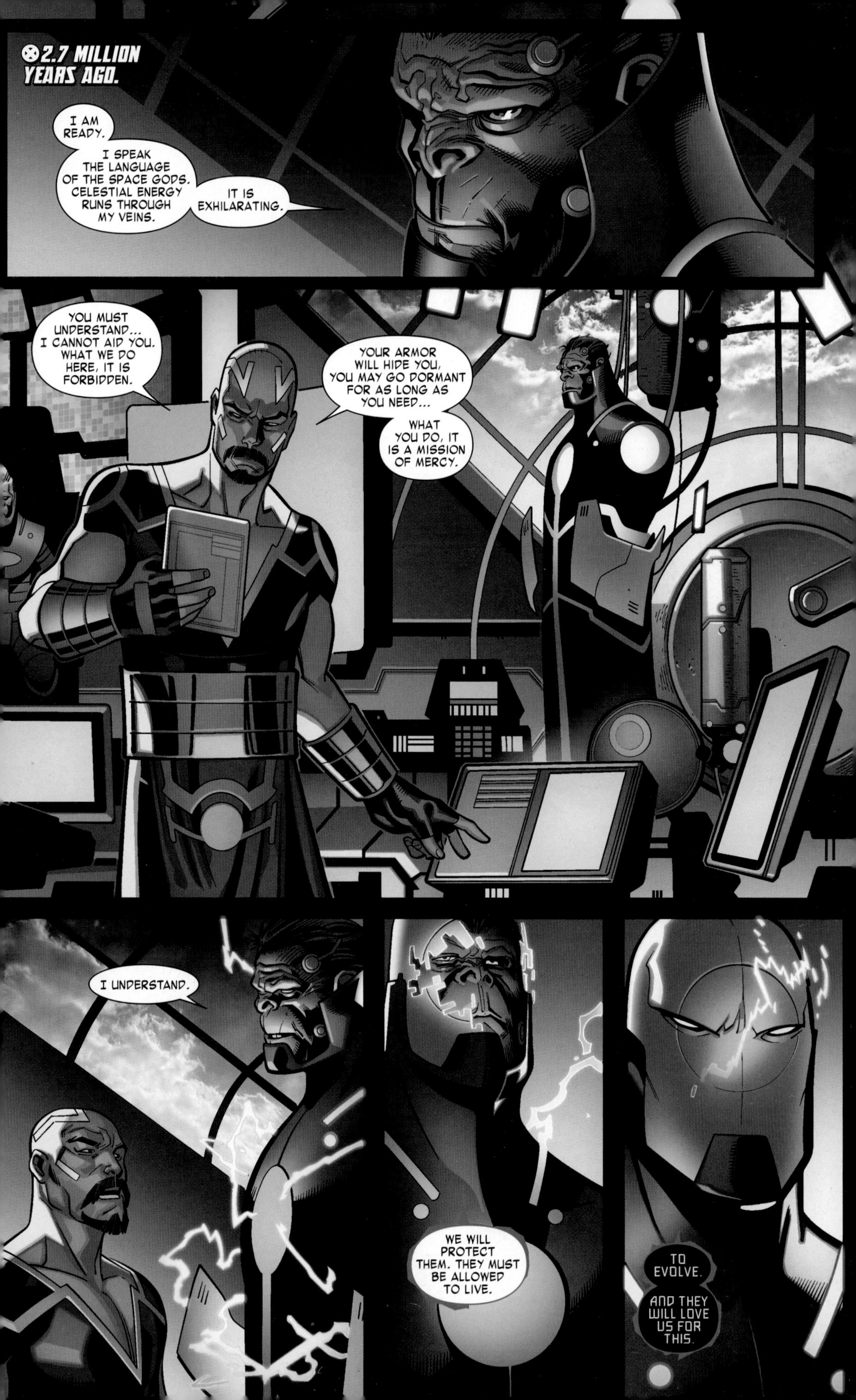
2.7 MILLION YEARS AGO.
I AM READY.
I SPEAK THE LANGUAGE OF THE SPACE GODS. CELESTIAL ENERGY RUNS THROUGH MY VEINS.
IT IS EXHILARATING.
YOU MUST UNDERSTAND... I CANNOT AID YOU. WHAT WE DO HERE, IT IS FORBIDDEN.
YOUR ARMOR WILL HIDE YOU, YOU MAY GO DORMANT FOR AS LONG AS YOU NEED...
WHAT YOU DO, IT IS A MISSION OF MERCY.
I UNDERSTAND.
WE WILL PROTECT THEM. THEY MUST BE ALLOWED TO LIVE.
TO EVOLVE.
AND THEY WILL LOVE US FOR THIS.

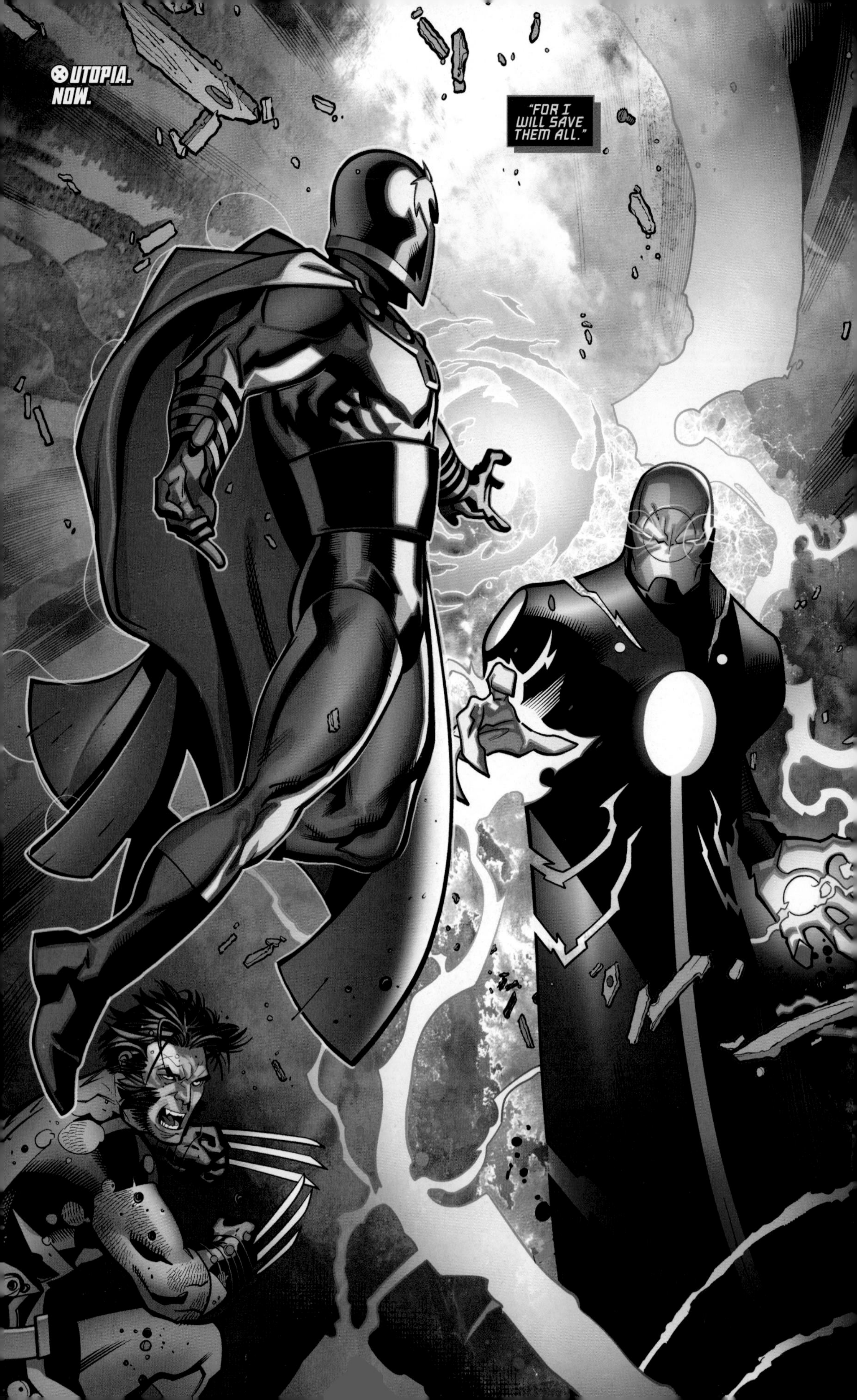
UTOPIA.
NOW.
"FOR I WILL SAVE THEM ALL."

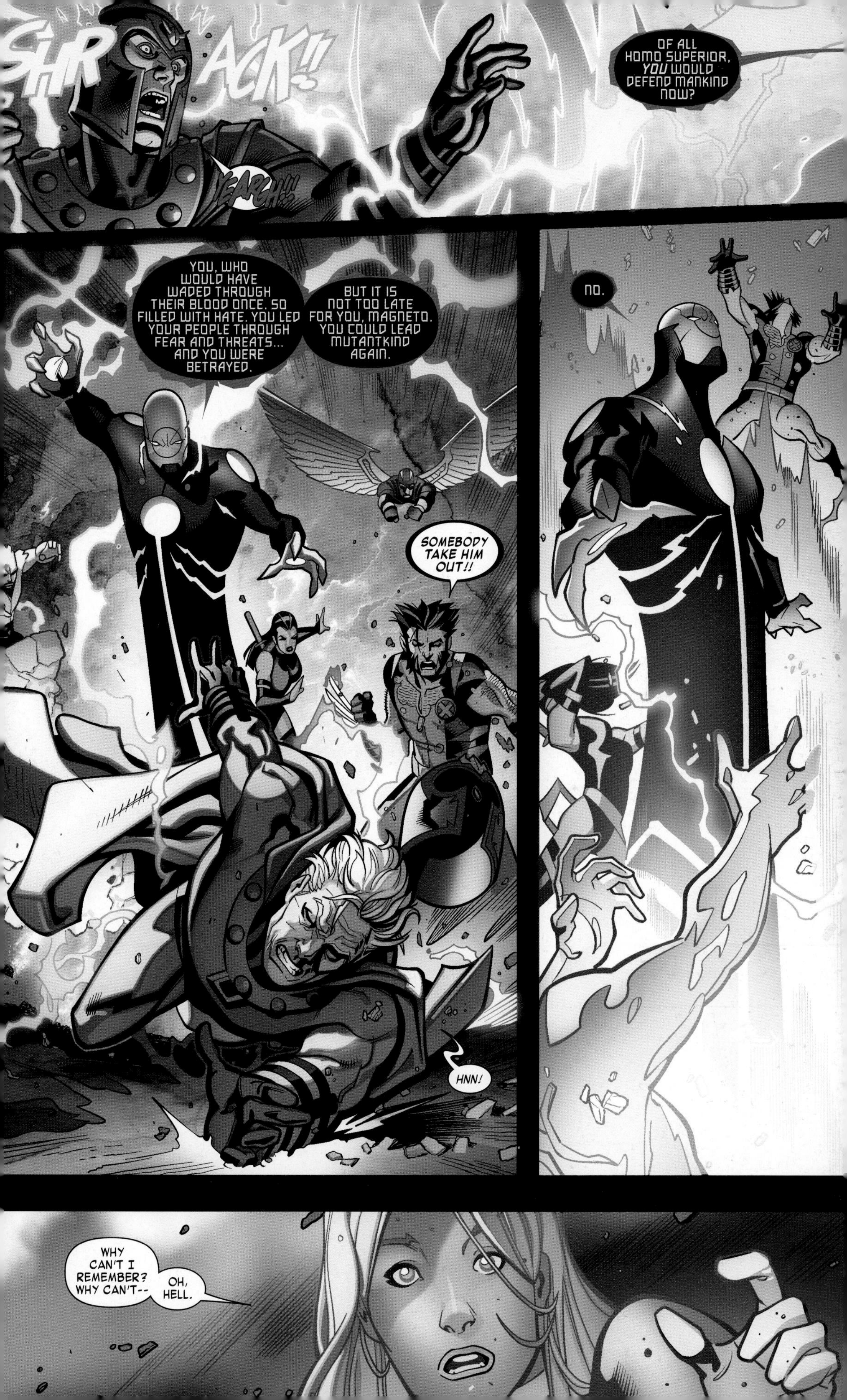
SHRACK!!
YEARGH!!
OF ALL HOMO SUPERIOR, YOU WOULD DEFEND MANKIND NOW?
YOU, WHO WOULD HAVE WADED THROUGH THEIR BLOOD ONCE. SO FILLED WITH HATE. YOU LED YOUR PEOPLE THROUGH FEAR AND THREATS... AND YOU WERE BETRAYED.
BUT IT IS NOT TOO LATE FOR YOU, MAGNETO. YOU COULD LEAD MUTANTKIND AGAIN.
NO.
SOMEBODY TAKE HIM OUT!!
HNN!
WHY CAN'T I REMEMBER? WHY CAN'T--
OH, HELL.

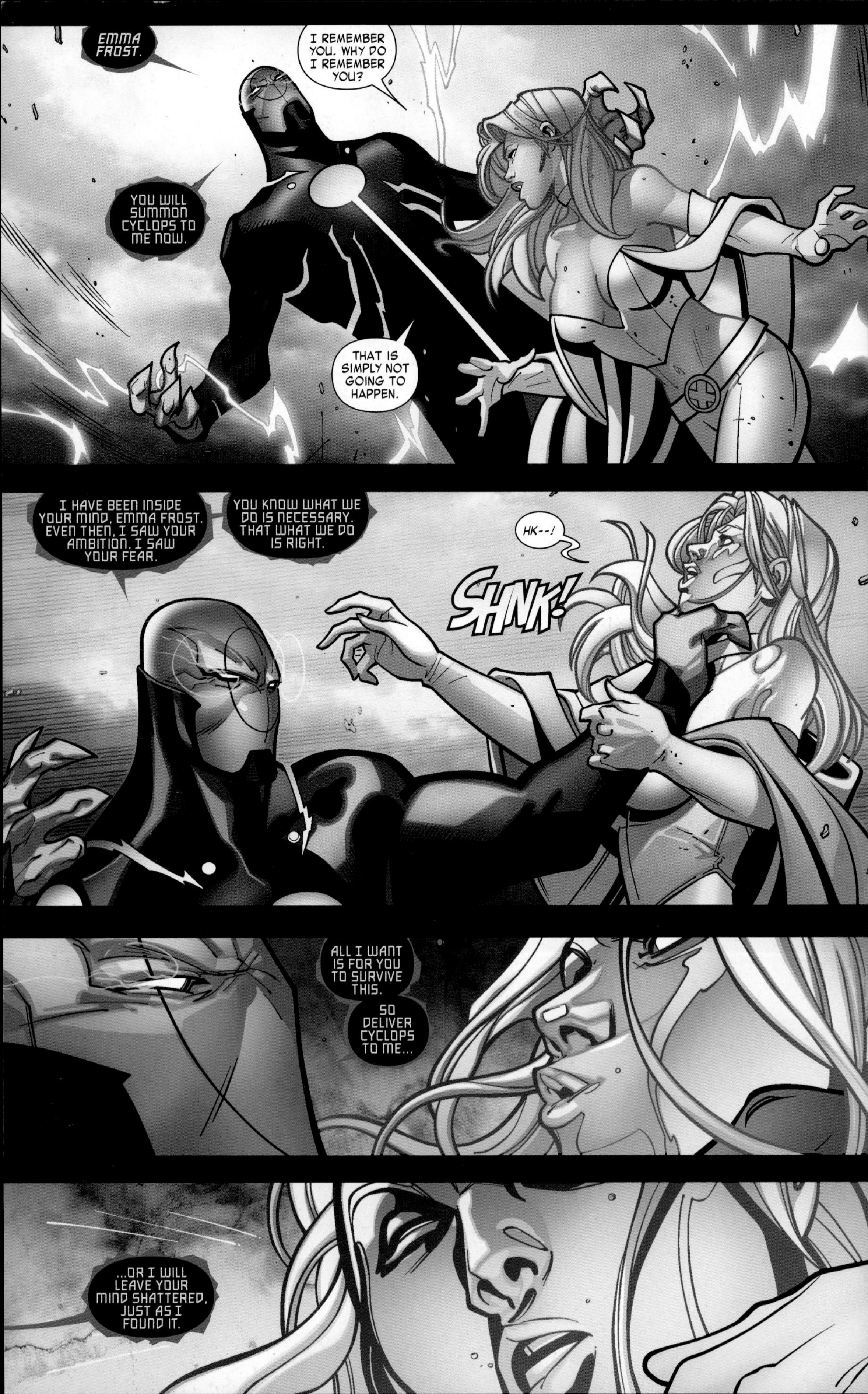
EMMA FROST.
I REMEMBER YOU. WHY DO I REMEMBER YOU?
YOU WILL SUMMON CYCLOPS TO ME NOW.
THAT IS SIMPLY NOT GOING TO HAPPEN.
I HAVE BEEN INSIDE YOUR MIND, EMMA FROST. EVEN THEN, I SAW YOUR AMBITION. I SAW YOUR FEAR.
YOU KNOW WHAT WE DO IS NECESSARY. THAT WHAT WE DO IS RIGHT.
HK--!
SHNK!
ALL I WANT IS FOR YOU TO SURVIVE THIS.
SO DELIVER CYCLOPS TO ME...
...OR I WILL LEAVE YOUR MIND SHATTERED, JUST AS I FOUND IT.

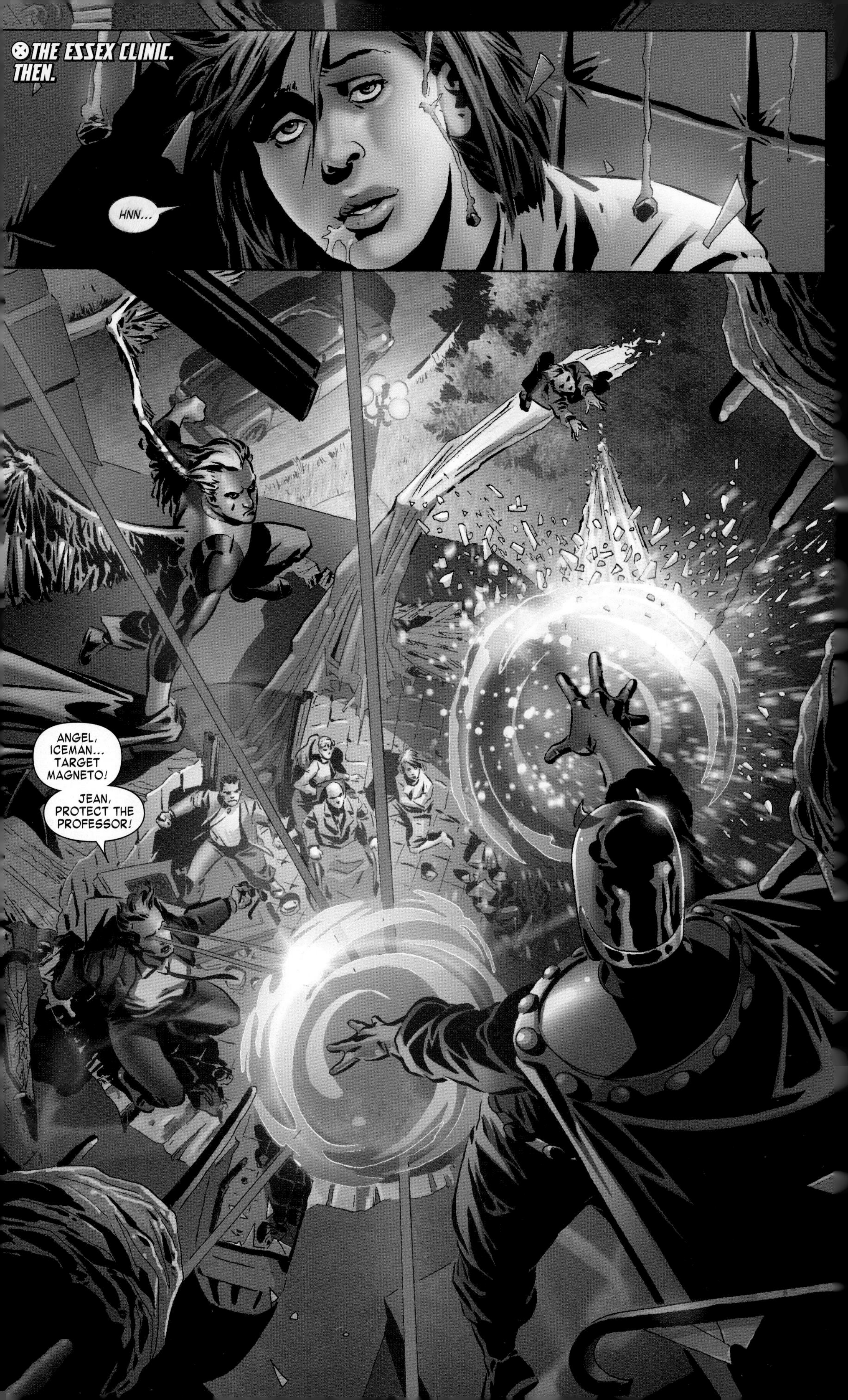
THE ESSEX CLINIC.
THEN.
HNN...
ANGEL, ICEMAN... TARGET MAGNETO!
JEAN, PROTECT THE PROFESSOR!

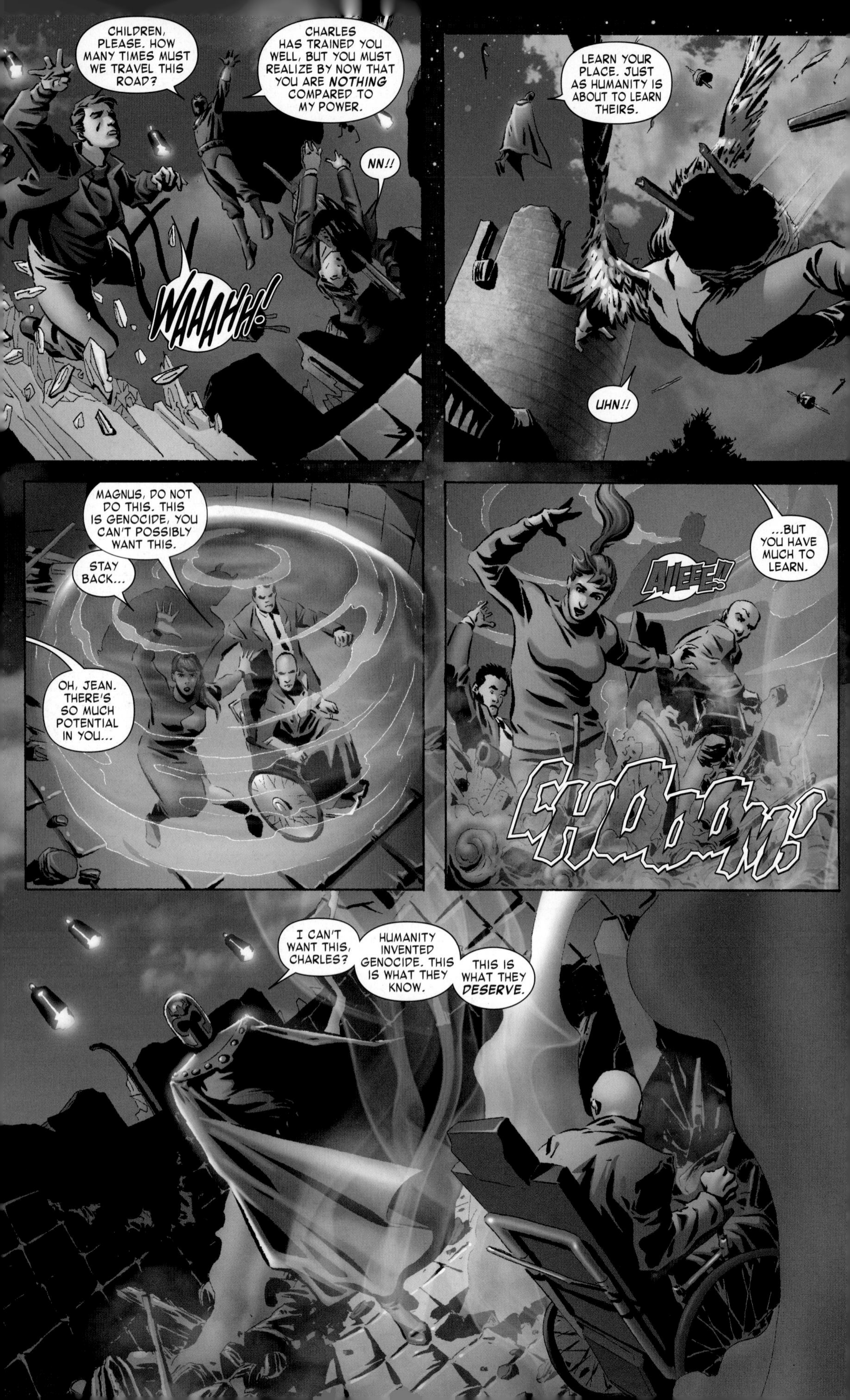
CHILDREN, PLEASE. HOW MANY TIMES MUST WE TRAVEL THIS ROAD?
CHARLES HAS TRAINED YOU WELL, BUT YOU MUST REALIZE BY NOW THAT YOU ARE NOTHING COMPARED TO MY POWER.
NN!!
WAAAHH!
LEARN YOUR PLACE. JUST AS HUMANITY IS ABOUT TO LEARN THEIRS.
UHN!!
MAGNUS, DO NOT DO THIS. THIS IS GENOCIDE, YOU CAN'T POSSIBLY WANT THIS.
STAY BACK...
OH, JEAN. THERE'S SO MUCH POTENTIAL IN YOU...
...BUT YOU HAVE MUCH TO LEARN.
AIIEEE!!
CHOOOM!
I CAN'T WANT THIS, CHARLES?
HUMANITY INVENTED GENOCIDE. THIS IS WHAT THEY KNOW.
THIS IS WHAT THEY DESERVE.

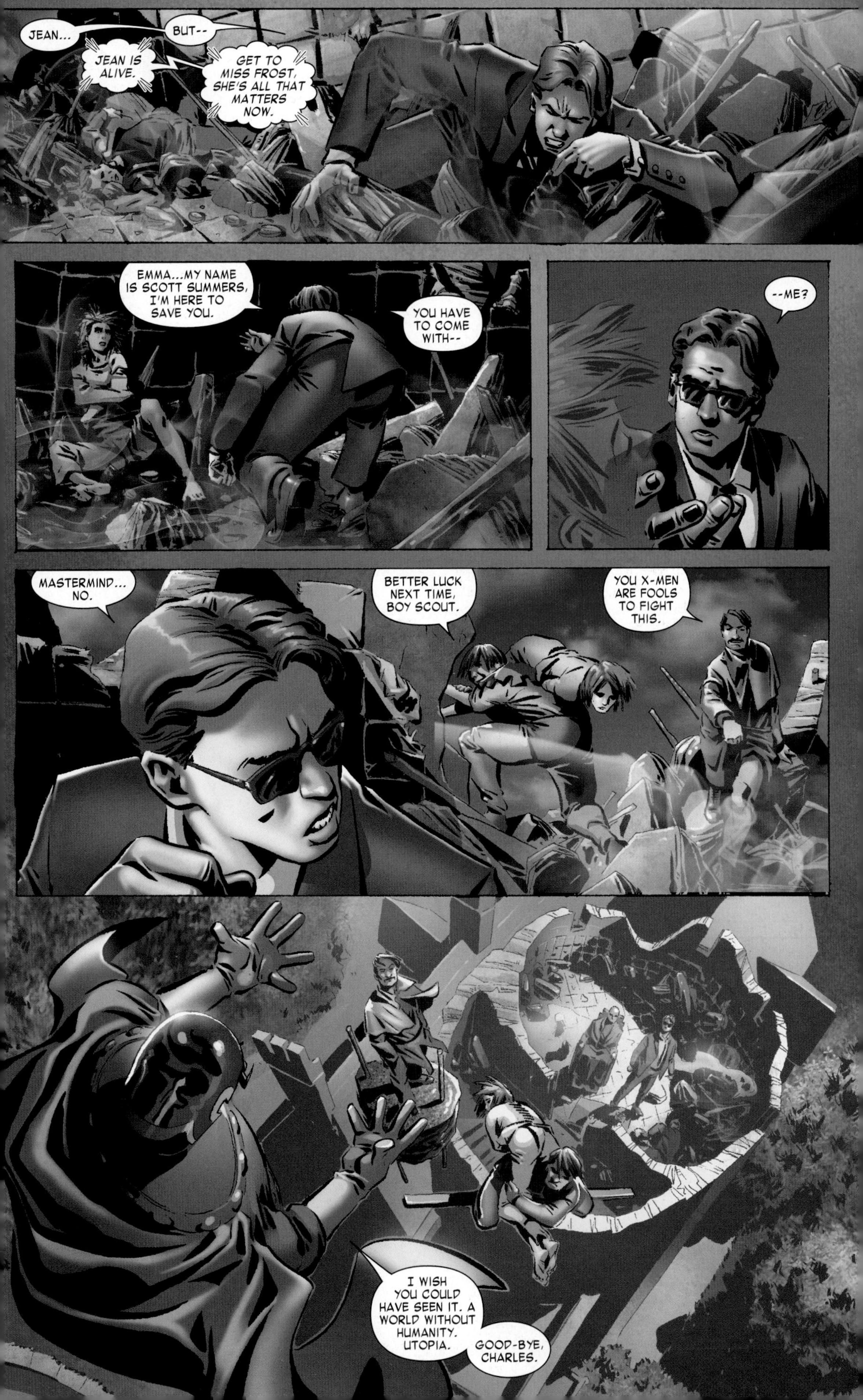
JEAN...
BUT--
JEAN IS ALIVE.
GET TO MISS FROST, SHE'S ALL THAT MATTERS NOW.
EMMA...MY NAME IS SCOTT SUMMERS, I'M HERE TO SAVE YOU.
YOU HAVE TO COME WITH--
--ME?
MASTERMIND... NO.
BETTER LUCK NEXT TIME, BOY SCOUT.
YOU X-MEN ARE FOOLS TO FIGHT THIS.
I WISH YOU COULD HAVE SEEN IT. A WORLD WITHOUT HUMANITY. UTOPIA.
GOOD-BYE, CHARLES.

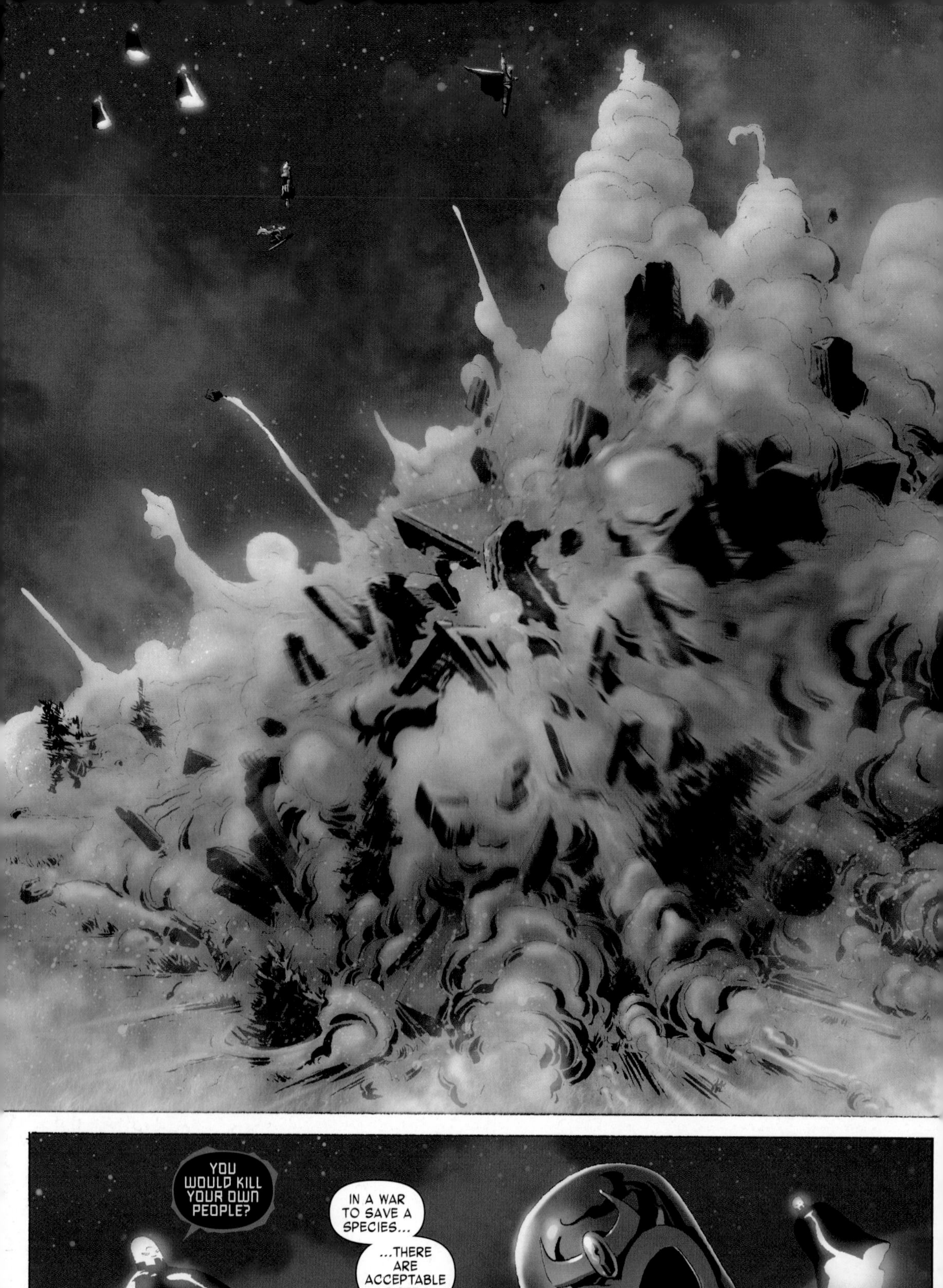

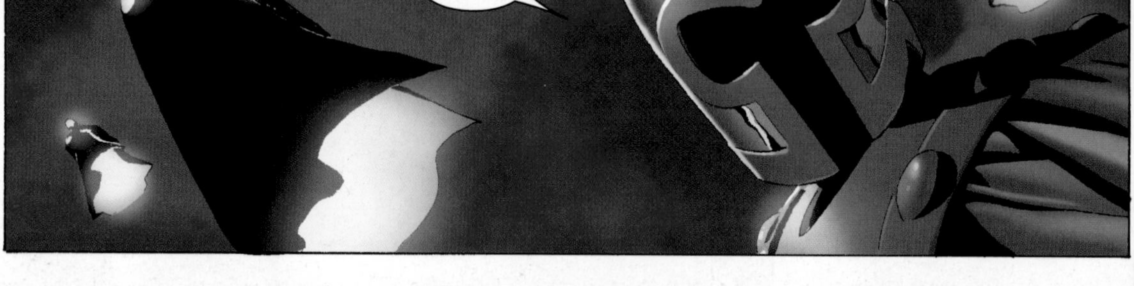
YOU WOULD KILL YOUR OWN PEOPLE?
IN A WAR TO SAVE A SPECIES...
...THERE ARE ACCEPTABLE LOSSES.

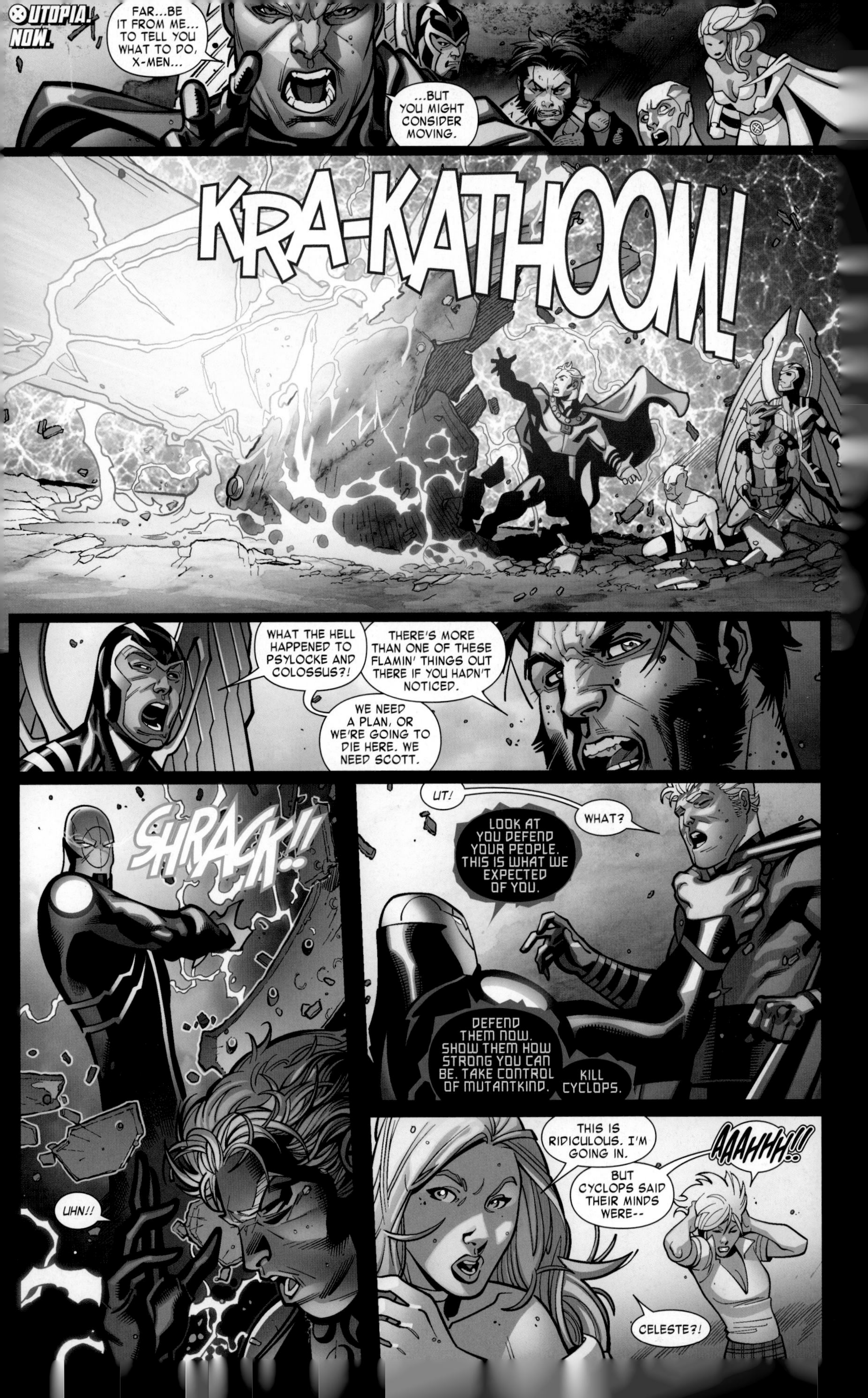
UTOPIA. NOW.
FAR...BE IT FROM ME... TO TELL YOU WHAT TO DO, X-MEN...
...BUT YOU MIGHT CONSIDER MOVING.
KRA-KATHOOM!
WHAT THE HELL HAPPENED TO PSYLOCKE AND COLOSSUS?!
THERE'S MORE THAN ONE OF THESE FLAMIN' THINGS OUT THERE IF YOU HADN'T NOTICED.
WE NEED A PLAN, OR WE'RE GOING TO DIE HERE. WE NEED SCOTT.
SHRACK!!
UHN!!
UT!
WHAT?
LOOK AT YOU DEFEND YOUR PEOPLE. THIS IS WHAT WE EXPECTED OF YOU.
DEFEND THEM NOW. SHOW THEM HOW STRONG YOU CAN BE. TAKE CONTROL OF MUTANTKIND.
KILL CYCLOPS.
THIS IS RIDICULOUS. I'M GOING IN.
BUT CYCLOPS SAID THEIR MINDS WERE--
AAAHHH!!
CELESTE?!

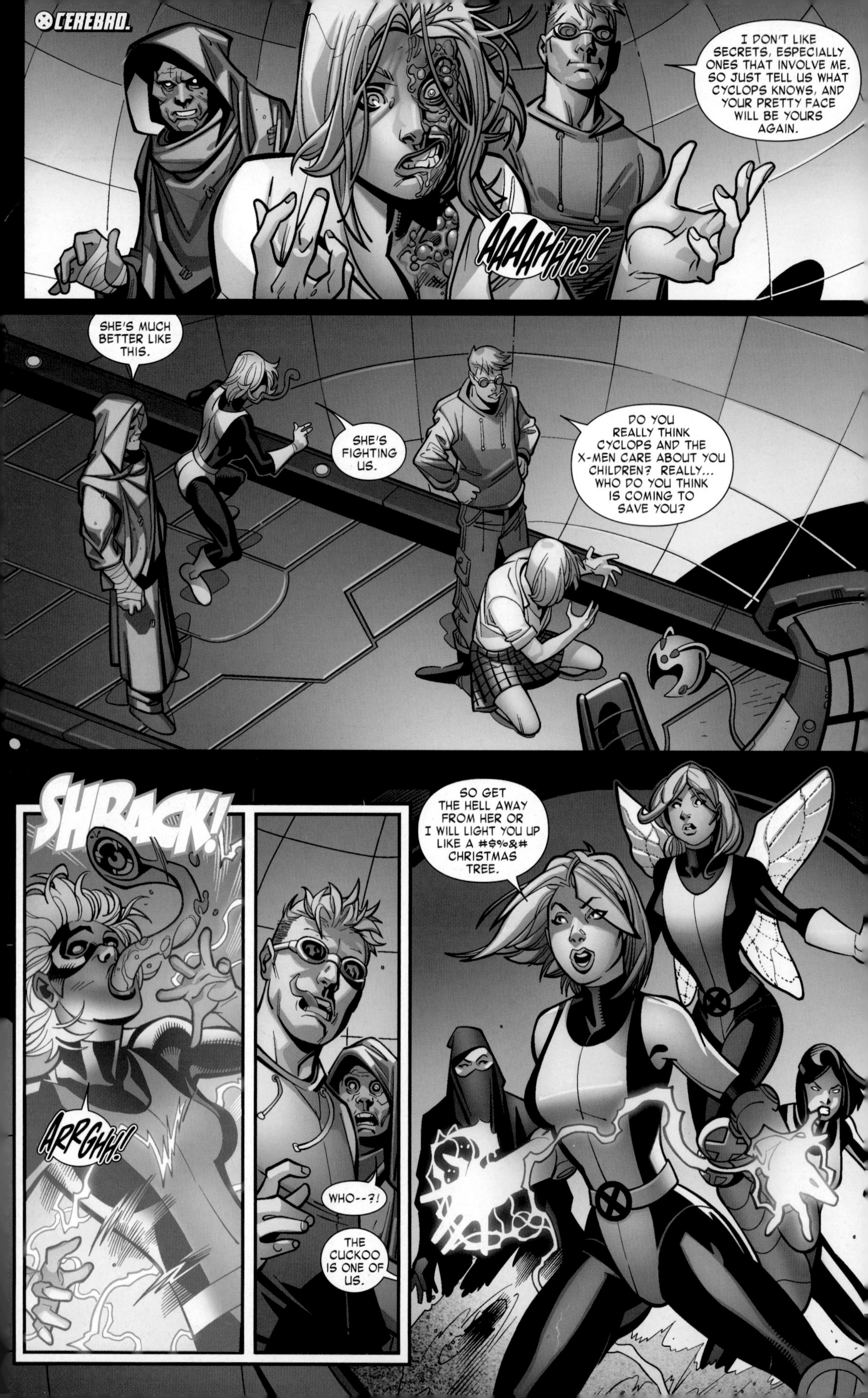
CEREBRO.
I DON'T LIKE SECRETS, ESPECIALLY ONES THAT INVOLVE ME. SO JUST TELL US WHAT CYCLOPS KNOWS, AND YOUR PRETTY FACE WILL BE YOURS AGAIN.
AAAAHHH!
SHE'S MUCH BETTER LIKE THIS.
SHE'S FIGHTING US.
DO YOU REALLY THINK CYCLOPS AND THE X-MEN CARE ABOUT YOU CHILDREN? REALLY... WHO DO YOU THINK IS COMING TO SAVE YOU?
SHRACK!
ARRGHH!
WHO--?!
THE CUCKOO IS ONE OF US.
SO GET THE HELL AWAY FROM HER OR I WILL LIGHT YOU UP LIKE A #$%&# CHRISTMAS TREE.

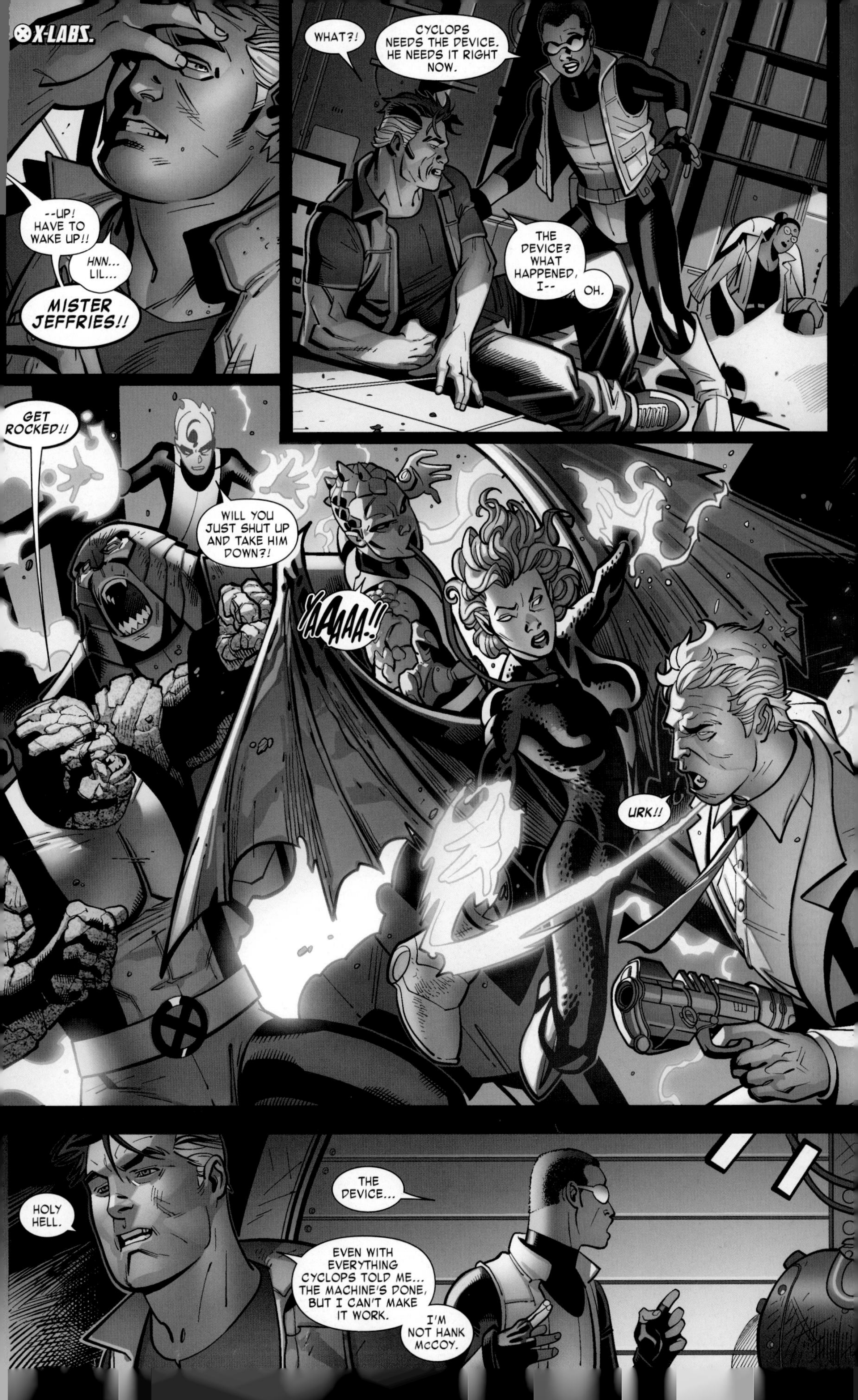
X-LABS.
--UP! HAVE TO WAKE UP!!
HNN... LIL...
MISTER JEFFRIES!!
WHAT?!
CYCLOPS NEEDS THE DEVICE. HE NEEDS IT RIGHT NOW.
THE DEVICE? WHAT HAPPENED, I--
OH.
GET ROCKED!!
WILL YOU JUST SHUT UP AND TAKE HIM DOWN?!
YAAAAAA!!
URK!!
HOLY HELL.
THE DEVICE...
EVEN WITH EVERYTHING CYCLOPS TOLD ME... THE MACHINE'S DONE, BUT I CAN'T MAKE IT WORK.
I'M NOT HANK McCOY.

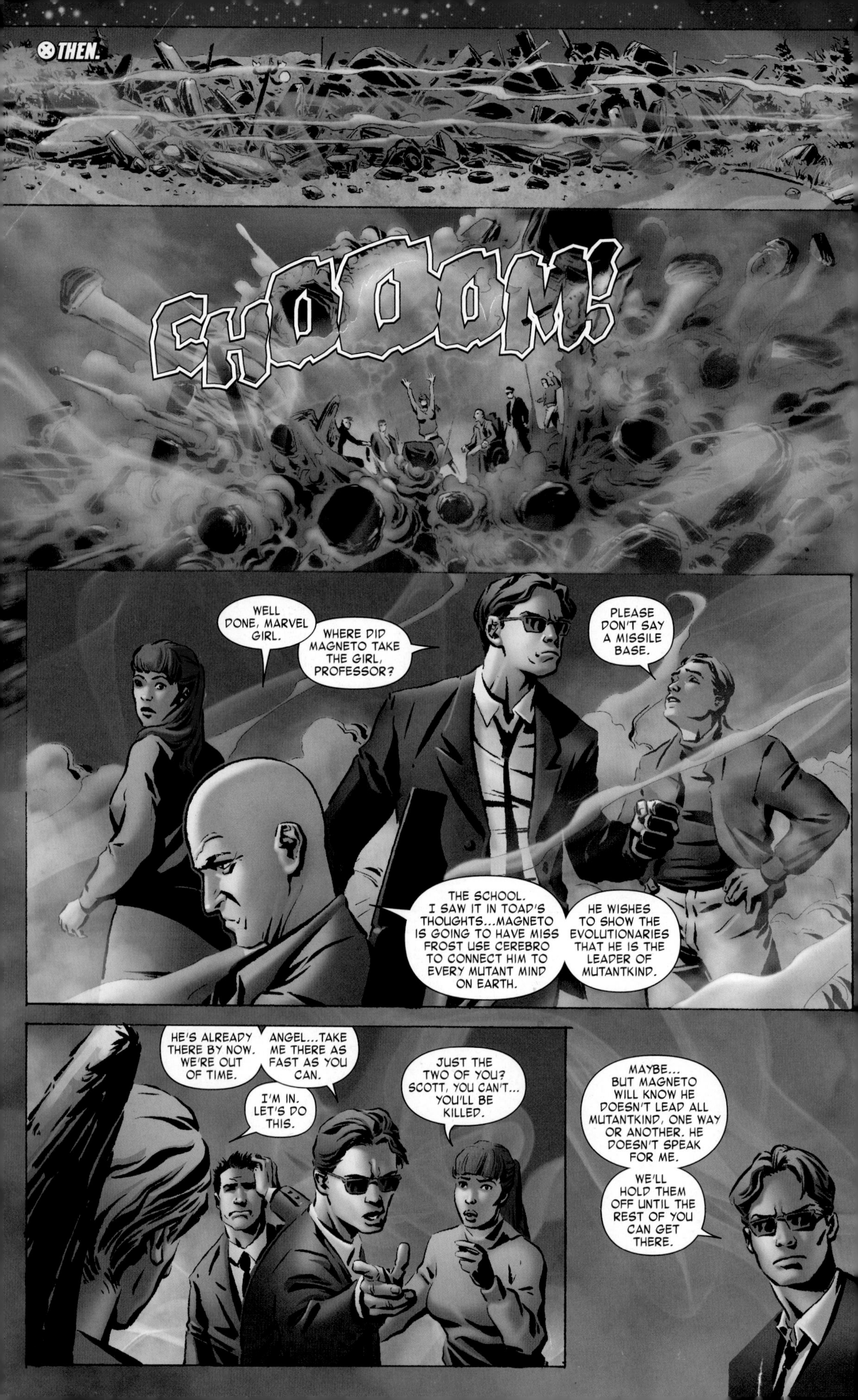
THEN.
CHOOOM!
WELL DONE, MARVEL GIRL.
WHERE DID MAGNETO TAKE THE GIRL, PROFESSOR?
PLEASE DON'T SAY A MISSILE BASE.
THE SCHOOL. I SAW IT IN TOAD'S THOUGHTS...MAGNETO IS GOING TO HAVE MISS FROST USE CEREBRO TO CONNECT HIM TO EVERY MUTANT MIND ON EARTH.
HE WISHES TO SHOW THE EVOLUTIONARIES THAT HE IS THE LEADER OF MUTANTKIND.
HE'S ALREADY THERE BY NOW. WE'RE OUT OF TIME.
ANGEL...TAKE ME THERE AS FAST AS YOU CAN.
I'M IN. LET'S DO THIS.
JUST THE TWO OF YOU? SCOTT, YOU CAN'T... YOU'LL BE KILLED.
MAYBE... BUT MAGNETO WILL KNOW HE DOESN'T LEAD ALL MUTANTKIND, ONE WAY OR ANOTHER. HE DOESN'T SPEAK FOR ME.
WE'LL HOLD THEM OFF UNTIL THE REST OF YOU CAN GET THERE.

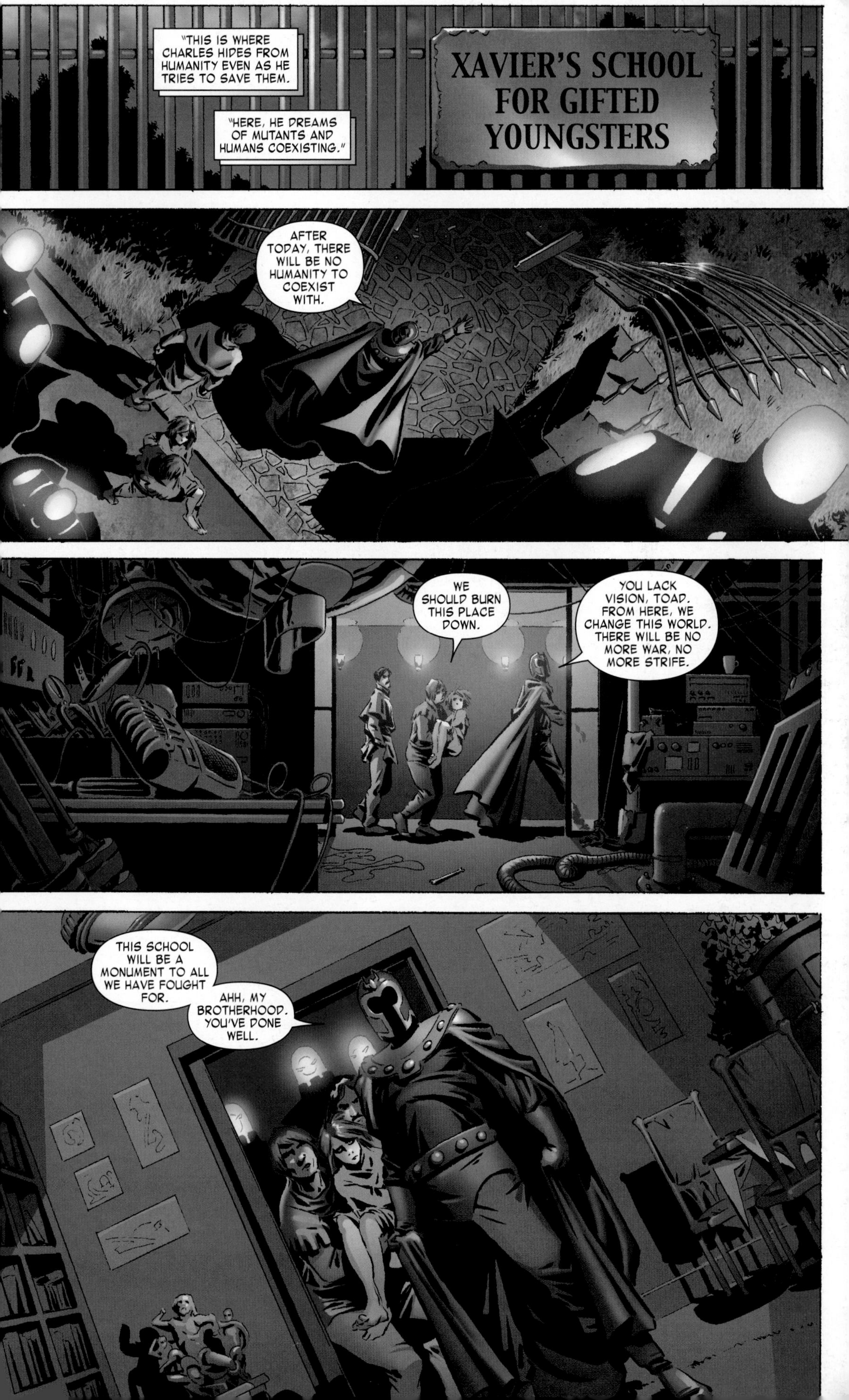
"THIS IS WHERE CHARLES HIDES FROM HUMANITY EVEN AS HE TRIES TO SAVE THEM.
XAVIER'S SCHOOL FOR GIFTED YOUNGSTERS
"HERE, HE DREAMS OF MUTANTS AND HUMANS COEXISTING."
AFTER TODAY, THERE WILL BE NO HUMANITY TO COEXIST WITH.
WE SHOULD BURN THIS PLACE DOWN.
YOU LACK VISION, TOAD. FROM HERE, WE CHANGE THIS WORLD. THERE WILL BE NO MORE WAR, NO MORE STRIFE.
THIS SCHOOL WILL BE A MONUMENT TO ALL WE HAVE FOUGHT FOR.
AHH, MY BROTHERHOOD. YOU'VE DONE WELL.

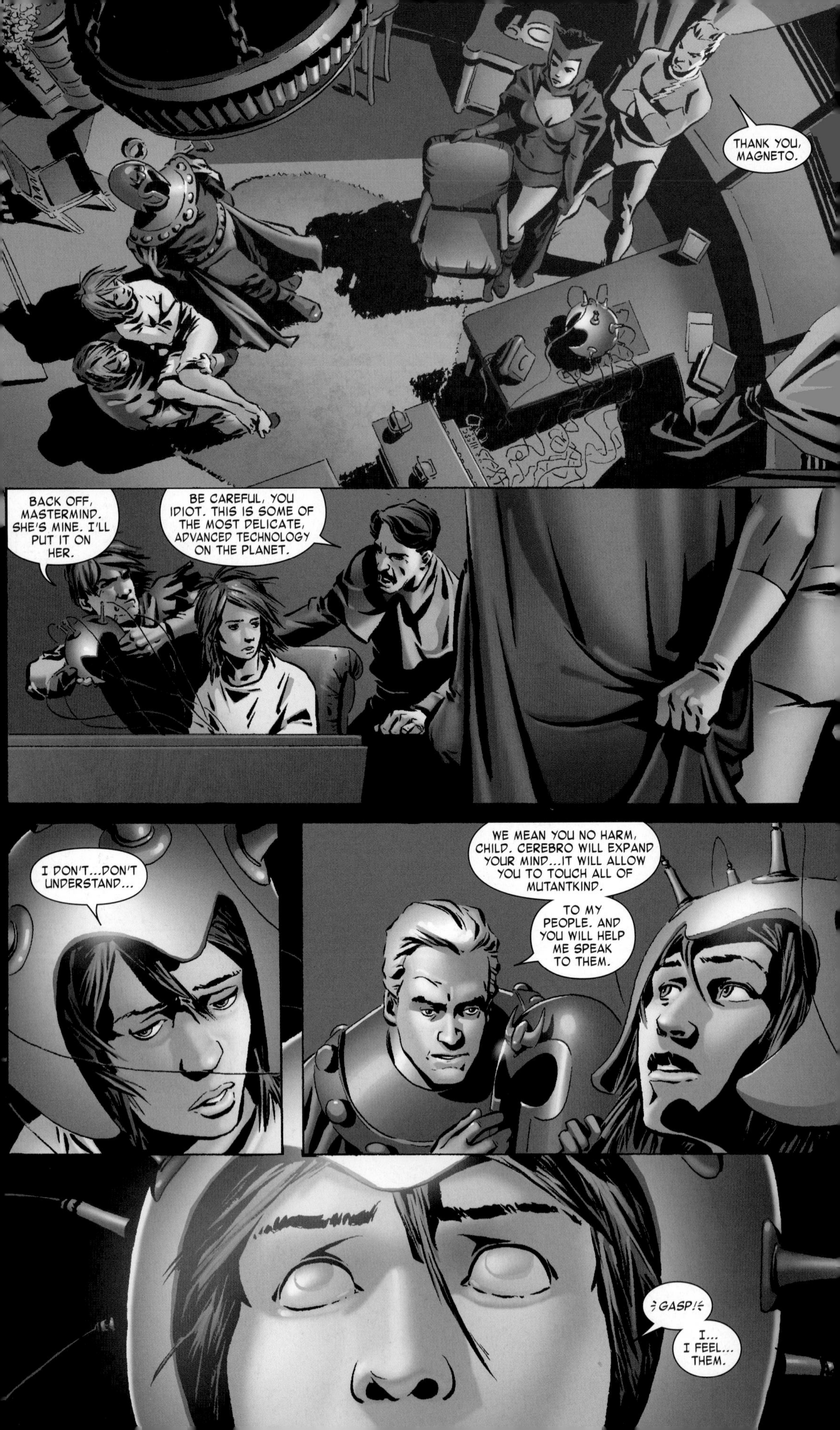
THANK YOU, MAGNETO.
BACK OFF, MASTERMIND. SHE'S MINE. I'LL PUT IT ON HER.
BE CAREFUL, YOU IDIOT. THIS IS SOME OF THE MOST DELICATE, ADVANCED TECHNOLOGY ON THE PLANET.
I DON'T...DON'T UNDERSTAND...
WE MEAN YOU NO HARM, CHILD. CEREBRO WILL EXPAND YOUR MIND...IT WILL ALLOW YOU TO TOUCH ALL OF MUTANTKIND.
TO MY PEOPLE. AND YOU WILL HELP ME SPEAK TO THEM.
GASP!
I... I FEEL... THEM.

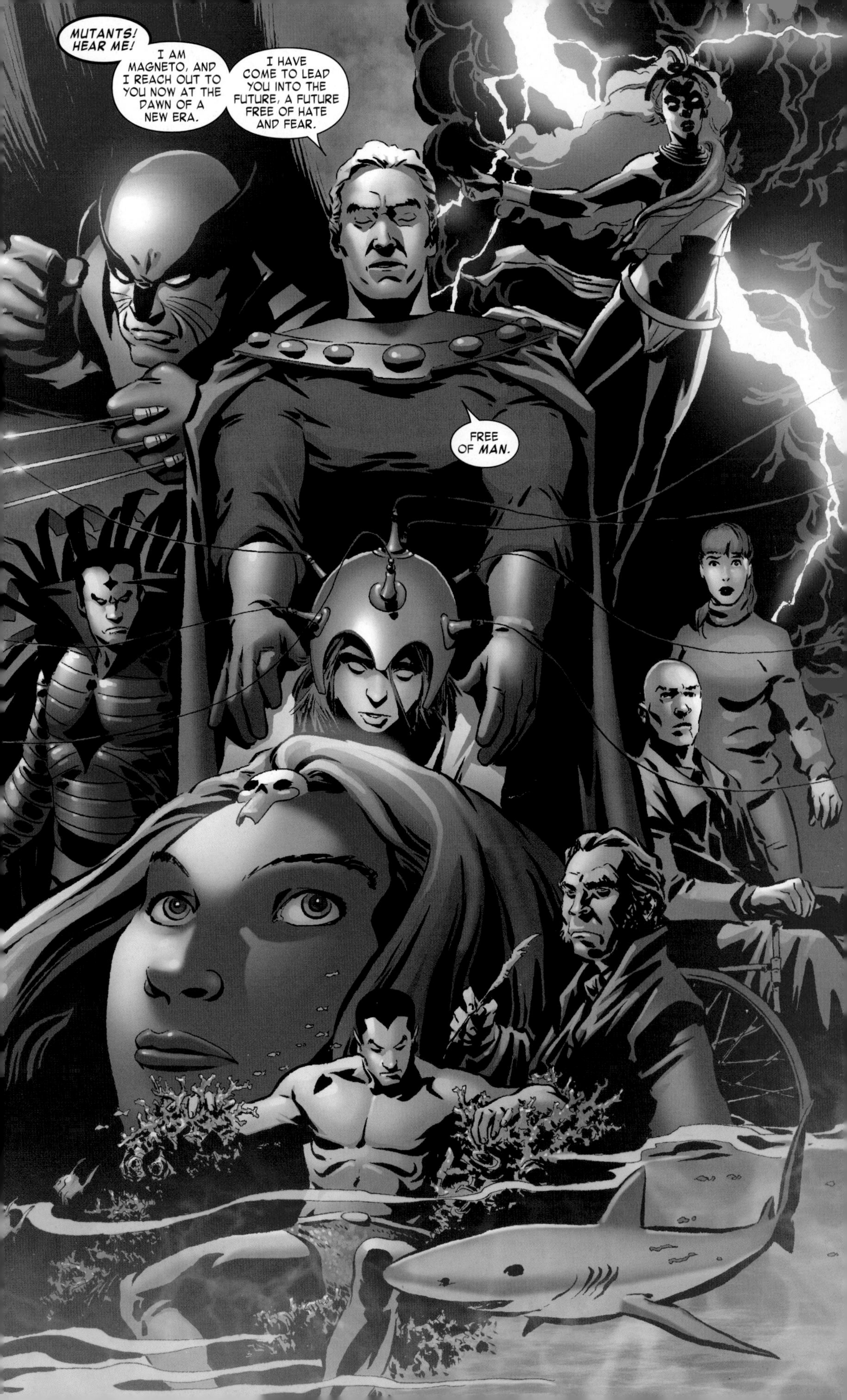
MUTANTS! HEAR ME!
I AM MAGNETO, AND I REACH OUT TO YOU NOW AT THE DAWN OF A NEW ERA.
I HAVE COME TO LEAD YOU INTO THE FUTURE, A FUTURE FREE OF HATE AND FEAR.
FREE OF MAN.

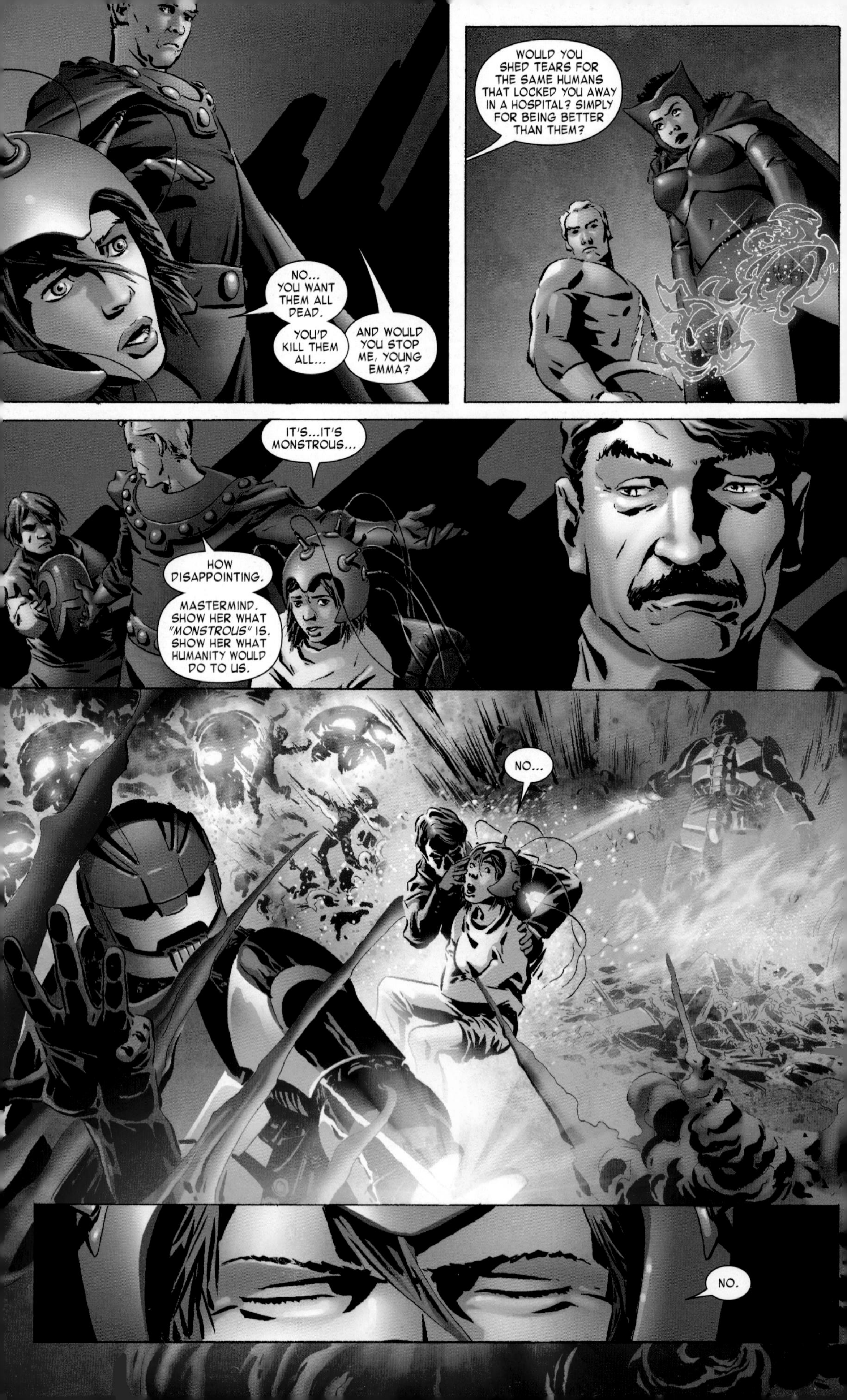
NO... YOU WANT THEM ALL DEAD.
YOU'D KILL THEM ALL...
AND WOULD YOU STOP ME, YOUNG EMMA?
WOULD YOU SHED TEARS FOR THE SAME HUMANS THAT LOCKED YOU AWAY IN A HOSPITAL? SIMPLY FOR BEING BETTER THAN THEM?
IT'S...IT'S MONSTROUS...
HOW DISAPPOINTING.
MASTERMIND. SHOW HER WHAT "MONSTROUS" IS. SHOW HER WHAT HUMANITY WOULD DO TO US.
NO...
NO.

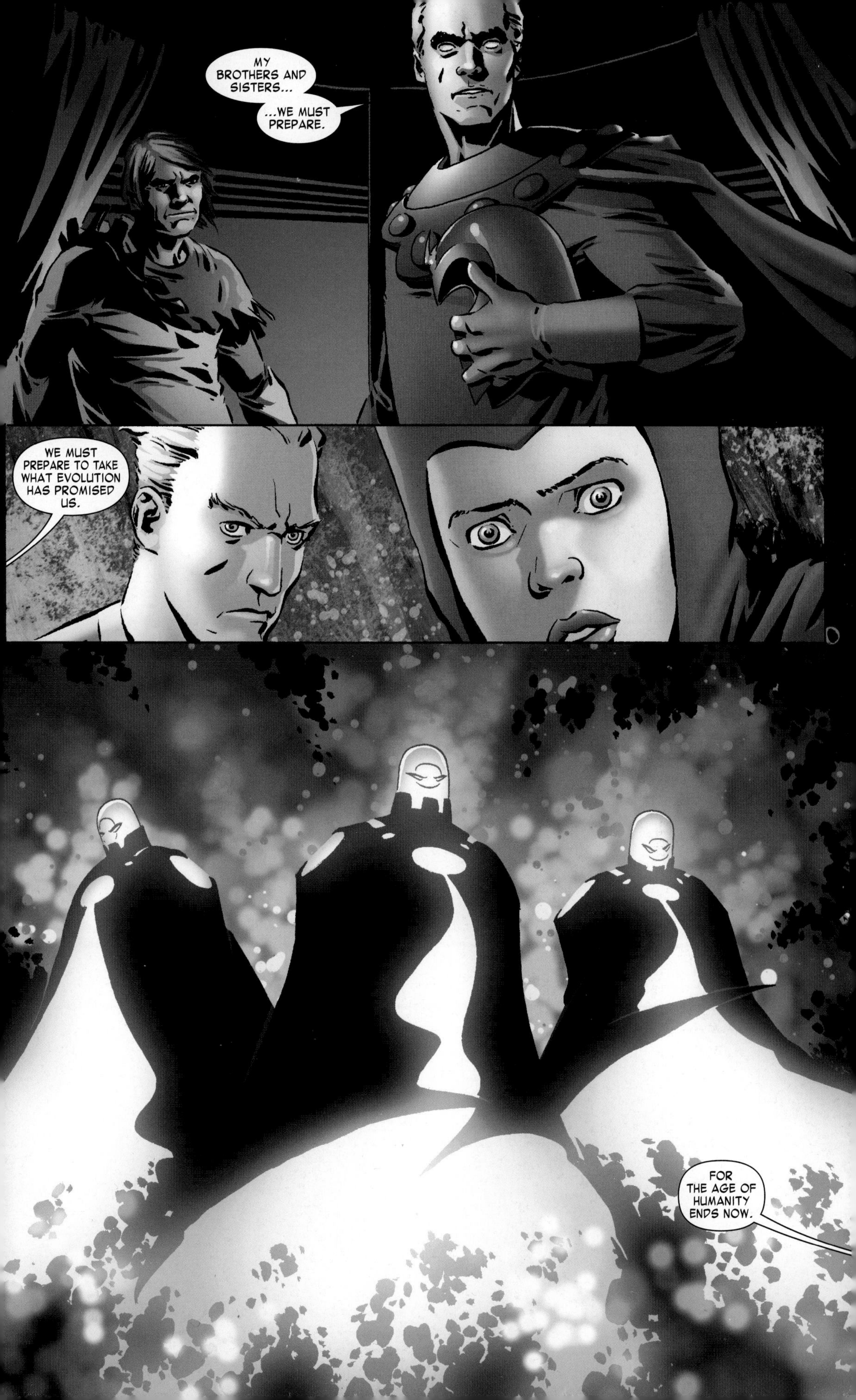
MY BROTHERS AND SISTERS...
...WE MUST PREPARE.
WE MUST PREPARE TO TAKE WHAT EVOLUTION HAS PROMISED US.
FOR THE AGE OF HUMANITY ENDS NOW.

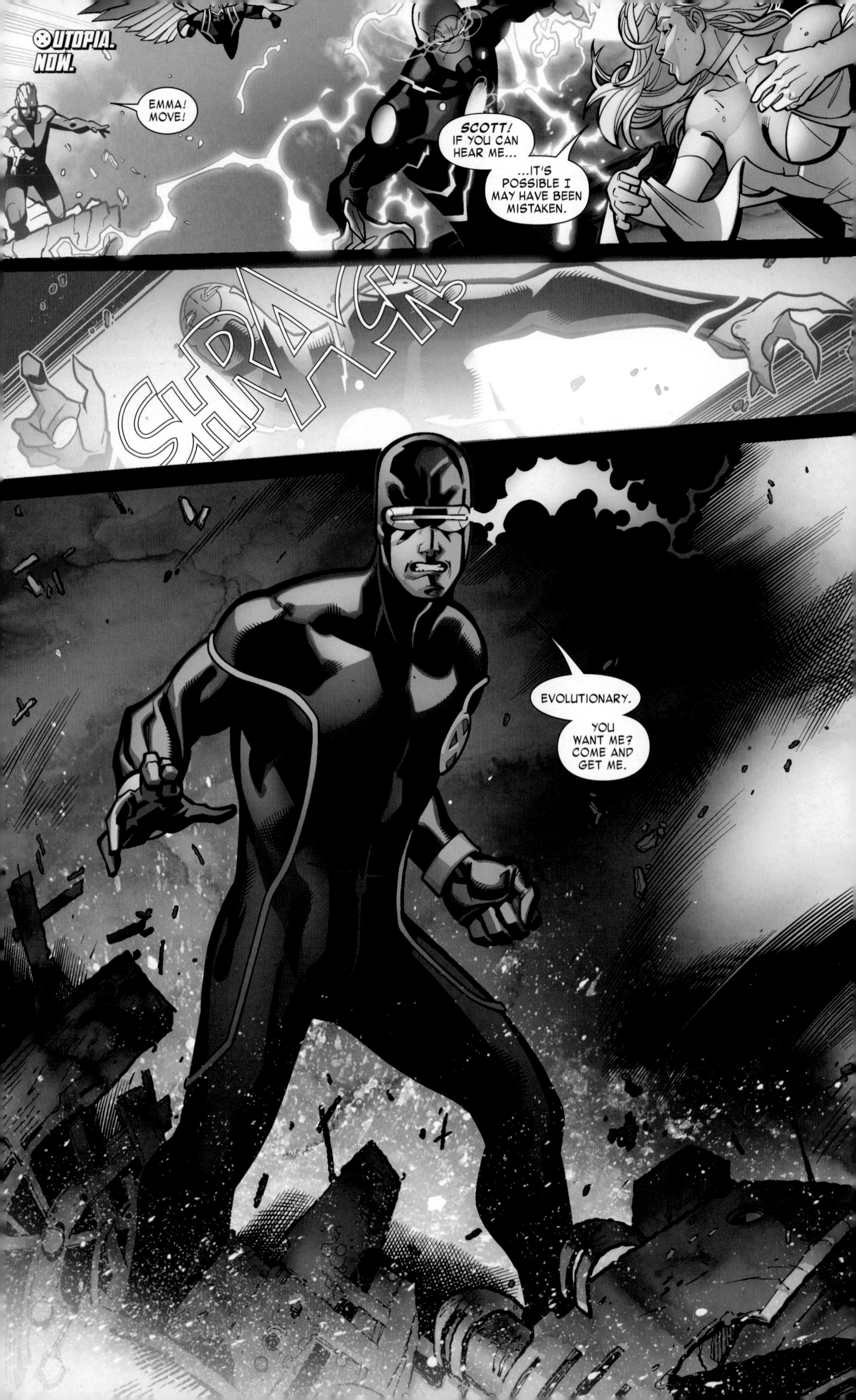
UTOPIA. NOW.
EMMA! MOVE!
SCOTT! IF YOU CAN HEAR ME...
...IT'S POSSIBLE I MAY HAVE BEEN MISTAKEN.
SHRAKK
EVOLUTIONARY.
YOU WANT ME? COME AND GET ME.

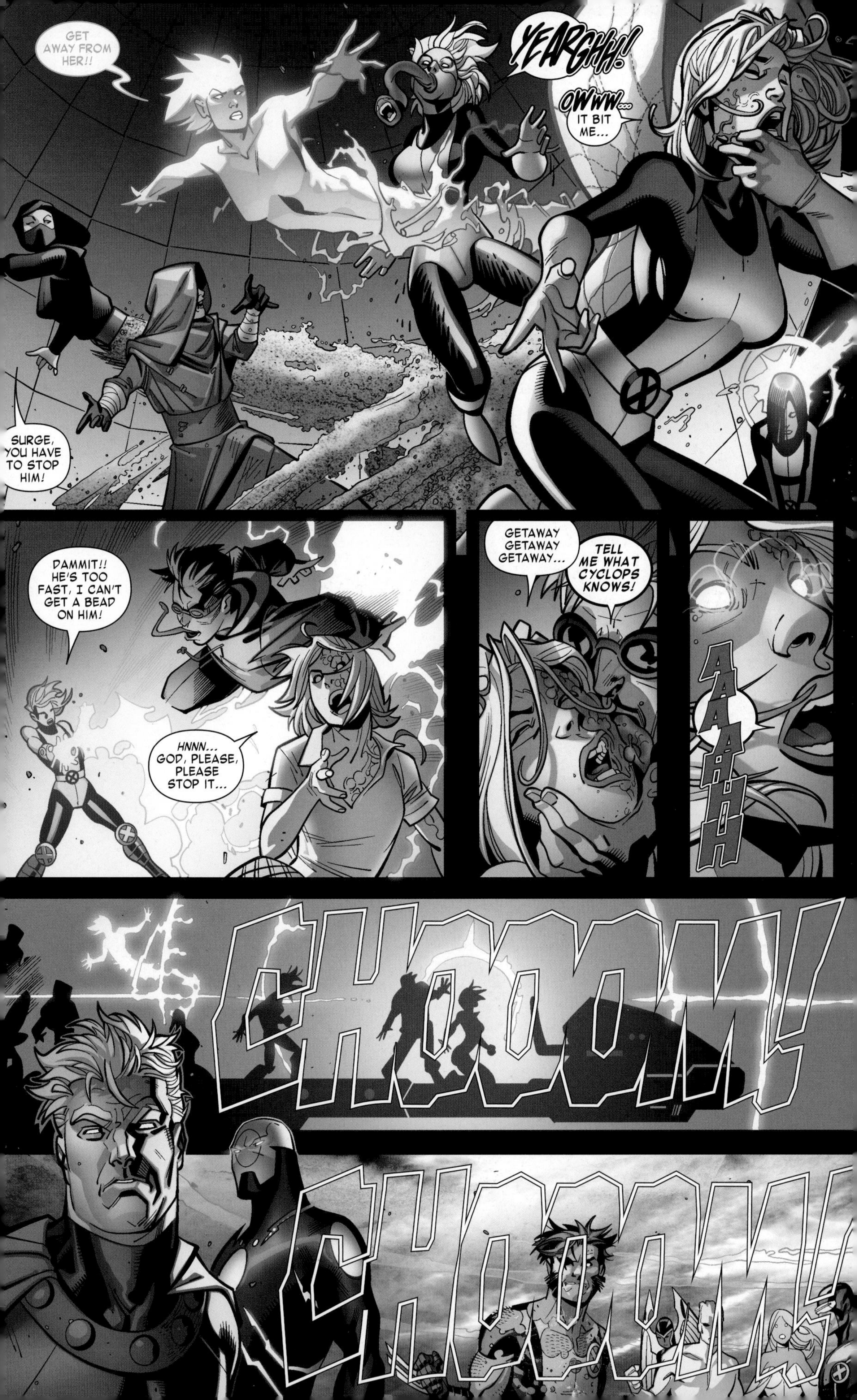
GET AWAY FROM HER!!
YEARGHH!
OWWW... IT BIT ME...
SURGE, YOU HAVE TO STOP HIM!
DAMMIT!! HE'S TOO FAST, I CAN'T GET A BEAD ON HIM!
HNNN... GOD, PLEASE, PLEASE STOP IT...
GETAWAY GETAWAY GETAWAY...
TELL ME WHAT CYCLOPS KNOWS!
AAAAAHHHH
CHOOOM!
CHOOOM!

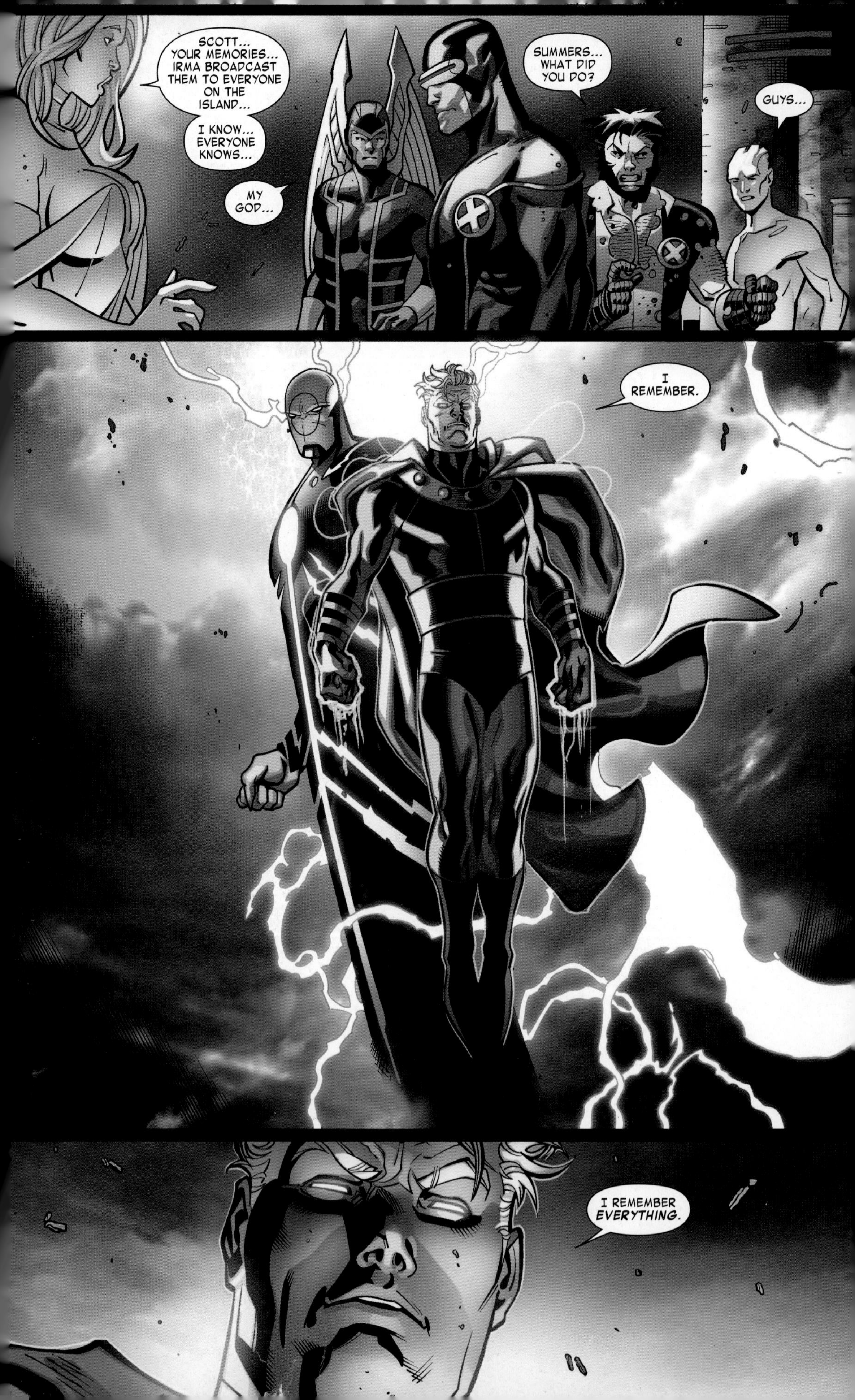
SCOTT... YOUR MEMORIES... IRMA BROADCAST THEM TO EVERYONE ON THE ISLAND...
I KNOW... EVERYONE KNOWS...
MY GOD...
SUMMERS... WHAT DID YOU DO?
GUYS...
I REMEMBER.
I REMEMBER EVERYTHING.

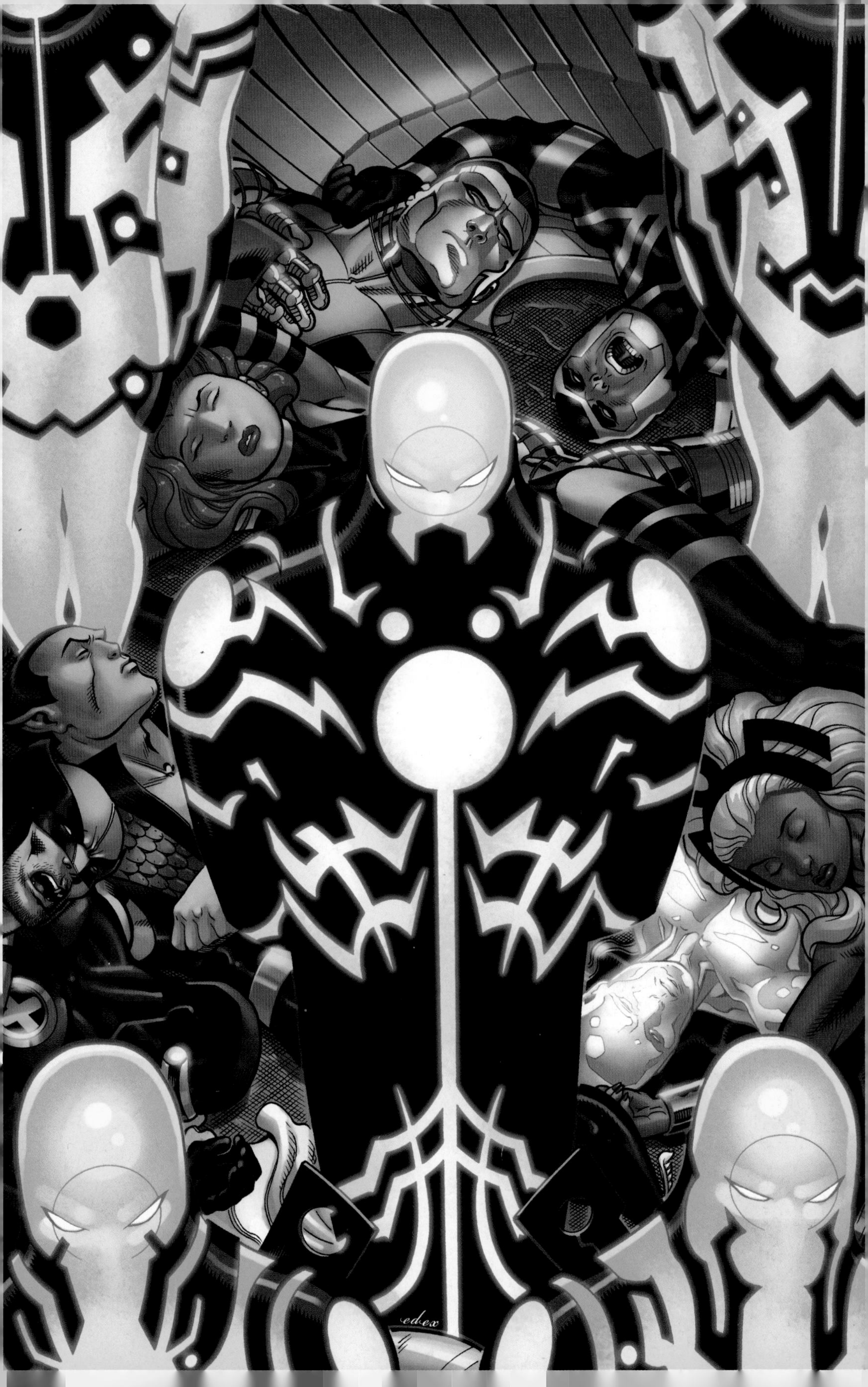
ed:ex

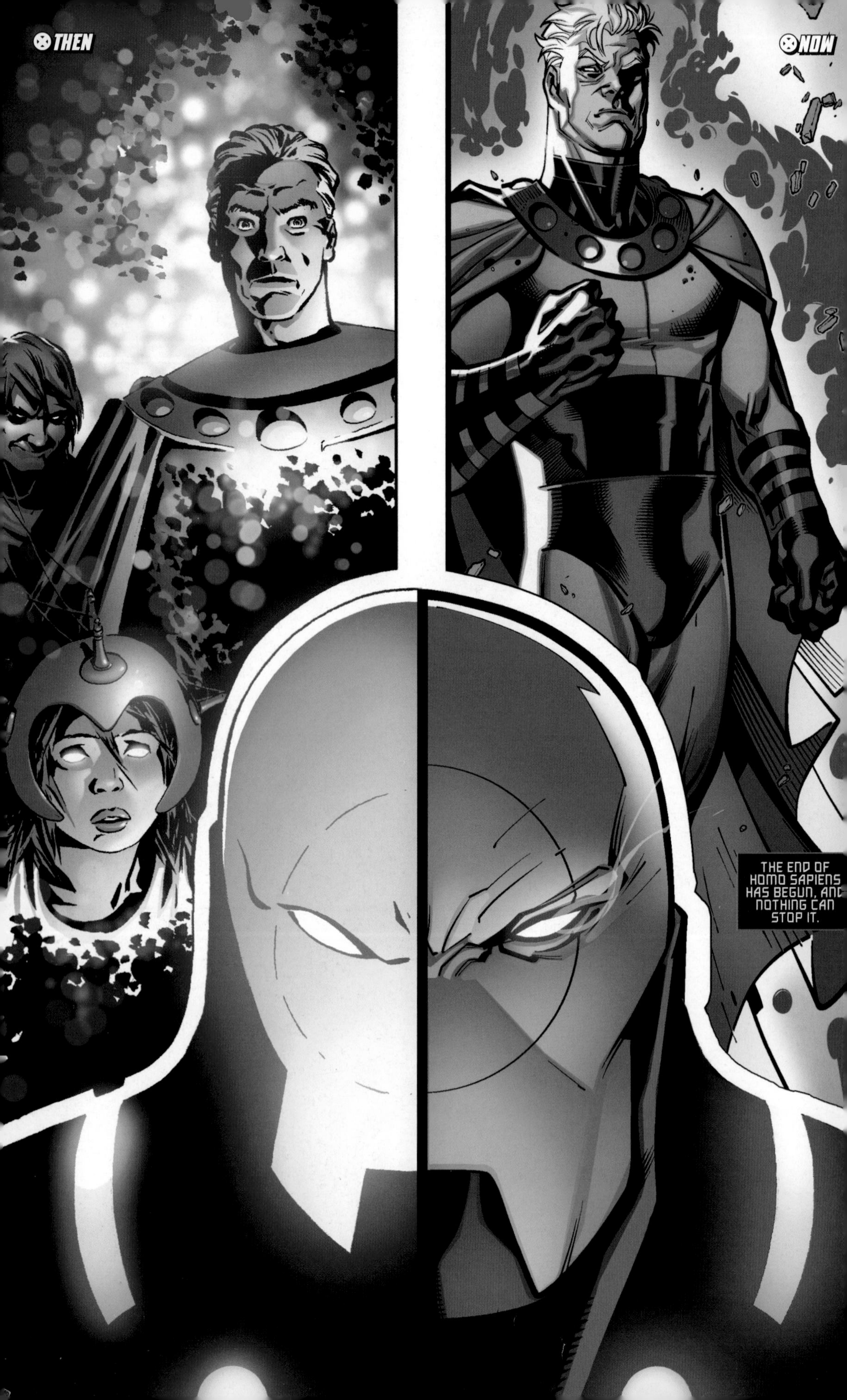
THEN
NOW
THE END OF HOMO SAPIENS HAS BEGUN, AND NOTHING CAN STOP IT.

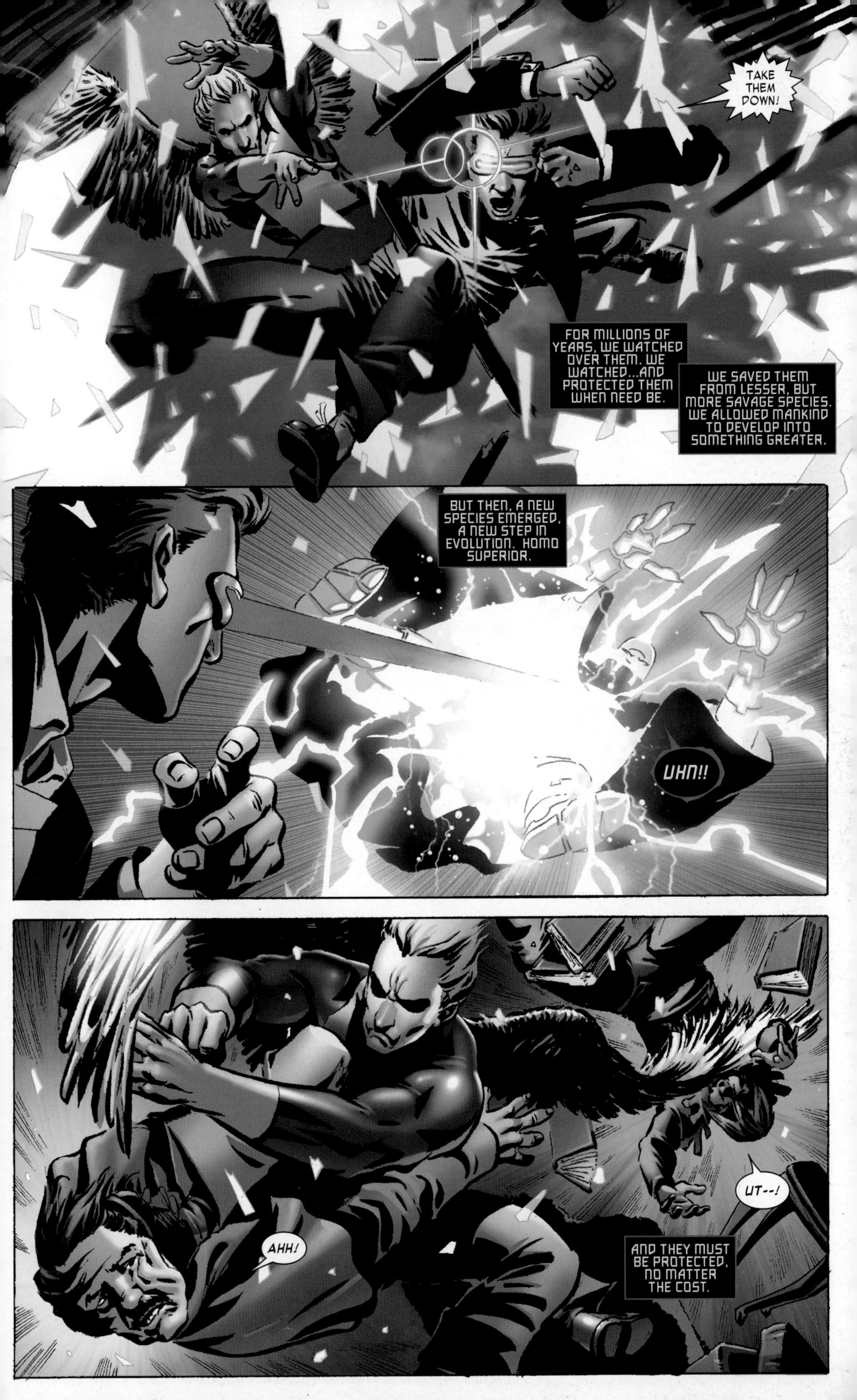
TAKE THEM DOWN!
FOR MILLIONS OF YEARS, WE WATCHED OVER THEM. WE WATCHED...AND PROTECTED THEM WHEN NEED BE.
WE SAVED THEM FROM LESSER, BUT MORE SAVAGE SPECIES. WE ALLOWED MANKIND TO DEVELOP INTO SOMETHING GREATER.
BUT THEN, A NEW SPECIES EMERGED, A NEW STEP IN EVOLUTION. HOMO SUPERIOR.
UHN!!
UT--!
AHH!
AND THEY MUST BE PROTECTED, NO MATTER THE COST.

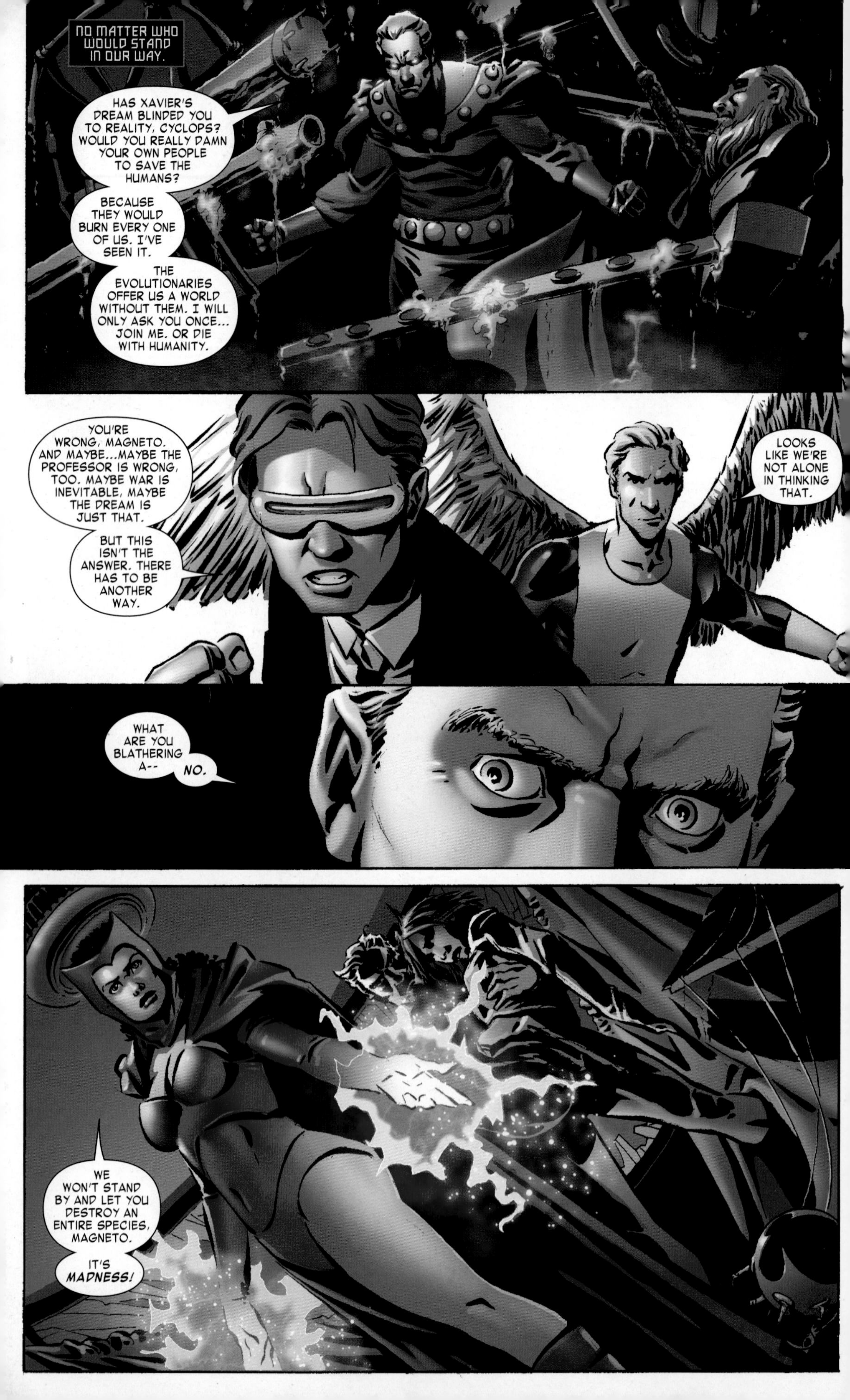
NO MATTER WHO WOULD STAND IN OUR WAY.
HAS XAVIER'S DREAM BLINDED YOU TO REALITY, CYCLOPS? WOULD YOU REALLY DAMN YOUR OWN PEOPLE TO SAVE THE HUMANS?
BECAUSE THEY WOULD BURN EVERY ONE OF US. I'VE SEEN IT.
THE EVOLUTIONARIES OFFER US A WORLD WITHOUT THEM. I WILL ONLY ASK YOU ONCE... JOIN ME. OR DIE WITH HUMANITY.
YOU'RE WRONG, MAGNETO. AND MAYBE...MAYBE THE PROFESSOR IS WRONG, TOO. MAYBE WAR IS INEVITABLE, MAYBE THE DREAM IS JUST THAT.
BUT THIS ISN'T THE ANSWER. THERE HAS TO BE ANOTHER WAY.
LOOKS LIKE WE'RE NOT ALONE IN THINKING THAT.
WHAT ARE YOU BLATHERING A--
NO.
WE WON'T STAND BY AND LET YOU DESTROY AN ENTIRE SPECIES, MAGNETO.
IT'S MADNESS!

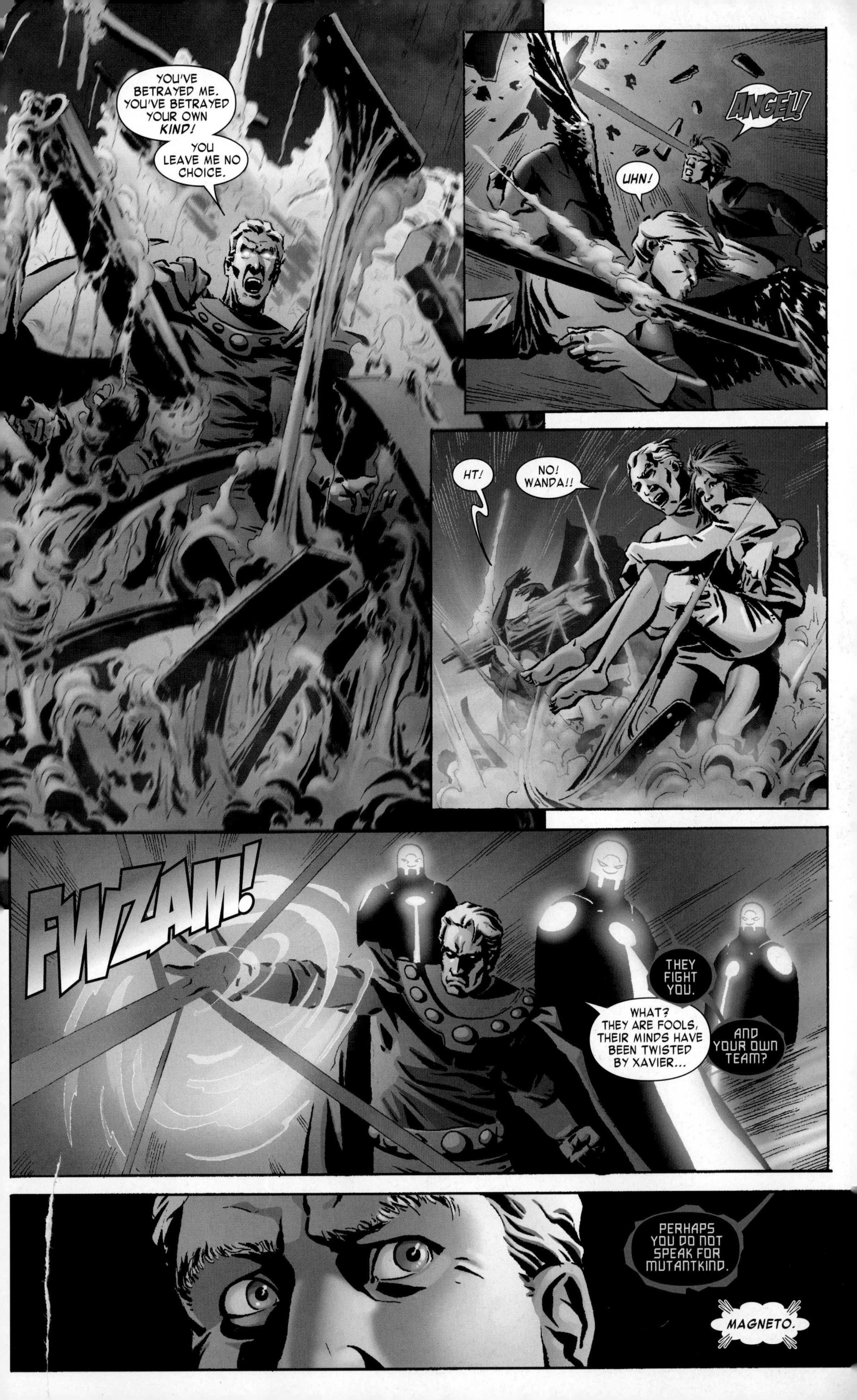
YOU'VE BETRAYED ME. YOU'VE BETRAYED YOUR OWN KIND!
YOU LEAVE ME NO CHOICE.
ANGEL!
UHN!
HT!
NO! WANDA!!
FWZAM!
THEY FIGHT YOU.
WHAT? THEY ARE FOOLS, THEIR MINDS HAVE BEEN TWISTED BY XAVIER...
AND YOUR OWN TEAM?
PERHAPS YOU DO NOT SPEAK FOR MUTANTKIND.
MAGNETO.

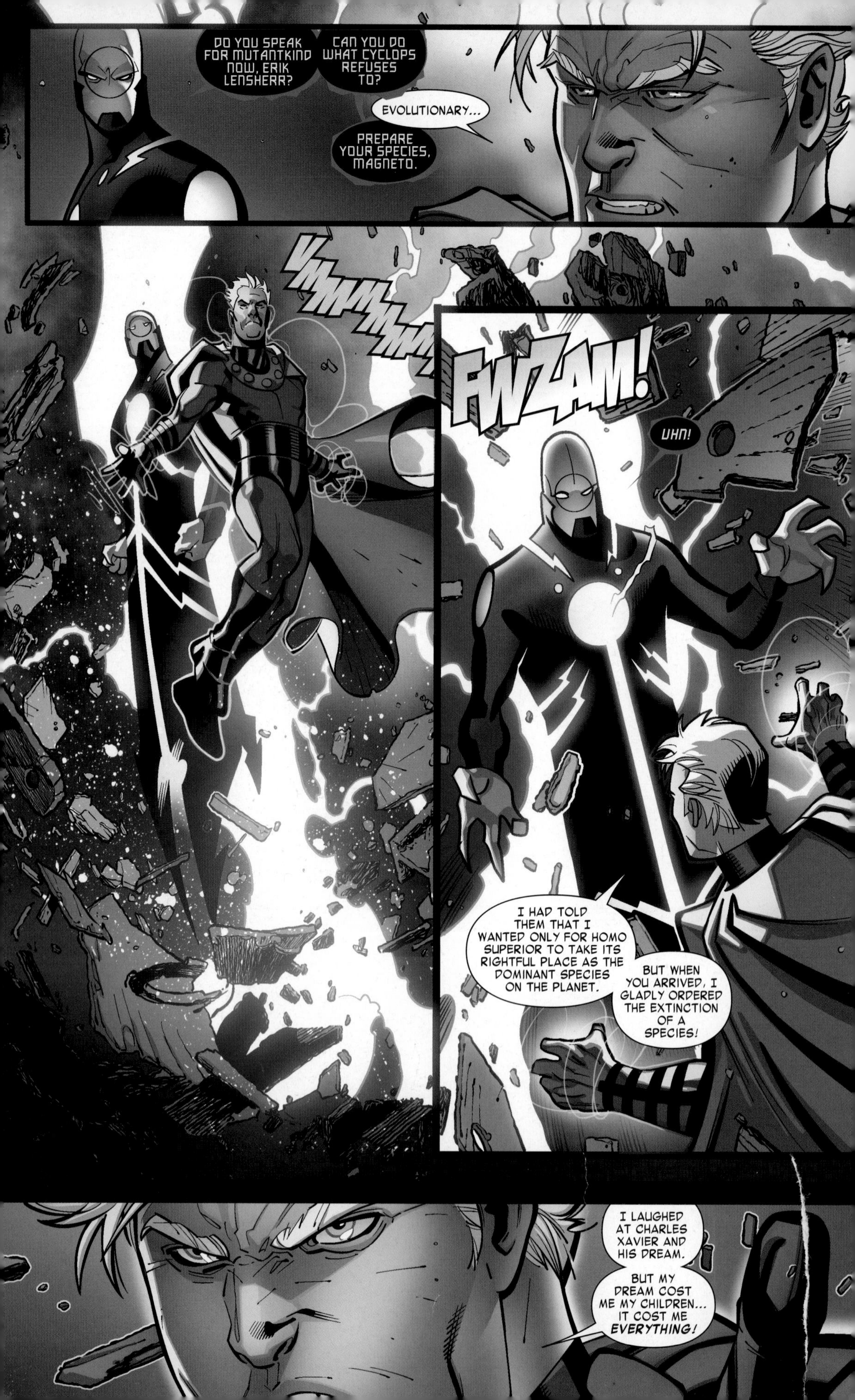
DO YOU SPEAK FOR MUTANTKIND NOW, ERIK LENSHERR?
CAN YOU DO WHAT CYCLOPS REFUSES TO?
EVOLUTIONARY...
PREPARE YOUR SPECIES, MAGNETO.
VMMMMMMMM
FWZAM!
UHN!
I HAD TOLD THEM THAT I WANTED ONLY FOR HOMO SUPERIOR TO TAKE ITS RIGHTFUL PLACE AS THE DOMINANT SPECIES ON THE PLANET.
BUT WHEN YOU ARRIVED, I GLADLY ORDERED THE EXTINCTION OF A SPECIES!
I LAUGHED AT CHARLES XAVIER AND HIS DREAM.
BUT MY DREAM COST ME MY CHILDREN... IT COST ME *EVERYTHING!*

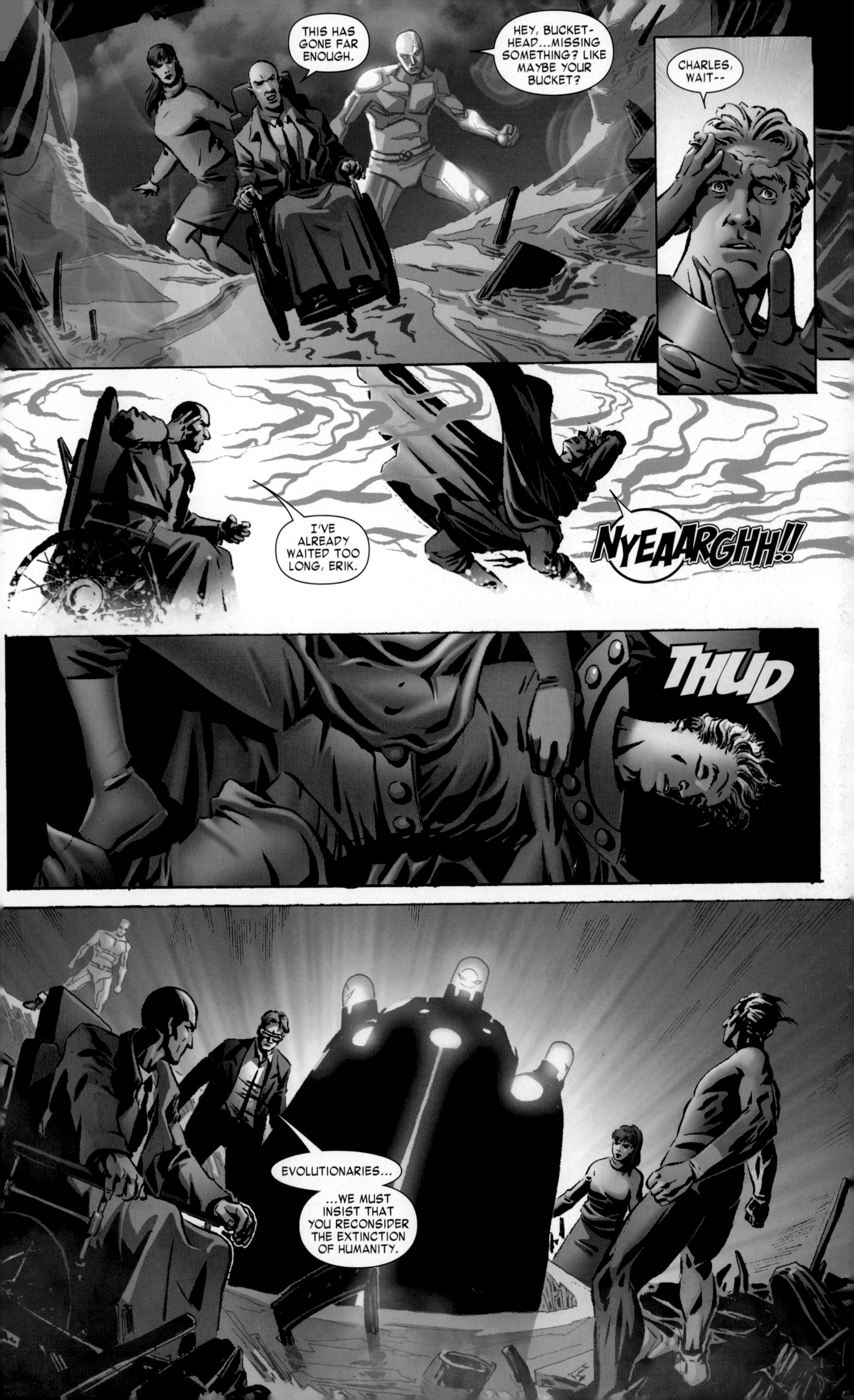
THIS HAS GONE FAR ENOUGH.
HEY, BUCKET-HEAD...MISSING SOMETHING? LIKE MAYBE YOUR BUCKET?
CHARLES, WAIT--
I'VE ALREADY WAITED TOO LONG, ERIK.
NYEAARGHH!!
THUD
EVOLUTIONARIES...
...WE MUST INSIST THAT YOU RECONSIDER THE EXTINCTION OF HUMANITY.

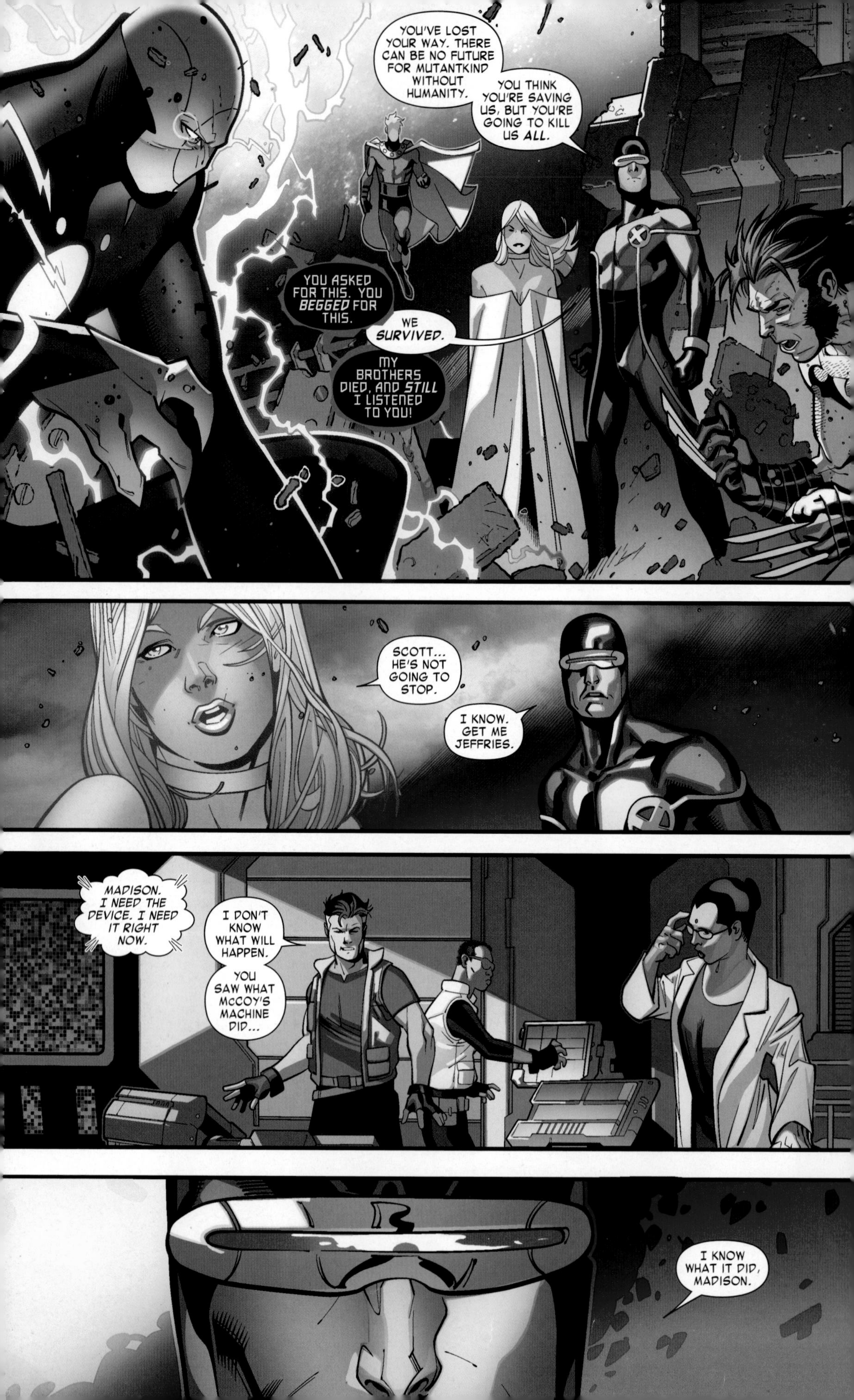
YOU'VE LOST YOUR WAY. THERE CAN BE NO FUTURE FOR MUTANTKIND WITHOUT HUMANITY.
YOU THINK YOU'RE SAVING US, BUT YOU'RE GOING TO KILL US ALL.
YOU ASKED FOR THIS. YOU BEGGED FOR THIS.
WE SURVIVED.
MY BROTHERS DIED, AND STILL I LISTENED TO YOU!
SCOTT... HE'S NOT GOING TO STOP.
I KNOW. GET ME JEFFRIES.
MADISON. I NEED THE DEVICE. I NEED IT RIGHT NOW.
I DON'T KNOW WHAT WILL HAPPEN.
YOU SAW WHAT McCOY'S MACHINE DID...
I KNOW WHAT IT DID, MADISON.

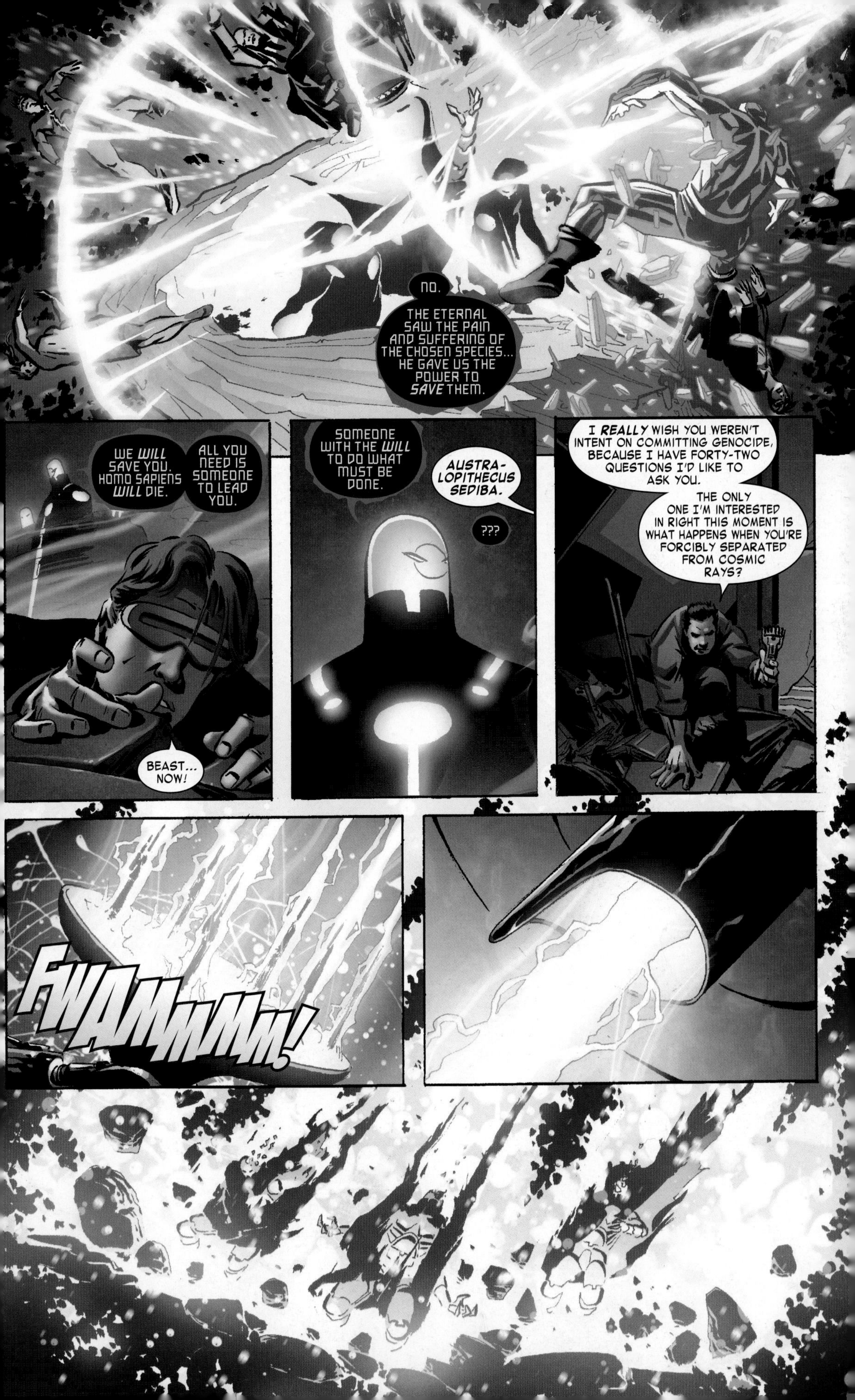

NO.
THE ETERNAL SAW THE PAIN AND SUFFERING OF THE CHOSEN SPECIES... HE GAVE US THE POWER TO *SAVE* THEM.
WE *WILL* SAVE YOU. HOMO SAPIENS *WILL* DIE.
ALL YOU NEED IS SOMEONE TO LEAD YOU.
BEAST... NOW!
SOMEONE WITH THE *WILL* TO DO WHAT MUST BE DONE.
AUSTRA-LOPITHECUS SEDIBA.
???
I *REALLY* WISH YOU WEREN'T INTENT ON COMMITTING GENOCIDE, BECAUSE I HAVE FORTY-TWO QUESTIONS I'D LIKE TO ASK YOU.
THE ONLY ONE I'M INTERESTED IN RIGHT THIS MOMENT IS WHAT HAPPENS WHEN YOU'RE FORCIBLY SEPARATED FROM COSMIC RAYS?
FWAMMMMM!

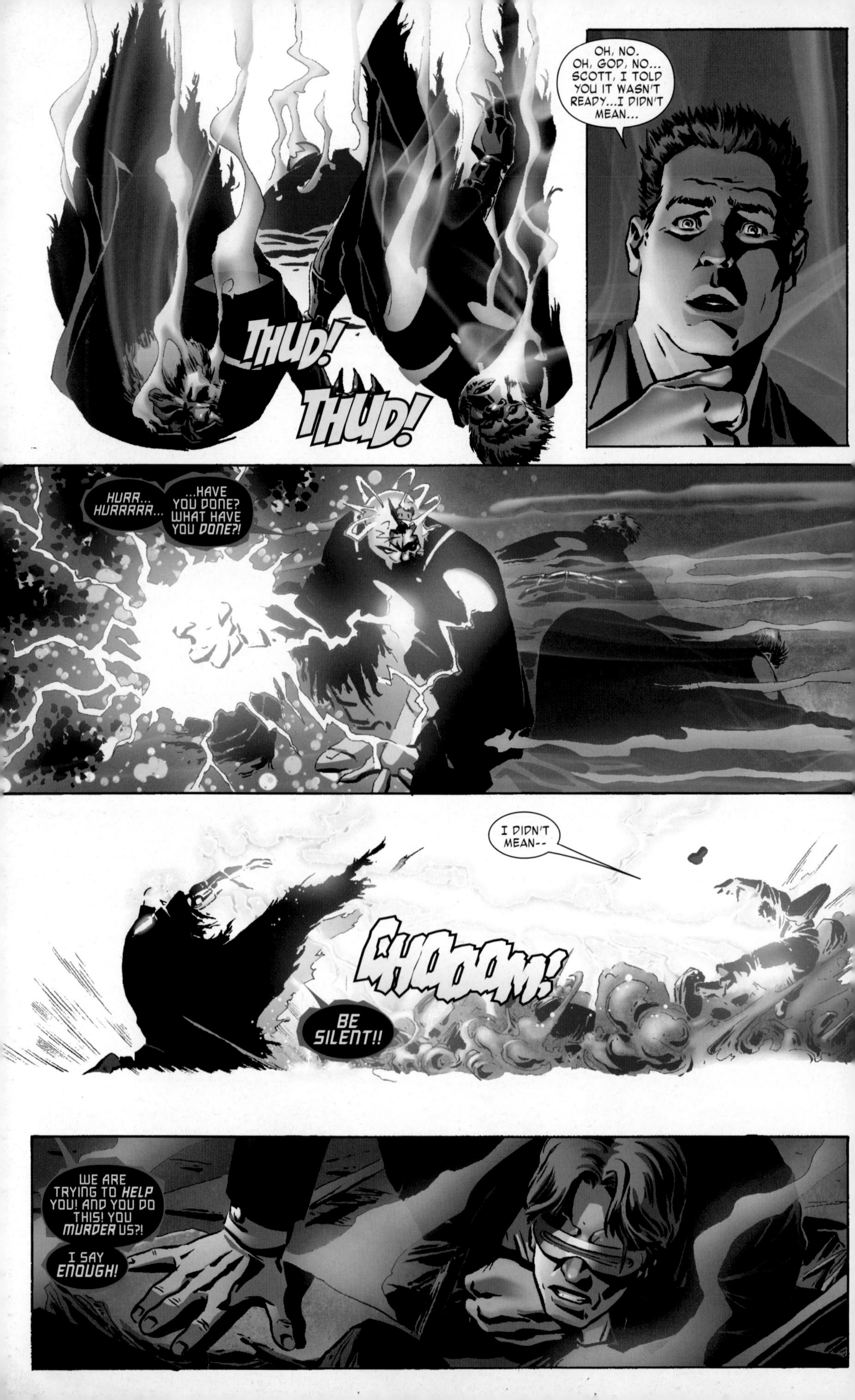
THUD!
THUD!
OH, NO. OH, GOD, NO... SCOTT, I TOLD YOU IT WASN'T READY...I DIDN'T MEAN...
HURR... HURRRRR...
...HAVE YOU DONE? WHAT HAVE YOU DONE?!
I DIDN'T MEAN--
CHOOOM!
BE SILENT!!
WE ARE TRYING TO HELP YOU! AND YOU DO THIS! YOU MURDER US?!
I SAY ENOUGH!

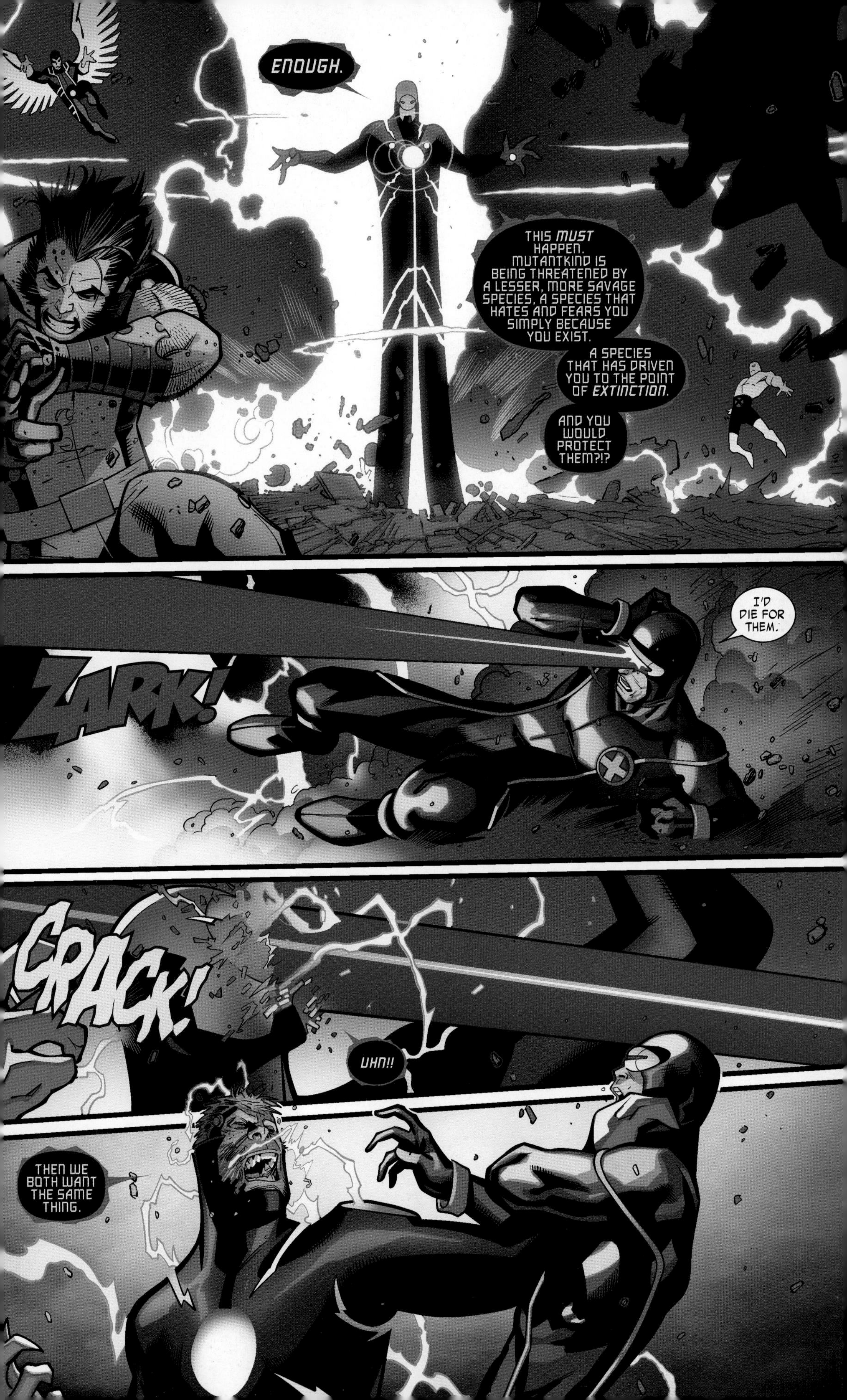

ENOUGH.
THIS MUST HAPPEN. MUTANTKIND IS BEING THREATENED BY A LESSER, MORE SAVAGE SPECIES, A SPECIES THAT HATES AND FEARS YOU SIMPLY BECAUSE YOU EXIST.
A SPECIES THAT HAS DRIVEN YOU TO THE POINT OF EXTINCTION.
AND YOU WOULD PROTECT THEM?!?
I'D DIE FOR THEM.
ZARK!
CRACK!
UHN!!
THEN WE BOTH WANT THE SAME THING.

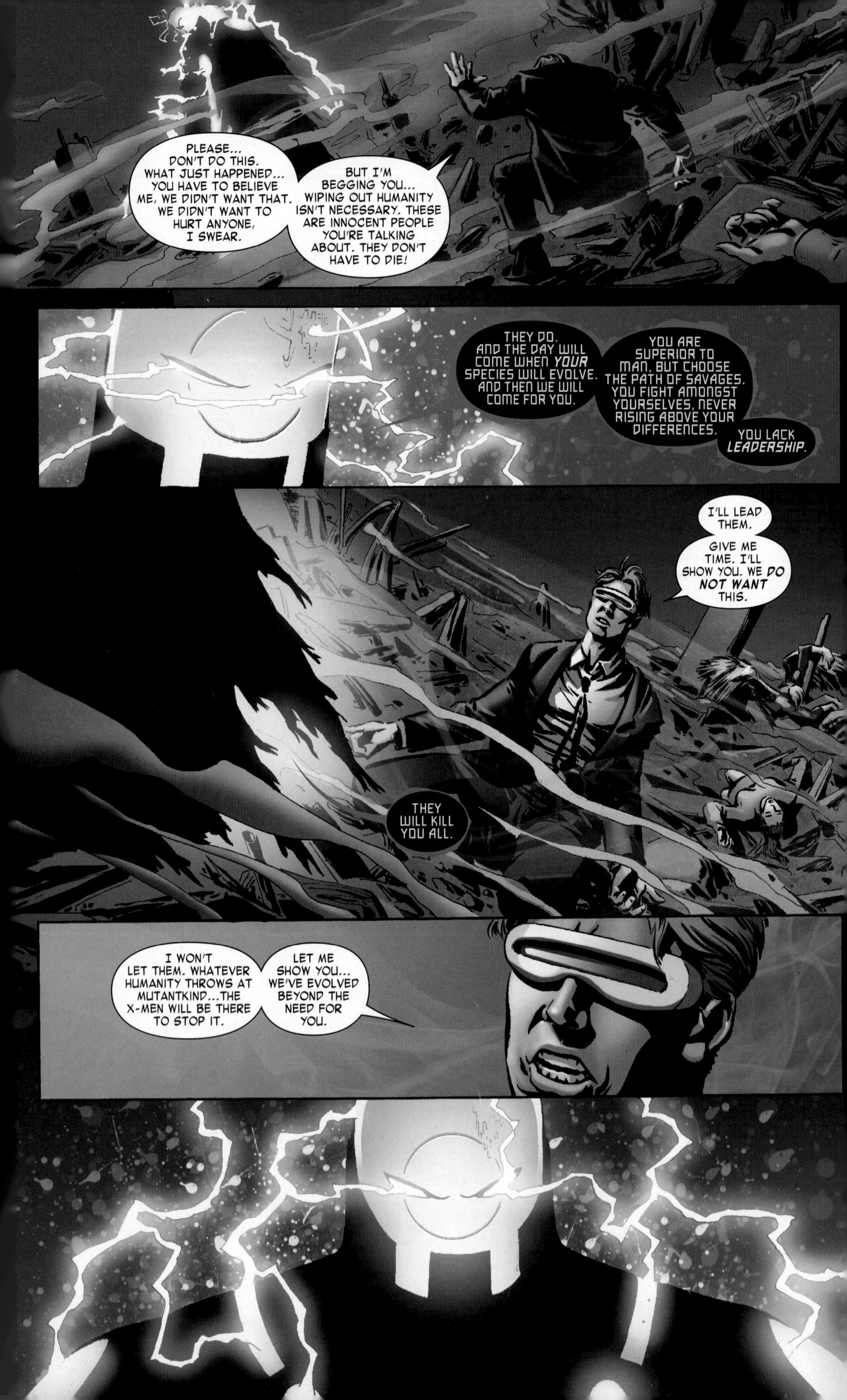
PLEASE... DON'T DO THIS. WHAT JUST HAPPENED... YOU HAVE TO BELIEVE ME, WE DIDN'T WANT THAT. WE DIDN'T WANT TO HURT ANYONE, I SWEAR.
BUT I'M BEGGING YOU... WIPING OUT HUMANITY ISN'T NECESSARY. THESE ARE INNOCENT PEOPLE YOU'RE TALKING ABOUT. THEY DON'T HAVE TO DIE!
THEY DO. AND THE DAY WILL COME WHEN YOUR SPECIES WILL EVOLVE. AND THEN WE WILL COME FOR YOU.
YOU ARE SUPERIOR TO MAN, BUT CHOOSE THE PATH OF SAVAGES. YOU FIGHT AMONGST YOURSELVES, NEVER RISING ABOVE YOUR DIFFERENCES.
YOU LACK LEADERSHIP.
I'LL LEAD THEM.
GIVE ME TIME. I'LL SHOW YOU. WE DO NOT WANT THIS.
THEY WILL KILL YOU ALL.
I WON'T LET THEM. WHATEVER HUMANITY THROWS AT MUTANTKIND...THE X-MEN WILL BE THERE TO STOP IT.
LET ME SHOW YOU... WE'VE EVOLVED BEYOND THE NEED FOR YOU.

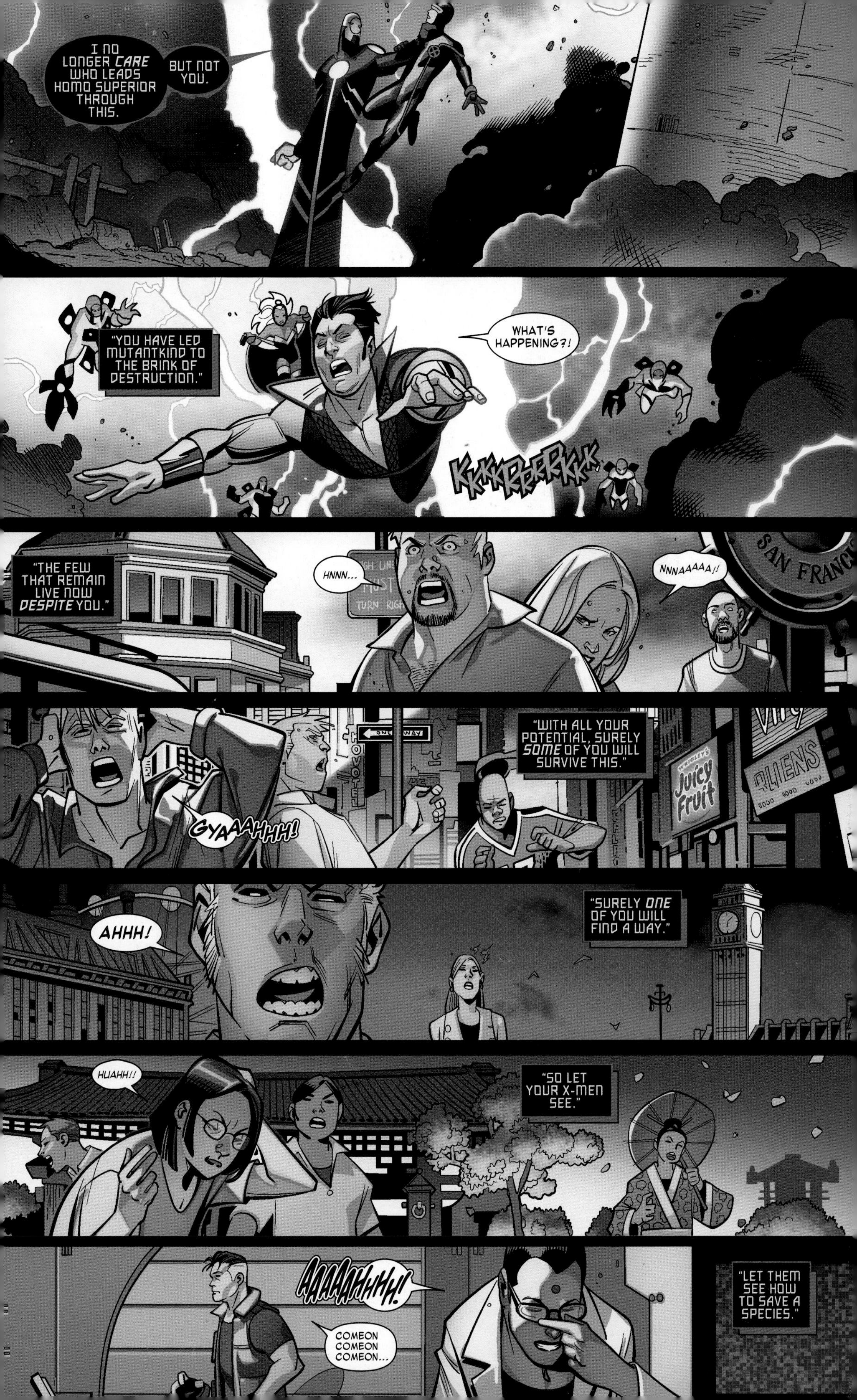
I NO LONGER CARE WHO LEADS HOMO SUPERIOR THROUGH THIS.
BUT NOT YOU.
"YOU HAVE LED MUTANTKIND TO THE BRINK OF DESTRUCTION."
WHAT'S HAPPENING?!
KKKKRRRRKKK
"THE FEW THAT REMAIN LIVE NOW DESPITE YOU."
HNNN...
NNNAAAAA!!
SAN FRANC
TURN RIGHT
"WITH ALL YOUR POTENTIAL, SURELY SOME OF YOU WILL SURVIVE THIS."
GYAAAHHH!
ONE WAY
Juicy Fruit
"SURELY ONE OF YOU WILL FIND A WAY."
AHHH!
HUAHH!!
"SO LET YOUR X-MEN SEE."
AAAAAHHHH!
COMEON COMEON COMEON...
"LET THEM SEE HOW TO SAVE A SPECIES."

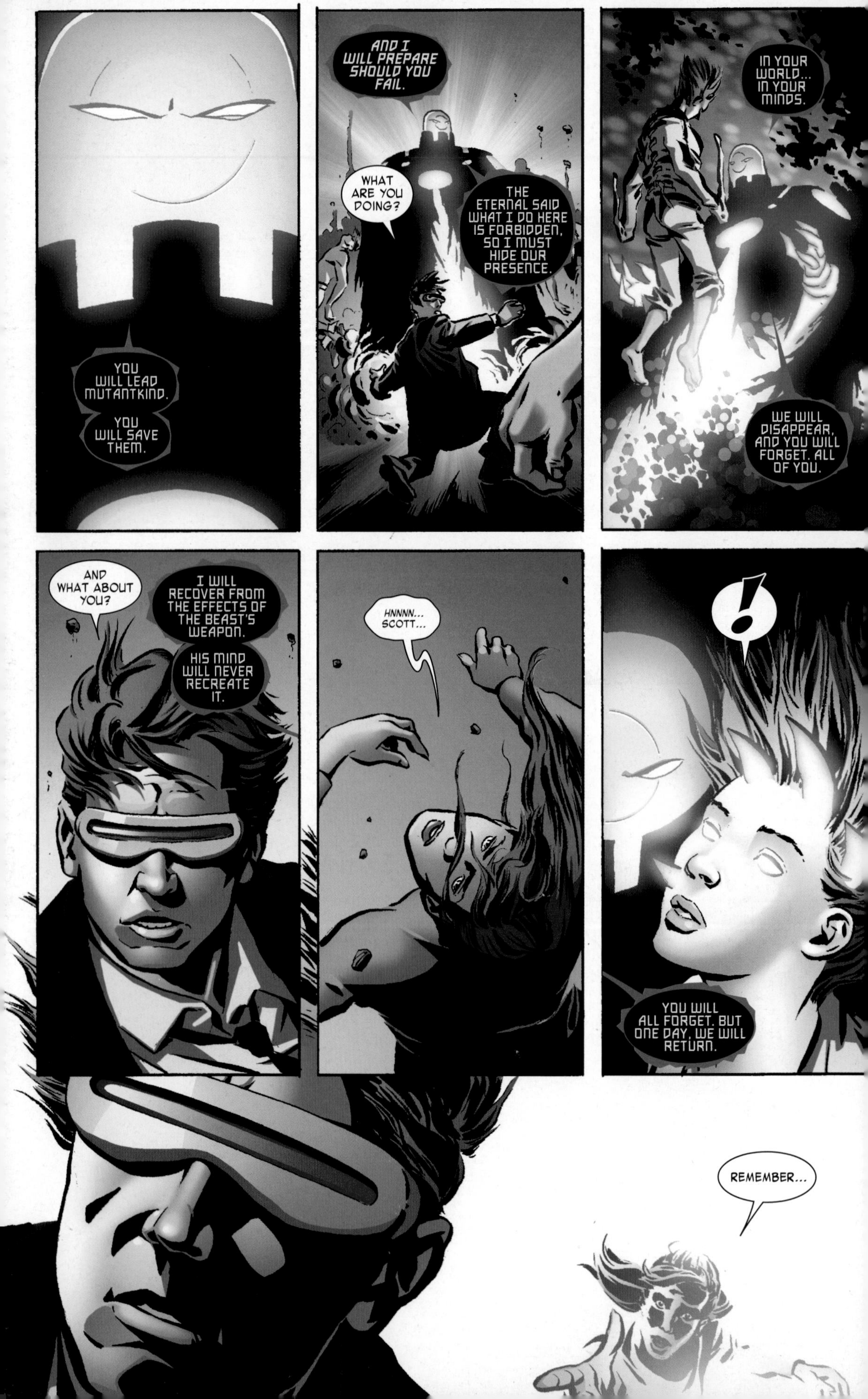
YOU WILL LEAD MUTANTKIND.
YOU WILL SAVE THEM.
AND I WILL PREPARE SHOULD YOU FAIL.
WHAT ARE YOU DOING?
THE ETERNAL SAID WHAT I DO HERE IS FORBIDDEN, SO I MUST HIDE OUR PRESENCE.
IN YOUR WORLD... IN YOUR MINDS.
WE WILL DISAPPEAR, AND YOU WILL FORGET. ALL OF YOU.
AND WHAT ABOUT YOU?
I WILL RECOVER FROM THE EFFECTS OF THE BEAST'S WEAPON.
HIS MIND WILL NEVER RECREATE IT.
HNNNN... SCOTT...
!
YOU WILL ALL FORGET. BUT ONE DAY, WE WILL RETURN.
REMEMBER...

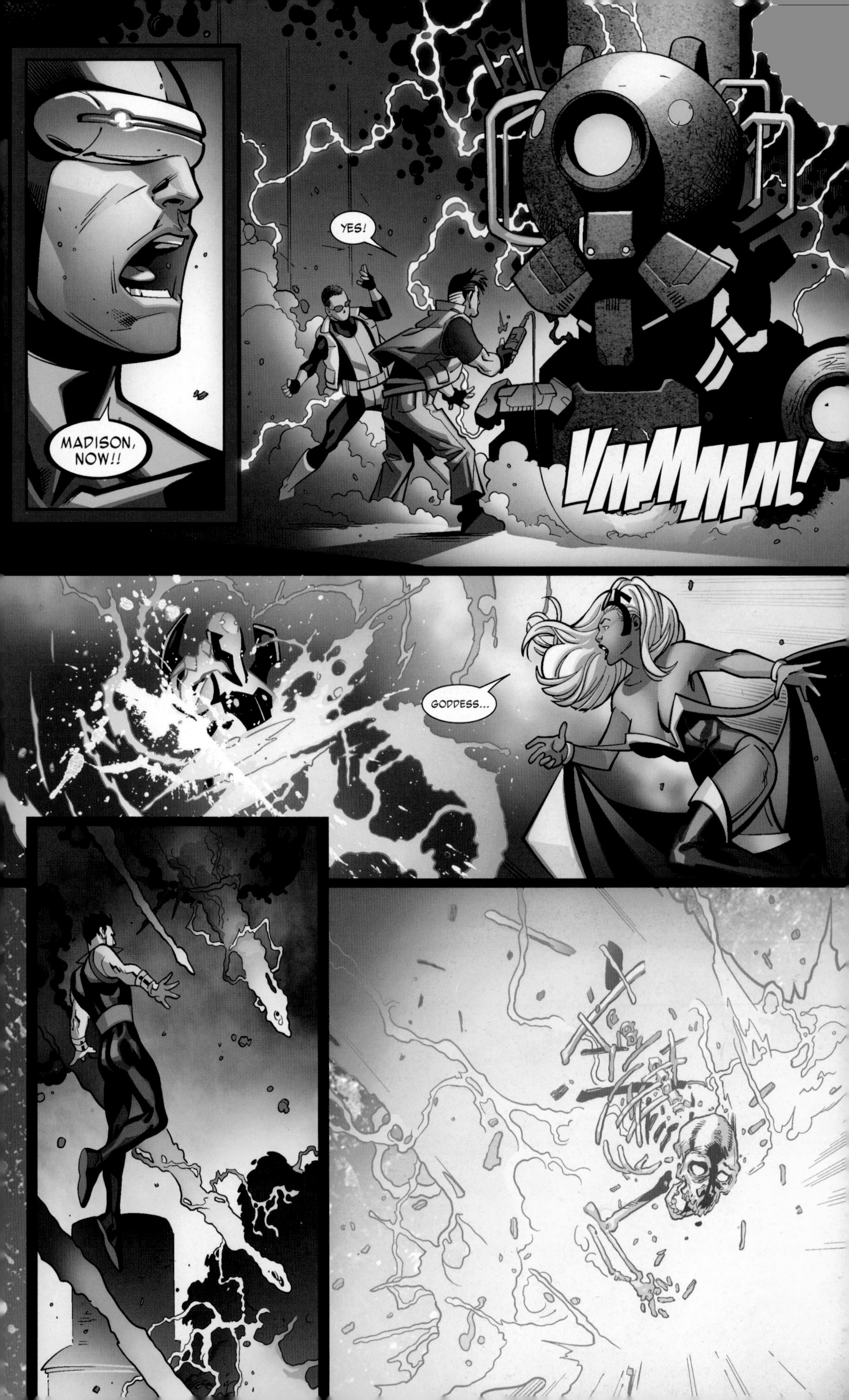
MADISON, NOW!!
YES!
VMMMMM!
GODDESS...

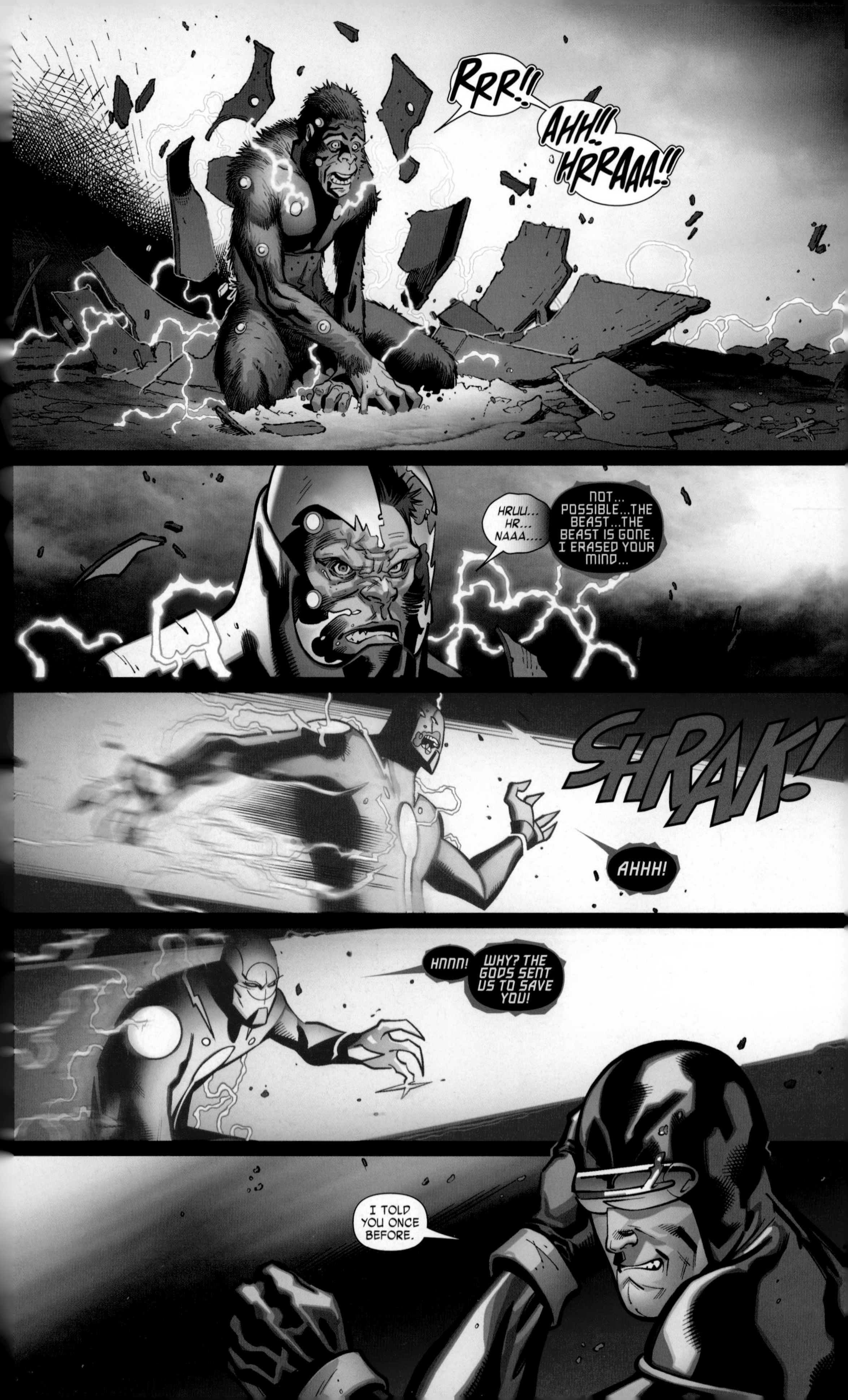
RRR!!
AHH!!
HRRAAA!!
HRUU... HR... NAAA....
NOT... POSSIBLE...THE BEAST...THE BEAST IS GONE. I ERASED YOUR MIND...
SHRAK!
AHHH!
HNNN!
WHY? THE GODS SENT US TO SAVE YOU!
I TOLD YOU ONCE BEFORE.

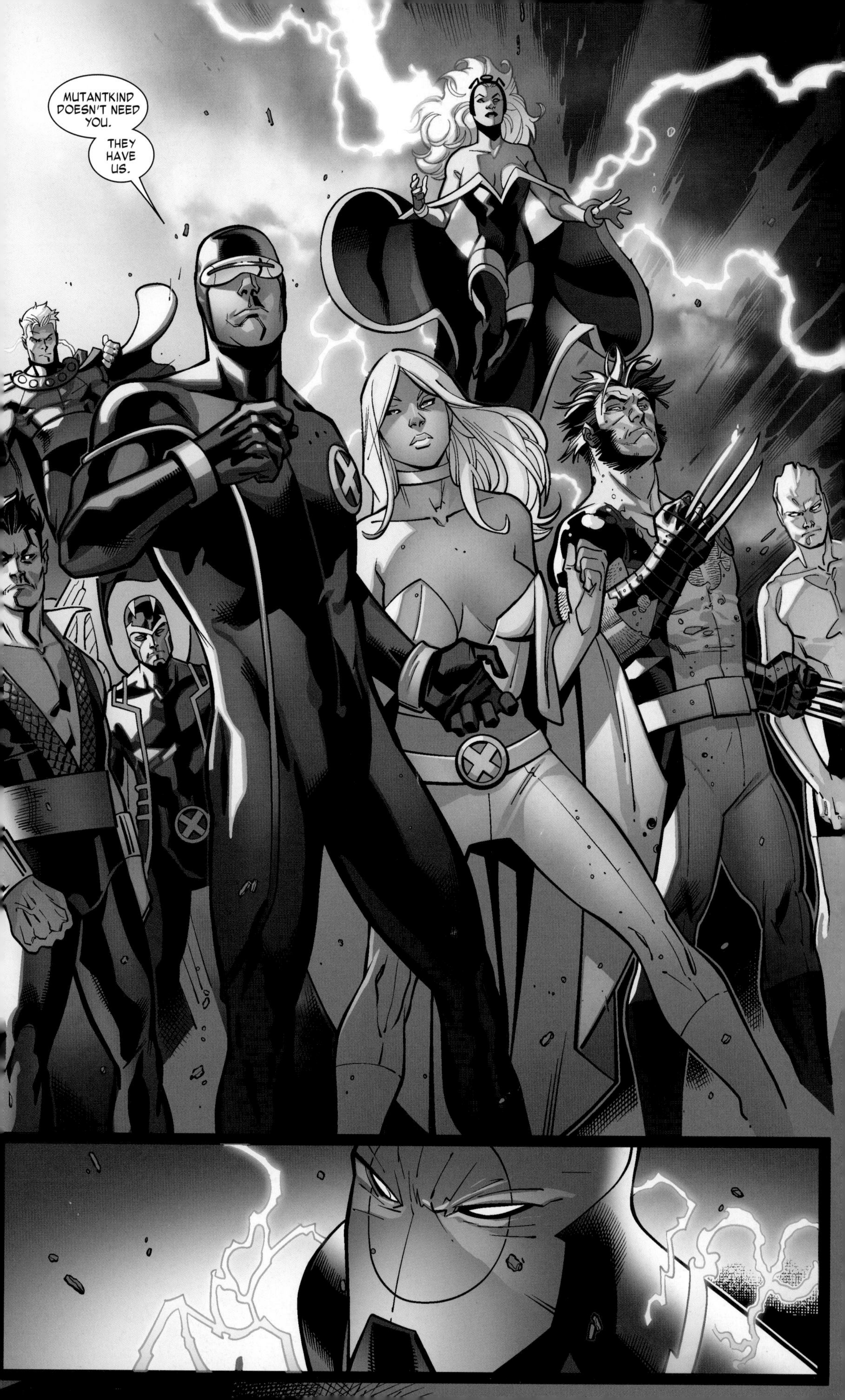
MUTANTKIND DOESN'T NEED YOU.
THEY HAVE US.

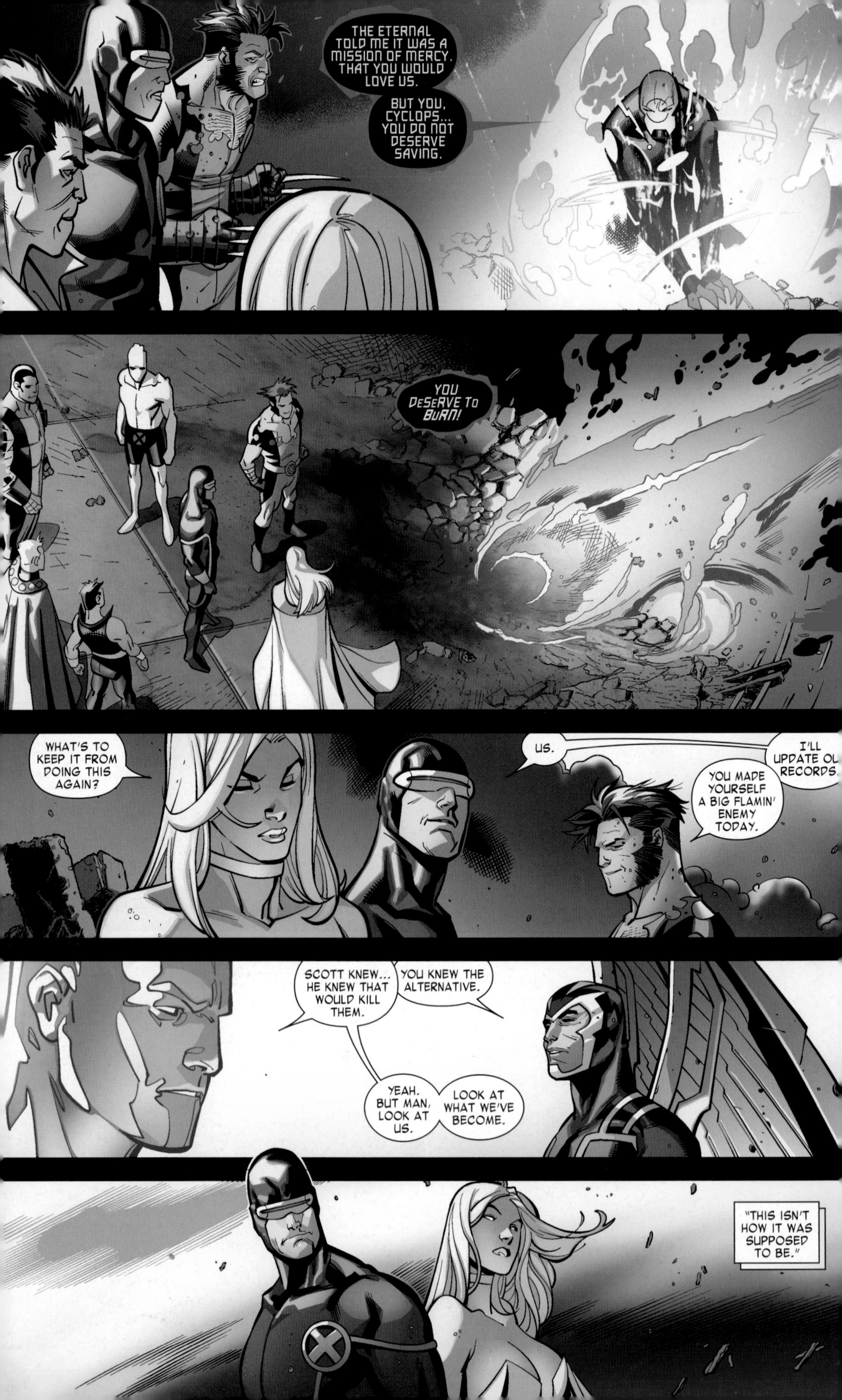

THE ETERNAL TOLD ME IT WAS A MISSION OF MERCY. THAT YOU WOULD LOVE US.
BUT YOU, CYCLOPS... YOU DO NOT DESERVE SAVING.
YOU DESERVE TO BURN!
WHAT'S TO KEEP IT FROM DOING THIS AGAIN?
US.
I'LL UPDATE OU RECORDS.
YOU MADE YOURSELF A BIG FLAMIN' ENEMY TODAY.
SCOTT KNEW... HE KNEW THAT WOULD KILL THEM.
YOU KNEW THE ALTERNATIVE.
YEAH. BUT MAN, LOOK AT US.
LOOK AT WHAT WE'VE BECOME.
"THIS ISN'T HOW IT WAS SUPPOSED TO BE."

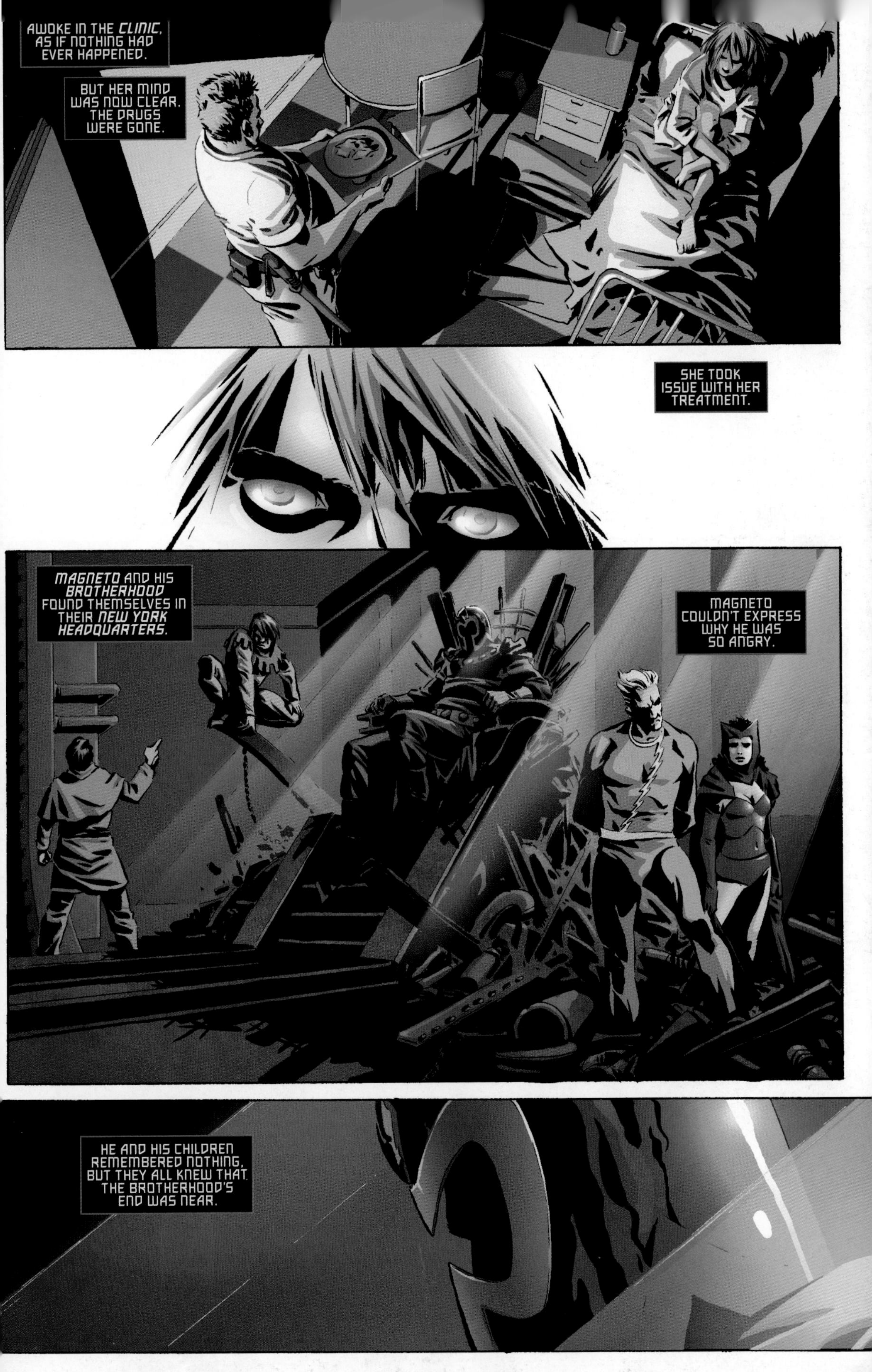
AWOKE IN THE CLINIC, AS IF NOTHING HAD EVER HAPPENED.
BUT HER MIND WAS NOW CLEAR. THE DRUGS WERE GONE.
SHE TOOK ISSUE WITH HER TREATMENT.
MAGNETO AND HIS BROTHERHOOD FOUND THEMSELVES IN THEIR NEW YORK HEADQUARTERS.
MAGNETO COULDN'T EXPRESS WHY HE WAS SO ANGRY.
HE AND HIS CHILDREN REMEMBERED NOTHING, BUT THEY ALL KNEW THAT THE BROTHERHOOD'S END WAS NEAR.

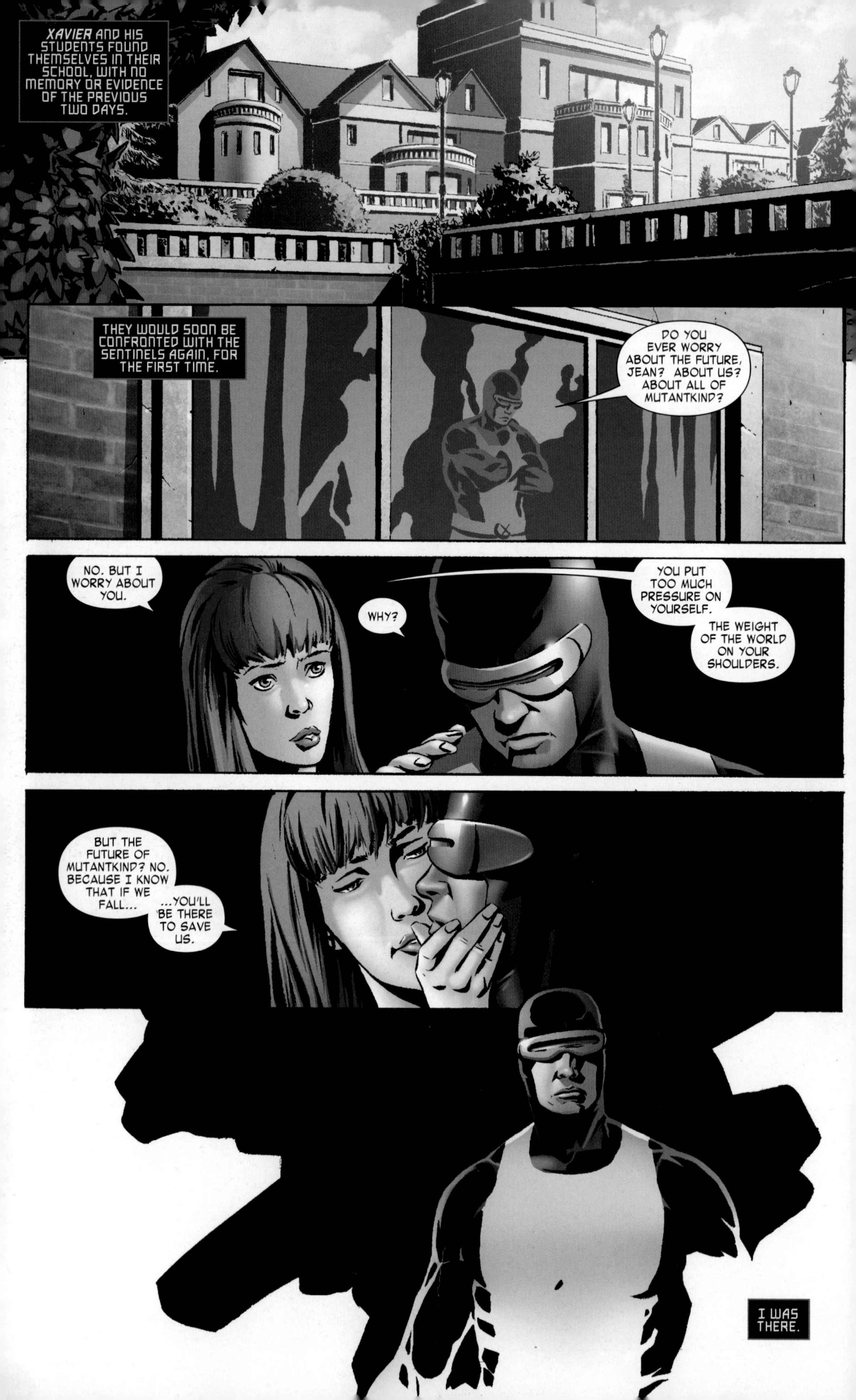
XAVIER AND HIS STUDENTS FOUND THEMSELVES IN THEIR SCHOOL, WITH NO MEMORY OR EVIDENCE OF THE PREVIOUS TWO DAYS.
THEY WOULD SOON BE CONFRONTED WITH THE SENTINELS AGAIN, FOR THE FIRST TIME.
DO YOU EVER WORRY ABOUT THE FUTURE, JEAN? ABOUT US? ABOUT ALL OF MUTANTKIND?
NO. BUT I WORRY ABOUT YOU.
WHY?
YOU PUT TOO MUCH PRESSURE ON YOURSELF.
THE WEIGHT OF THE WORLD ON YOUR SHOULDERS.
BUT THE FUTURE OF MUTANTKIND? NO. BECAUSE I KNOW THAT IF WE FALL...
...YOU'LL BE THERE TO SAVE US.
I WAS THERE.

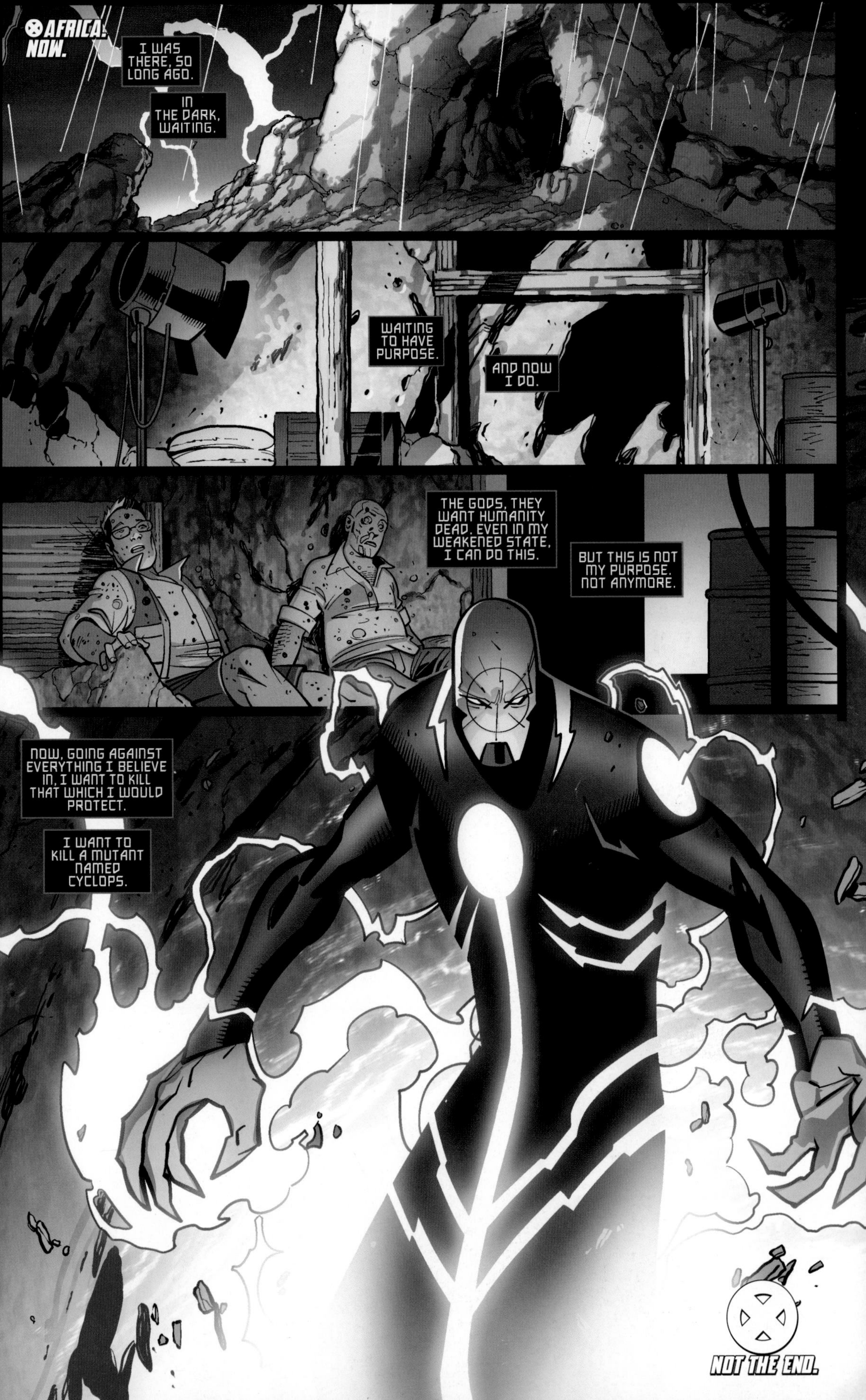
AFRICA. NOW.
I WAS THERE, SO LONG AGO.
IN THE DARK, WAITING.
WAITING TO HAVE PURPOSE.
AND NOW I DO.
THE GODS, THEY WANT HUMANITY DEAD. EVEN IN MY WEAKENED STATE, I CAN DO THIS.
BUT THIS IS NOT MY PURPOSE. NOT ANYMORE.
NOW, GOING AGAINST EVERYTHING I BELIEVE IN, I WANT TO KILL THAT WHICH I WOULD PROTECT.
I WANT TO KILL A MUTANT NAMED CYCLOPS.
NOT THE END.

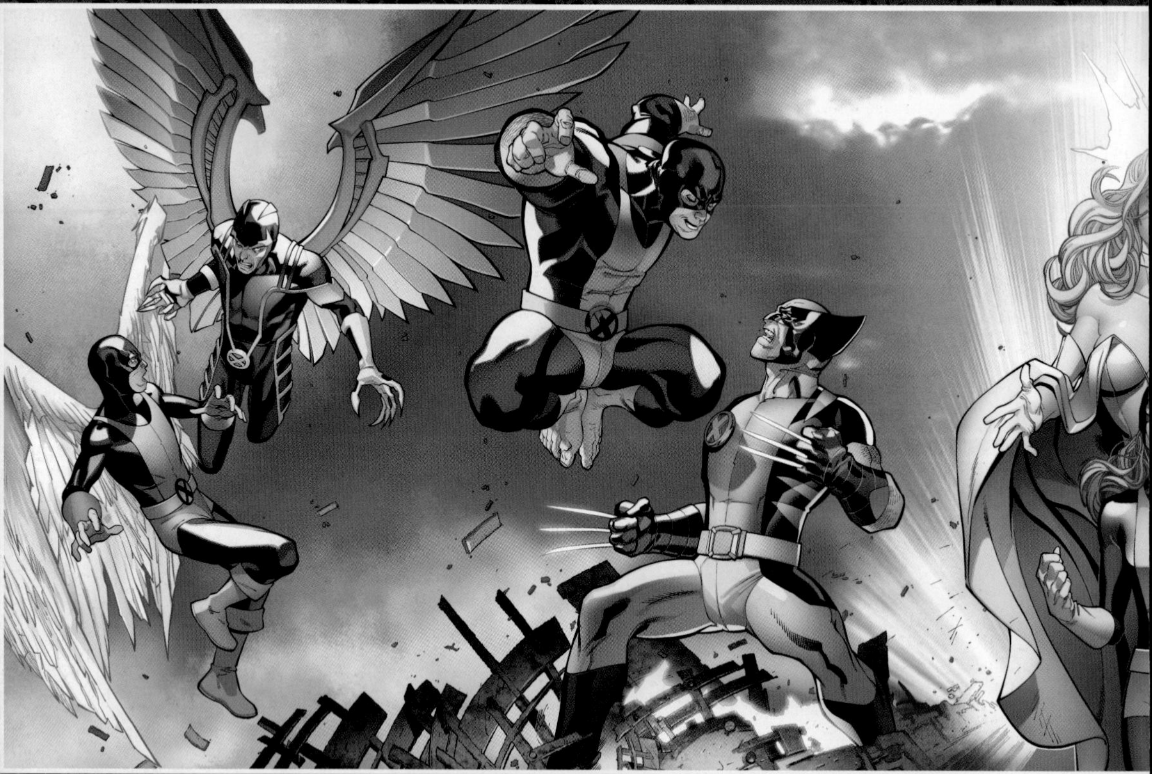

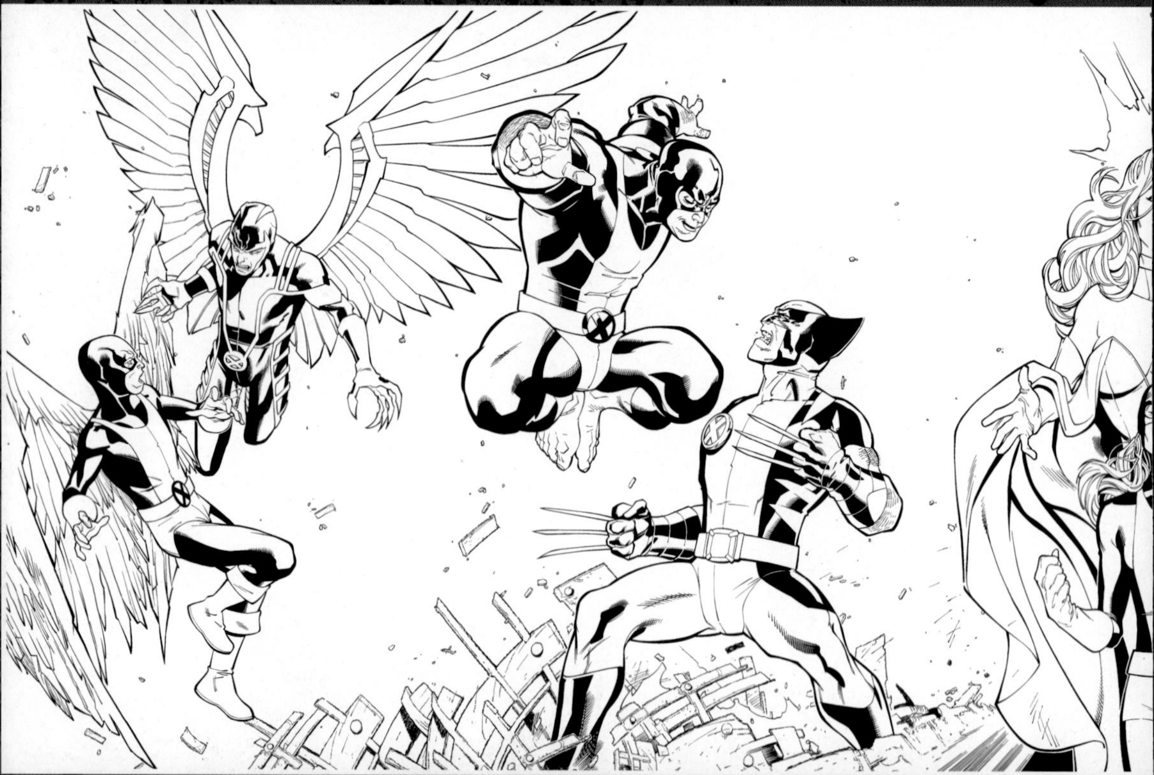

\#12-15 COMBINED VARIANTS BY
PACO MEDINA, JUAN VLASCO & MARTE GRACIA

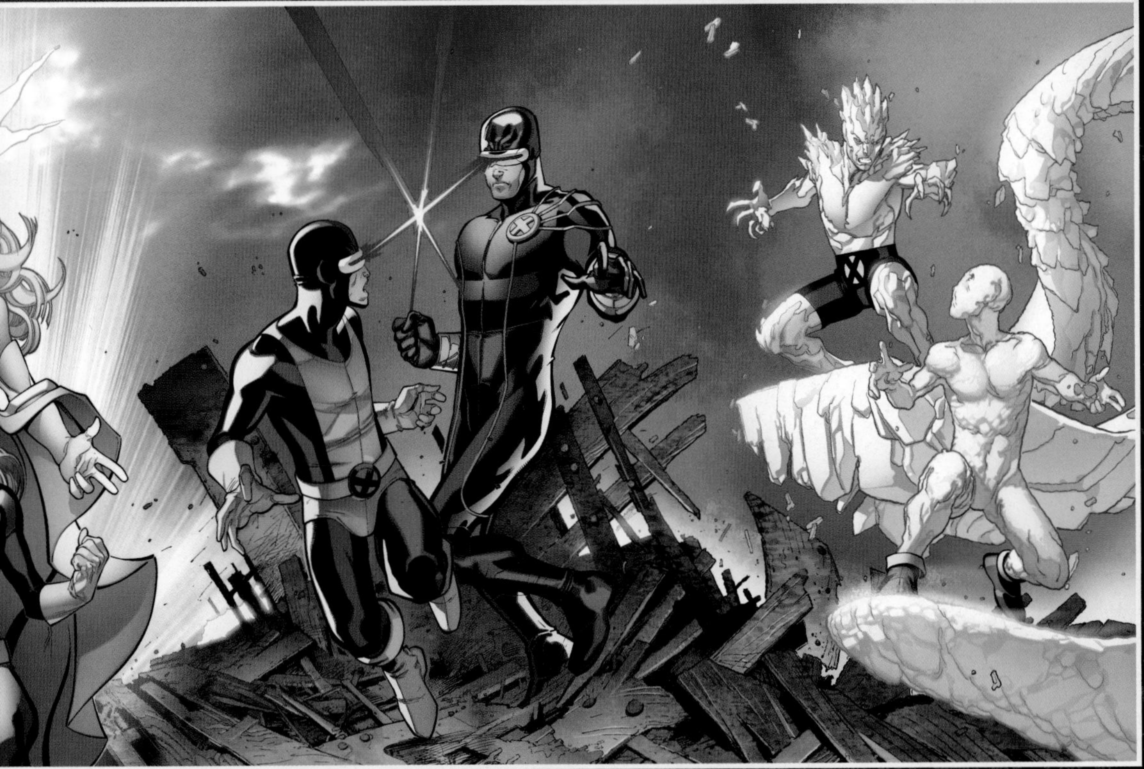

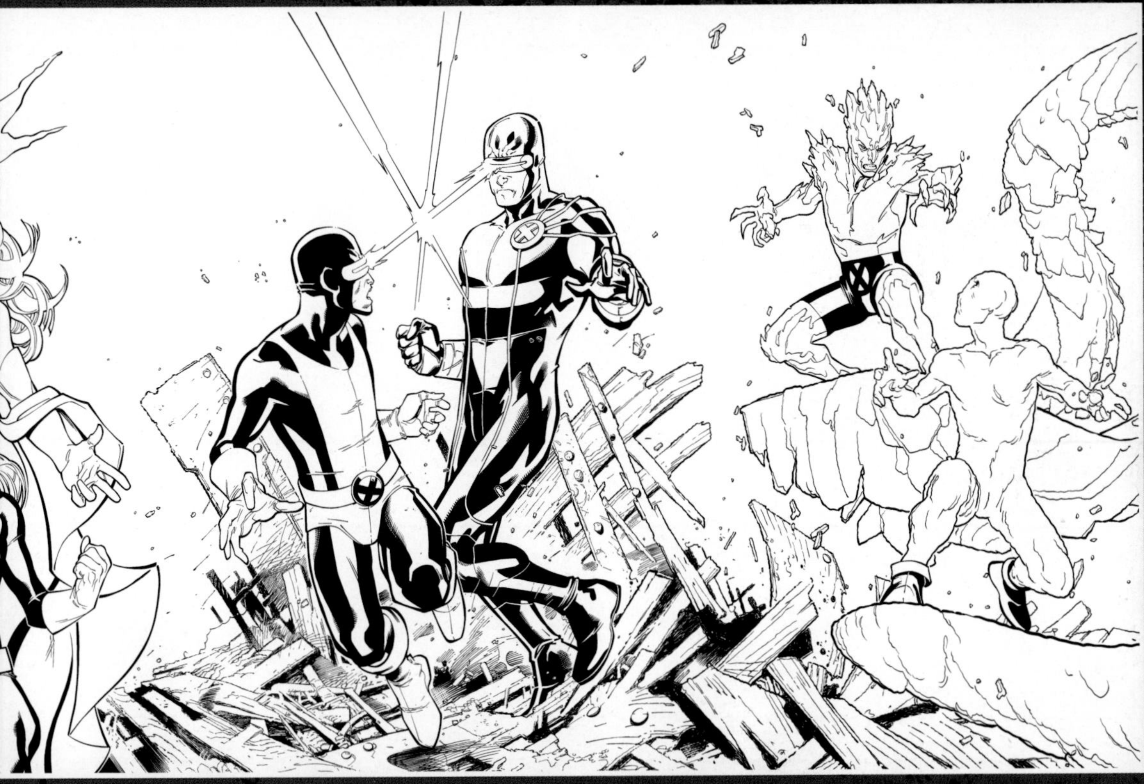

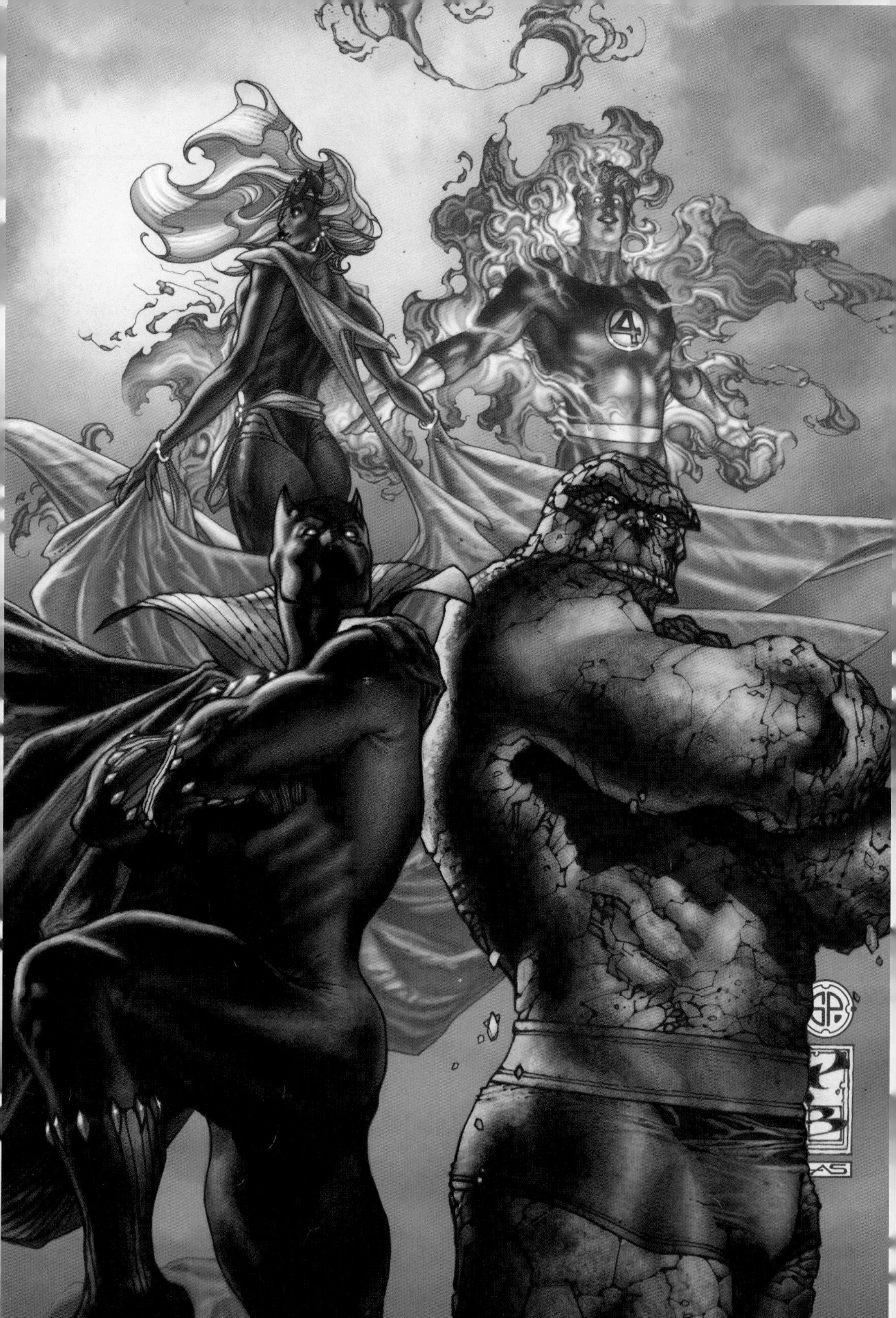

X-MEN GIANT-SIZE #1 FANTASTIC FOUR ANNIVERSARY VARIANT BY **SIMONE BIANCHI**

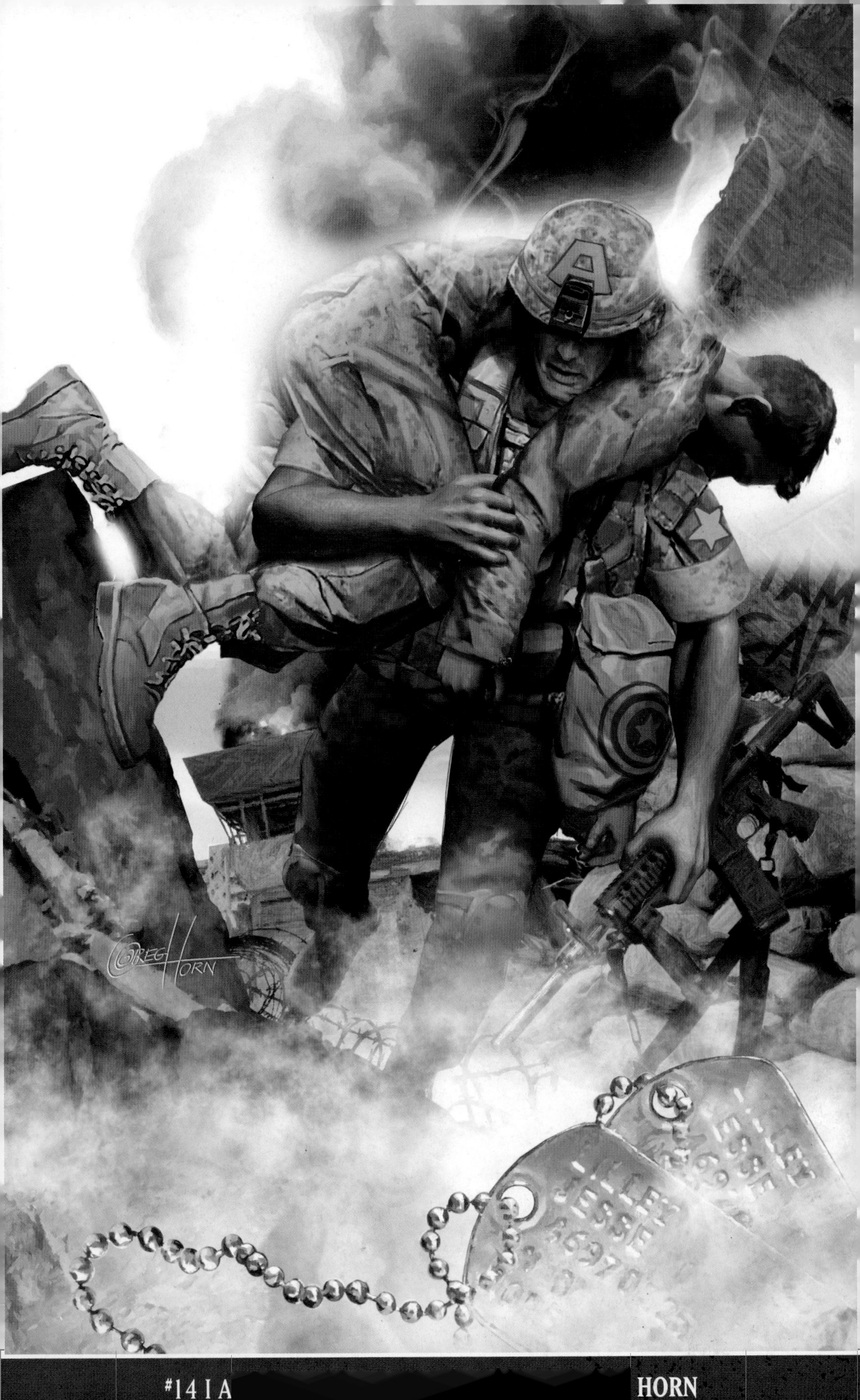
GREG HORN

#14 I A [redacted] HORN

EXERCISE IN DESIGN
WITH EDITOR DANIEL KETCHUM

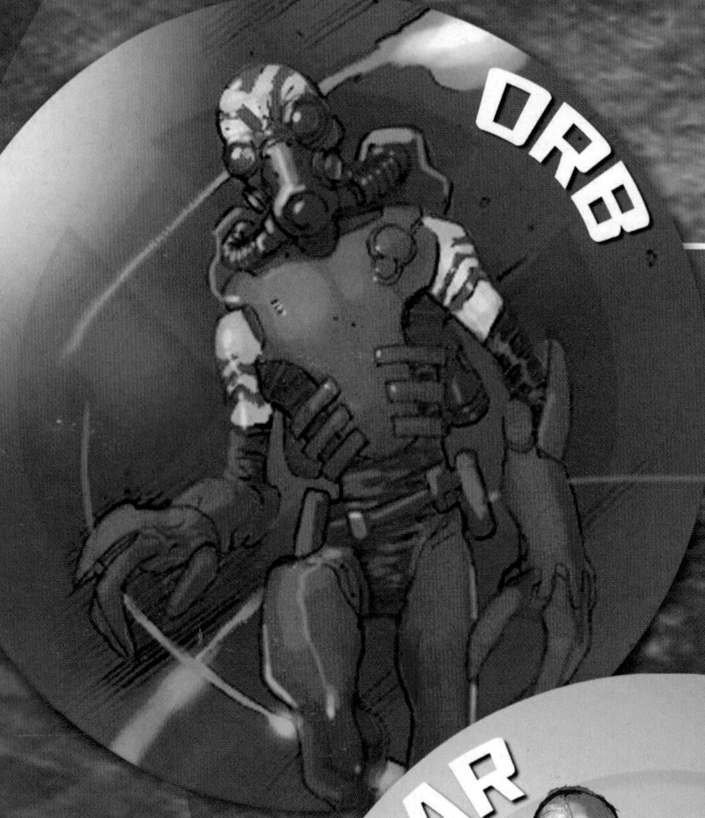
ORB

"Believe it or not, looking CREEPY isn't his power… it's manipulating spheres of energy."

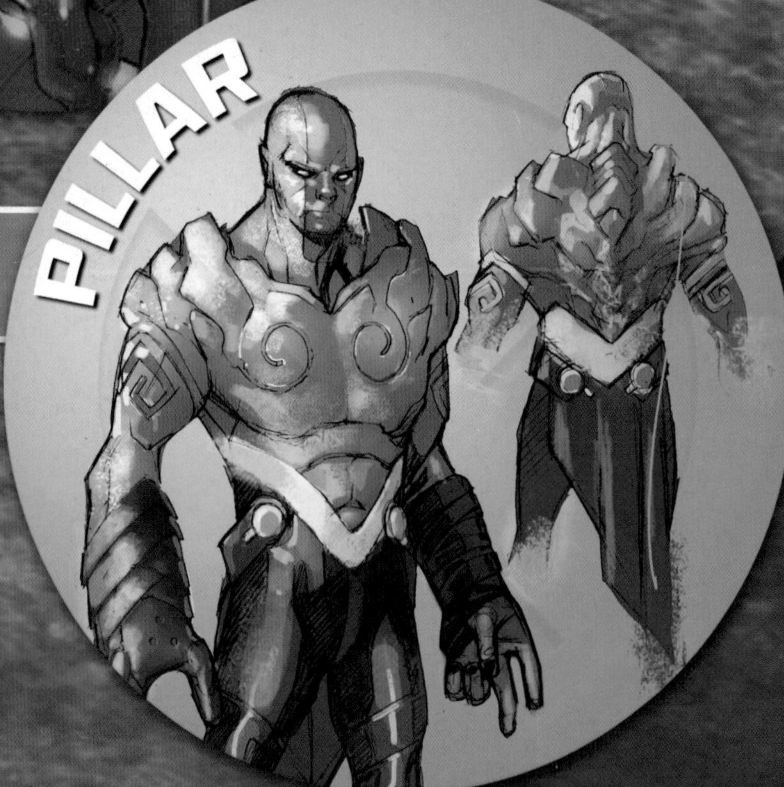
PILLAR

"He's tall. REALLY tall."

The *Neo* are an offshoot species of mutantkind, one that's more powerful than its evolutionary counterpart...but still equally susceptible to extermination. When the Scarlet Witch decimated mutantkind, the Neo also found themselves effected--their number greatly reduced, with no new members of their species being born.

Upon learning that mutantkind has witnessed a spate of new mutant manifestations, the Neo confront the X-Men demanding to know how they managed to save their species so that they may do the same. Unfortunately for the X-Men, they possess no easy answer that will satisfy the Neo... and fisticuffs ensue.

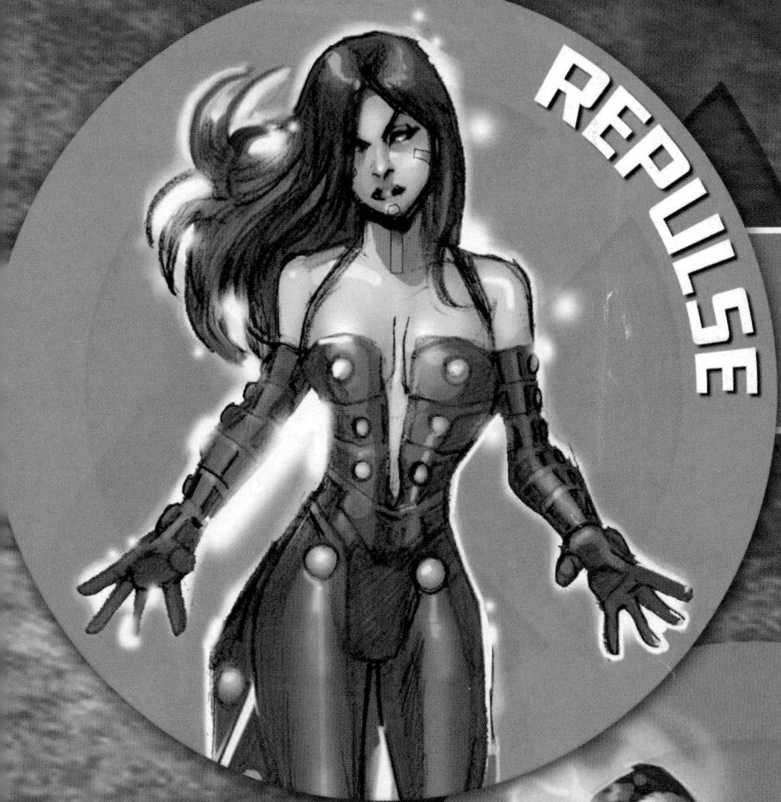
REPULSE

"A beautiful raven-haired woman who will do exactly what her name says... via her psionic force field."

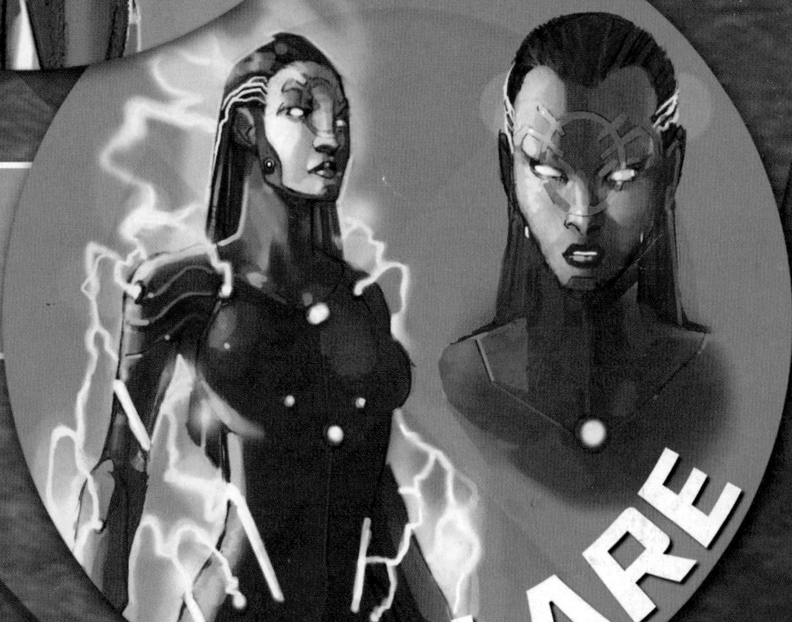
FLARE

"You can look, but certainly don't touch... this lady's too hot to handle. Literally!"

CHARACTER DESIGNS BY
PACO MEDINA

X-Men: First to Last

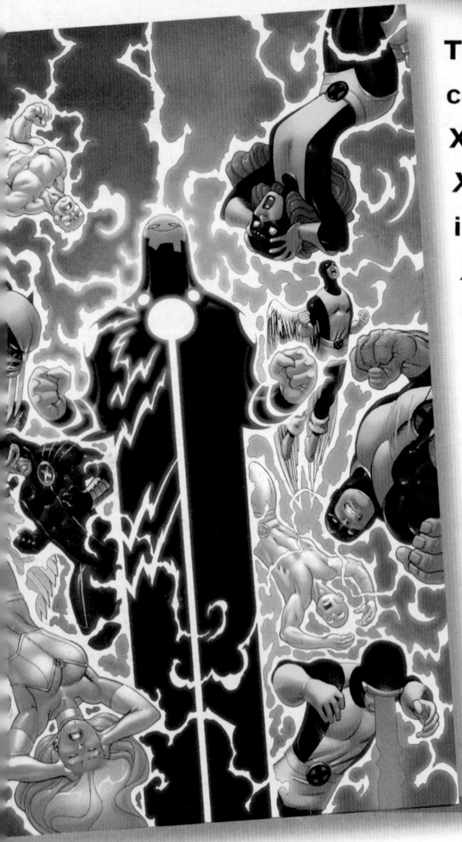

The mutant action isn't solely confined to the stories of the X-Men's past. Starting in May's *X-Men Giant Size #1* and continuing in June with an arc that begins in *X-Men #12*, writer Chris Yost will bridge the gap between the First Class era and the modern day with the "X-Men: First To Last" story. Focusing on a powerful group of mystery villains known as The Evolutionaries, the story involves every major character from the classic X-Men franchise, and below the writer describes how he'll bring a threat to all of mutantkind. • KIEL PHEGLEY

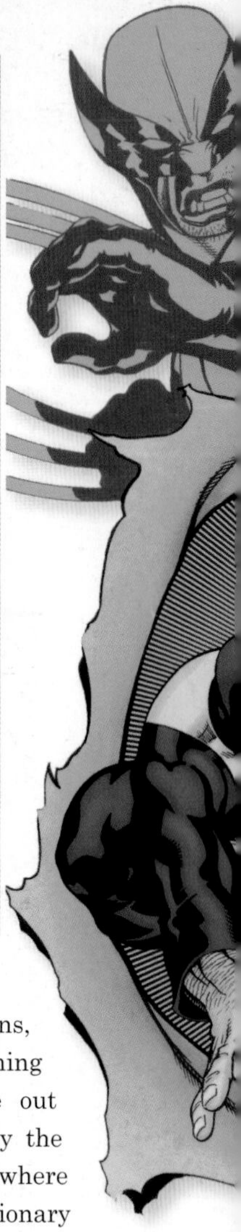

KIEL PHEGLEY: **With the past of the X-Men being such a popular topic these days, what drew you in specifically in telling the story of "First To Last"?**

CHRIS YOST: Well, I've always been a big fan of the X-Men from day one. Cyclops and Jean Grey are *the* X-Men power couple and I jumped at the chance to work with them. But the thing we talked about most of all for this series was how these people have changed over time. The story is set back in the First Class days and in the present, and it explores the changes in Cyclops, Iceman, Beast and Archangel and everything they've been through over the years. It's been pretty fun to explore that.

KP: **You're creating a new set of villains with the Evolutionaries. One thing that always interests me about writers on the X-Men is that you can pick what theme you want to play with from social outcasts to soap operatics. It feels as though these villains will challenge the idea of mutants as the next step in human life. How do they work as X-Men-specific villains?**

CY: That's a good question. The Evolutionaries kind of started with a Charles Darwin quote about how more advanced species will eventually take over. But in the case of mutants and humans, humans are doing everything they can to survive and take out the mutants who are essentially the future. So you get this situation where something lower down the evolutionary scale is trying to take someone out on the top — with a great degree of death. The Evolutionarie in some ways are a response to that.

That probably doesn't make a lot of sense at first [*Laughs*] But they're certainly big, scary guys. An they have a purpose they're here to carry out. They fi so well into the X-Men's idea of "To Protect And Serv Those That Hate And Fear You." The X-Men are ther to protect mutants, of course, but to protect human too. That's always been their thing. The Evolutionarie are going to challenge that in a big way.

KP: **This story starts out in the *X-Men Giant-Size #* How did you decide where in the team's past to begi the story?**

CY: It starts about 2.7 million years ago and goes a the way to today, so you're going to see [the X-Men' current base] of Utopia from Matt Fraction and Kiero Gillen's *Uncanny X-Men*, but you're also going to se

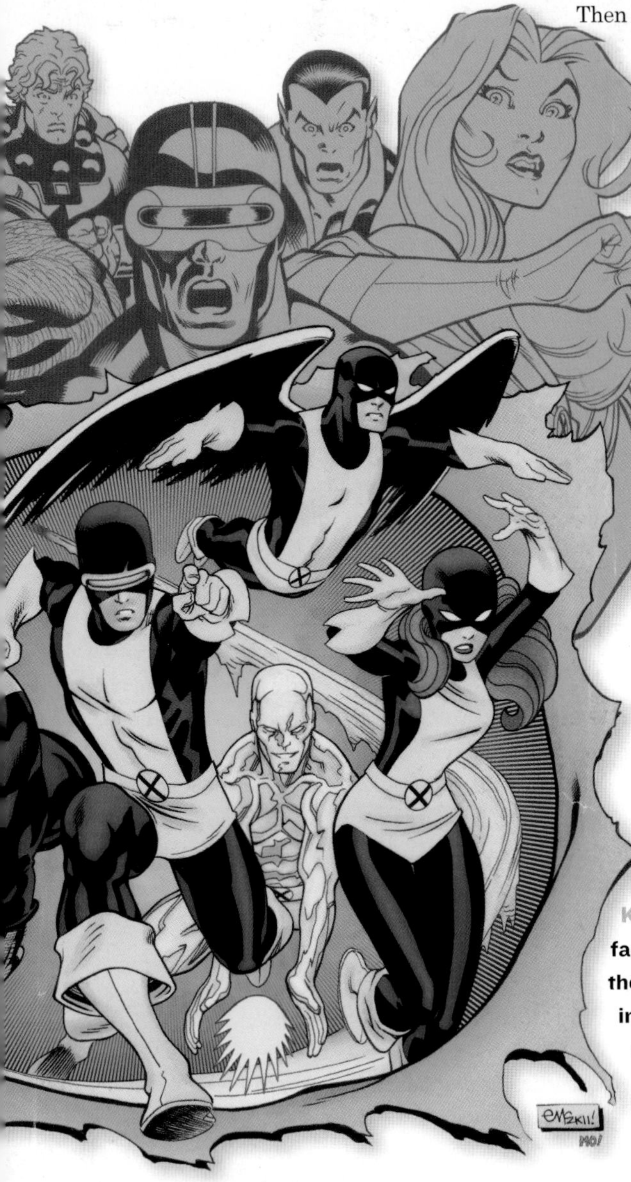

he team back in the First Class days. I think I pegged hat around the original *The X-Men #11* — that's the imeline we're talking about. You'll see the cool five original members. You're going to see Professor Xavier and the School For Gifted Youngsters as it was in its heyday. There's no Danger Room and Cerebro is this crazy computer at the Professor's desk. You're going to see Magneto and the Brotherhood as they were at the very beginning. This is all the Stan Lee/Jack Kirby stuff. Then on the flipside, you're seeing Utopia and what the X-Men have become. Everything is changed.

KP: **Looking at the team members, Cyclops is a central figure in both the origins of the X-Men and as the leader of the mutants of Utopia now. He's changed so much over the years. Was it harder to get a handle on him in two eras?**

CY: In the present day I've been able to work with him quite a bit, and a large part of what the X-Men books are now are in some ways shaped by Cyclops and his drive to keep them alive. Mutantkind has hit the biggest crisis they've ever seen. They're literally an endangered species and are being hunted and killed on a daily basis. It's all been put on Cyclops' shoulders to get them through that, more or less, where as in the First Class days the stakes weren't as high. But you can kind of see in him that need to be the leader and to be perfect — to really please Professor Xavier to a certain extent as well. All the makings of what Cyclops becomes in our time are there in the past.

KP: **And a major change for him and everyone is the fact that Jean Grey is alive in the past but dead in the present. Is it a challenge to tell an exciting story in the past when you know where these characters will go?**

CY: It's definitely something you think about because Jean Grey is fighting to save a future that she herself will not see. That's something the character may now know, but as a writer you can't help but have those moments where there's a little bit of sadness. For example, Warren in the First Class days is Angel, but in the future he's going to be much, much darker. Beast too has not got his blue fur yet and is still part of the X-Men where in the future he's changed physically and changed teams. He left the X-Men because of moral objections. And even with Iceman you'll see some fairly big differences. He was

> "*MUTANTKIND* ***has hit the biggest crisis they've ever seen. They're literally an endangered species and are being hunted and killed on a daily basis.***"

kind of the snowman joker in the past, and he's still a lot of fun in the present though things have changed for him. The other big idea here is power. The X-Men are a lot more powerful than they were in the past.

KP: The story also features characters like Emma Frost and Wolverine in today's world. Is part of the story about exploring the way the X-Men have grown?

CY: Absolutely. And how has the tone changed? If the past X-Men were to see themselves in the future, what would they think? I've got to think that they'd have some reservations. From that point of view, the world is so different. I mean, things got dark. Back in the day, the biggest villains the X-Men fought were the Blob or Unus the Untouchable. Today, they're facing down the extinction of their entire species.

KP: What's it been like writing scripts for two artists with Paco Medina covering the present day pages and Dalibor Talajic covering the First Class era?

CY: I think in some regards the art worked itself out. Dalibor's got such a specific kind of retro style and so does Paco with his fairly modern style that to see them go back and forth has been amazing. There's not going to be any mistake for readers to know what era they're in because those styles come through in everything from the pencils right on to the colors. It's

been amazing and looks pretty great. You can real[l] see the differences.

KP: Overall, the Evolutionaries are showing up in the pas[t] and the present. Are the X-Men of today going to be mor[e] prepared for this threat because they've encountered thi[s] force once before?

CY: It's a pretty equal problem for each era. In th[e] present, these things show up and nobody knows quit[e] what they are. They're a mystery. The only perso[n] who quite knows is Cyclops, and because of the wa[y] everything plays out, nobody's got the upper hand.

KP: From the *Giant-Size* kick off, the story runs throug[h] the monthly *X-Men* title. How has that format helpe[d] shape your story?

CY: The *Giant-Size* is huge. I think it's actually th[e] longest physical comic book I've ever written. It's lik[e] 34 pages of story. We really sat down and tried to mak[e] it worth it — to have something big enough happe[n] to get everyone's attention. You'll see the past stor[y] and the present one there, and how everything shake[s] out in the first issue has to be accessible. At the sam[e] time, since I'm such a big fan of continuity and usin[g] everything you can, we tried to have some fun with i[t] for the fans who are longtime readers. ■

Chris Yost explores how the members of the first class have evolved over the years and how the team has expanded to include dynamic new members like Wolverine and Emma Frost